Cracking the GRE

with Four Complete Practice Tests on CD-ROM

The Princeton Review

Cracking the GRE

with Four Complete Practice Tests on CD-ROM

By
Karen Lurie, Magda Pecsenye, and Adam Robinson

2003 EDITION

Random House, Inc.
New York

www.PrincetonReview.com

Princeton Review Publishing, L.L.C.
2315 Broadway
New York, NY   10024
E-mail: booksupport@review.com

ISBN: 0-375-76248-5

Editor: Jeff Soloway
Production Editor: Maria Dente
Production Coordinator: Raymond Asencio
Illustrations by: The Production Department of The Princeton Review

Manufactured in the United States of America.

9 8 7 6 5 4 3 2 1

2003 Edition

ACKNOWLEDGMENTS

The following people deserve thanks for their help with this book:

Jeff Soloway, Robert "Precious" McCormack, Jennifer Arias, Maria Dente, Dan Edmonds, Joe Reddy, Becky Oliver-Remshifski, Ken Riley, Rena Rosenthal, Cathryn Still, and Clare Zagrecki.

CONTENTS

GET MORE FROM *CRACKING THE GRE* BY USING OUR FREE ONLINE TOOLS

Buyers of this book receive access to the latest in interactive test-preparation tools. The **CD-ROM** included at the back of the book allows you to take four full-length GRE tests at your computer. Upon completion of each test, you'll receive a personalized score report identifying your strengths and weaknesses. Afterwards, you'll know exactly where you should be concentrating your preparation efforts.

Furthermore, by buying this book you'll also get a subscription to *Cracking the GRE*'s **online companion course**. Go to www.review.com/cracking to register for all the free online services we offer to help you improve your test score and find the right graduate program. Once you've logged on, you'll be able to:

- **Learn Key Test-Taking Skills Through Our Distance Learning Tools.** Some of the key lessons of *Cracking the GRE* will be even clearer after you've spent a few hours seeing and hearing them presented online.

- **Practice New Techniques with Online Exercises and Drills.** Once you've learned a new technique or concept, you can gauge your mastery by trying out the sample questions in our online review modules. You'll also have online access to some of the tests included in the CD-ROM at the back of this book.

- **Research and Apply to the Best Graduate Programs for You.** Through Review.com, our award-winning search site, you can access our complete library of information on graduate programs, degrees, and financial aid.

YOU'RE IN COMPLETE CONTROL

Here's what you'll see once you've registered.

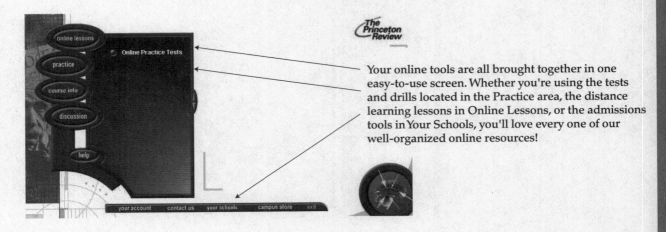

Your online tools are all brought together in one easy-to-use screen. Whether you're using the tests and drills located in the Practice area, the distance learning lessons in Online Lessons, or the admissions tools in Your Schools, you'll love every one of our well-organized online resources!

READING YOUR SCORE REPORT

After you take your extra diagnostic exams, here's how to use your score report:

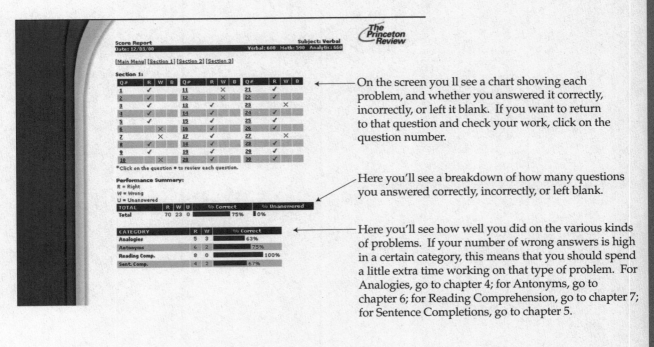

On the screen you ll see a chart showing each problem, and whether you answered it correctly, incorrectly, or left it blank. If you want to return to that question and check your work, click on the question number.

Here you'll see a breakdown of how many questions you answered correctly, incorrectly, or left blank.

Here you'll see how well you did on the various kinds of problems. If your number of wrong answers is high in a certain category, this means that you should spend a little extra time working on that type of problem. For Analogies, go to chapter 4; for Antonyms, go to chapter 6; for Reading Comprehension, go to chapter 7; for Sentence Completions, go to chapter 5.

ONLINE TOOLS

PART I

Orientation

1
Introduction

WHAT IS THE GRE?

The Graduate Record Examination (GRE) is a multiple-choice admissions test intended for applicants to graduate schools. The three sections that count toward your score are (not necessarily in this order):

- One 30-minute, 30-question "Verbal Ability" (vocabulary and reading) section
- One 45-minute, 28-question "Quantitative Ability" (math) section
- One 75-minute, 2-question "Analytical Writing" (essay) section

As you can see, you won't be incredibly pressed for time on the GRE. You shouldn't feel as rushed on this test as you might have on other standardized tests.

The Verbal section of the GRE contains four types of questions, which pop up in no particular order:

- Antonyms
- Sentence Completions
- Analogies
- Reading Comprehension

The Quantitative, or Math, section contains two types of questions, which pop up in no particular order:

- Four-choice Quantitative Comparisons
- Five-choice Problem Solving questions

The Analytical Writing section contains two essay questions, one of each of the following types:

- Analyze an Issue
- Analyze an Argument

Each of these question types will be dealt with in detail later in the book.

EXPERIMENTAL SECTION

You will probably have a fourth, unidentified experimental section. It can be anywhere on the test. This section will not count toward your score. You can't *not* do it, and you won't even recognize it. If you get two Verbal sections, then one of them is experimental, but you won't know which one. So, don't worry about it. Just do your best on all questions.

What Does a GRE Score Look Like?

You will receive separate Verbal and Quantitative scores. They are reported on a scale that runs from 200 to 800, and can rise or fall only by multiples of ten. The third digit is thus always a zero. You can't receive a score of 409 or 715 on a section of the GRE. Your Analytical Writing section will be listed separately, and is scored on a scale of 0 to 6.

Why is this test on a 200–800 scale? ETS didn't want it to look like the 0–100 scale used in schools.

Where Does the GRE Come From?

Like most standardized tests in this country, the GRE is administered by ETS, a big, tax-exempt private company in New Jersey. ETS publishes the GRE under the sponsorship of the Graduate Record Examinations Board, which is an organization affiliated with the Association of Graduate Schools and the Council of Graduate Schools in the United States.

ETS is the organization that brings you the Scholastic Aptitude Test (SAT), the Graduate Management Admissions Test (GMAT), the National Teacher Examination (NTE), and licensing and certification exams in dozens of fields, including hair styling, plumbing, and golf.

Scheduling a Test

You can schedule a test session for the GRE (which, by the way, will cost you $105) by calling 800-GRE-CALL. Or, you can register online at www.gre.org. General inquiries about the GRE can be made by calling Educational Testing Services at 609-921-9000. You may also call your local test center to set up an appointment (a list of centers is available from ETS). In order to schedule your test by phone, you must pay by VISA, American Express, or Mastercard.

Stay Current

The information in this book is accurate right now and will be updated yearly. However, the publishing business is such that if the test changed tomorrow (which it won't), the book might be a little behind.

Therefore, obtain the most current information possible on your test by visiting GRE's website at www.gre.org, or checking our website, www.PrincetonReview.com.

HOW THE VERBAL AND QUANTITATIVE SECTIONS WORK

The GRE is a computer-adaptive test. Computer-adaptive tests use your performance on one question to determine which question you will be asked next. The GRE begins with ETS assuming that you have the average score in a particular category—for example, a 480 in Verbal. You'll be asked a question of difficulty appropriate to this score level: If you answer correctly, the computer adjusts your score to a new level, say 550, and your next question is more difficult. If you answer incorrectly, your score will drop and your next question will be less difficult. In addition to adjusting your score, the amount your score will change with each new correct or incorrect answer is reduced as you move further into the test, so by the end the computer will have effectively zeroed in on your GRE score. That's the theory, anyway.

WHAT DOES ALL THIS MEAN?

It means that how much credit you get for a harder question depends on what you've done on the questions before you get to that harder question. If you've correctly answered all the questions before it, you're going to get more credit for answering a hard question correctly than you would if you had missed a bunch of questions before the hard question. In a nutshell: **Your responses to the first questions in a section will have a greater impact on your final score than will your responses to questions later in the section**, after the computer has already determined your score range. So be EXTRA careful in the beginning of each section. Also, you will be penalized for not giving an answer to every question in a section. So you must **answer every question**, whether you do any actual work on it or not (more on that in the next chapter).

Never try to figure out how difficult a question is. Just concentrate on working carefully on each question that you get. You'll learn a lot more about pacing, as well as other general strategy techniques, in the next chapter.

YOUR OWN PERSONAL GRE

The adaptive nature of the GRE means that no two people will have the same test. The question you're looking at on the screen at any given time has been "chosen" in response to how you did on the previous question.

Because the computer "decides" what to do next, based on how you answer the question on the screen, you MUST answer that question. There is no skipping a question and coming back to it later. And once you answer it, it's gone forever. The computer will ask you to confirm your choice, giving you one more chance to change your answer; once you confirm, that question is out of your life forever. That means you can't afford to make any careless errors. Throughout this book, you'll learn how to avoid making them.

COMPUTER TESTING FACTS

- You can take the GRE almost any day during the first three weeks of every month, morning or afternoon, weekday or weekend. Appointments are scheduled on a first-come, first-served basis. You may take the test only once per calendar month.

- There's no real deadline for registering for the test (technically, you can register the day before). But there's a limited number of seats available on any given day, and centers do fill up, sometimes weeks in advance. It's good to give yourself at least a couple of weeks of lead time to register.

- The GRE is technically simple: All you need to do is point a mouse arrow at the answer and click, then click a second box to confirm your choice and move to the next question.

- It's true that the lack of a physical test booklet makes it impossible to write directly on the problems themselves (to cross out incorrect answers, etc.). But you do get scratch paper, so your work space is limitless. No cramming your work into the margins of the test booklet. And you're going to find as you read this book that your use of scratch paper is one of the keys to scoring well on the GRE.

- You receive your Verbal and Quantitative raw scores right after you finish the exam (instantly!) and your Analytical Writing scores and "official" percentile scores for all three sections a few weeks later in the mail. But you will never see your actual test or the questions you got wrong. Disclosure is virtually non-existent for the GRE; all ETS offers is the GRE Diagnostic Service. The GRE Diagnostic Service (http://grediagnostic.ets.org:444/basic/gre.htm) allows you to review your test once you have received your official scores in the mail, but the method of review is very limited. You can see how many questions you missed, and where they fell on the test, but you cannot review the actual questions and so cannot learn from your mistakes. The diagnostic service also claims to let you know the level of difficulty of the questions you missed, but the scale used—a simple scale of 1–5—is neither particularly descriptive nor useful. So the bottom line is that while ETS has made some effort to provide limited disclosure for the GRE, the information that is actually disclosed is of questionable utility at best.

HOW TO USE THIS BOOK

This book is full of our tried-and-true GRE test-taking techniques, some of which, at first, might seem to violate your gut instincts. In order to take full advantage of our methods, you will have to trust them enough to make them automatic. So, besides telling you everything you need to know about scoring high on the GRE, we've provided you with sets of practice questions at the end of the book. The Verbal and Math "practice sets" are grouped according to difficulty: easy, medium, and difficult. There's no difficulty level for the Analytical Writing practice essay questions.

After you finish working through the instructional chapters of this book, work through the easy set of practice questions. Then check your answers and see how you did (explanations to each question follow in chapter 21). Use the questions you got wrong (if any!) as a guide to what topics you still need to review. Then go back through the book and review those topics. Afterward, move on to the medium sets, following the same process: Do the questions, check your answers, use the questions you got wrong (if any!) as a guide to what topics you still need to review, and go back through the book and review those topics. After that, follow the same process with the difficult question sets. Finally, write essays for each of the Analytical Writing topics given, and score your essays against the set of scoring criteria we give and the sample essay we've written for each question. Give your full attention to each essay while you're writing it, and don't go over the time limit of 45 minutes for the Analysis of an Issue essay and 30 minutes for the Analysis of an Argument essay. It's extremely important that you learn not only to answer Verbal and Quantitative questions under time constraints, but that you also learn to write a solid, high-scoring essay under time constraints. Practice is the only way to ensure that.

(Note: In case you've just gotten the brilliant idea to write an essay ahead of time for all the possible topics, all we can say is, "Don't do it." You will probably be able to write a great essay after practicing 5-10 times for both types of essay. The website contains over 120 topics for each essay type, so writing that many essays would be really redundant, not to mention a big time-waster! If you're feeling truly insecure about writing the essays, a better use of the official list from the website would be to spend five minutes doing the initial brainstorming process and writing the outline of the points you'll make—we'll go into this in detail in the Analytical Writing chapters later—for 20 or so of the topics from each list. That way, you'll be practicing how to attack a variety of topics without spending all the time to actually write an essay for each topic.)

REAL GREs

When you've finished with all the practice sets and essay questions, you're ready to practice what you've learned on our online practice GREs and "real GREs."

By "real GREs," we *don't* mean the practice tests in other coaching books, which often bear only a superficial resemblance to the questions actually used on the test; if you try our techniques on questions in other books, they might not work, because our techniques are designed for actual GREs. Even the questions in this book are not actual questions from real GREs, although we design our questions using the same methods as those used in designing real GREs. In addition, remember that any question you do in this book, even the practice questions in the back, will be unrealistic in at least one way: They're printed in a book, and not on a computer screen. So, to simulate the computer-based test experience as closely as possible, you should always do practice questions with scratch paper.

"Real GREs" are real questions from past GREs, and they provide the very best way to practice our techniques and to prepare for the test. The only source of real GREs is the publisher of the test, ETS, which so far has refused to let anyone (including us) license actual questions from old tests. We strongly recommend, therefore, that you purchase *GRE POWERPREP® Software—Test Preparation for the GRE General Test*, which includes a retired GRE question pool presented in the computer-adaptive mode. Or, you could purchase the book *Practicing to Take the GRE General Test*, 9th Edition, which also contains actual GRE questions. To order either of these, call the ETS publications office at 800-537-3160, or go to the website at www.gre.org. And don't forget that ETS also publishes all the possible essay topics for the analytical writing section on its GRE website.

(Note: In case you've just gotten the brilliant idea to write an essay ahead of time for all the possible topics, all we can say is, "Don't do it." You will probably be able to write a great essay after practicing 5-10 times for both types of essay. The website contains over 120 topics for each essay type, so writing that many essays would be really redundant, not to mention a big time-waster! If you're feeling truly insecure about writing the essays, a better use of the official list from the website would be to spend five minutes doing the initial brainstorming process and writing the outline of the points you'll make—we'll go into this in detail in the Analytical Writing chapters later—for 20 or so of the topics from each list. That way, you'll be practicing how to attack a variety of topics without spending all the time to actually write an essay for each topic.)

Remember, the real GREs available in the book are paper-and-pencil tests, so use them to practice content. *POWERPREP* allows you to practice on a computer in the computer-adaptive test style. Whatever you use, practice with scratch paper. As you prepare for the GRE, work through every question you do, in this book or anywhere else, as if the question is being presented on a computer screen. That means using scratch paper, copying things down on it, and not doing *anything* in your head. You'll learn more about how to do that throughout this book.

OUR ONLINE TOOLS

POWERPREP isn't the only way for you to practice taking the GRE on a computer. Don't forget that *Cracking the GRE* is more than just a book—it's also an interactive online test-preparation course. See page viii at the beginning of the book for information on how to register (there's no charge). You'll get access not only to online review modules designed to reinforce the lessons in this book, but also additional full-length practice GREs.

These tests look and act like the real computer-adaptive GRE, down to the time-clock clicking ominously away at the bottom of the screen. After you finish each test, you'll receive a personalized score report identifying your strengths and weaknesses, so you'll know which parts of the book you need to study a bit more and which parts you have down cold. You should take all four tests. The more you familiarize yourself with the computer-adaptive format, the better you'll feel when you're finally sitting in front of the computer screen at the testing center, ready to take the GRE.

2

General Strategy

CRACKING THE SYSTEM

Lesson One: The GRE definitely does NOT measure your intelligence, nor does it measure how well you will do in graduate school. The sooner you accept this, the better off you'll be. Despite what ETS says or admissions officers think, the GRE is less a measure of your intelligence than it is a measure of your ability to take ETS tests.

I THOUGHT THE GRE WAS COACH-PROOF

ETS has long claimed that one cannot be coached to do better on its tests. If the GRE was indeed a test of intelligence, that would be true. But, the GRE is NOT a measure of intelligence; it's a test of how well you handle standardized tests. And that's something that everyone can be taught. The first step in doing better on the GRE is realizing that.

THIS IS GOOD NEWS FOR YOU

This means that your ability to take ETS tests can be improved. With proper instruction and sufficient practice, virtually all test-takers can raise their scores, often substantially. You don't need to make yourself smarter in order to do this; you just need to make yourself better at taking ETS tests. That's why you bought this book.

WHY SHOULD I LISTEN TO THE PRINCETON REVIEW?

Quite simply, we monitor the GRE. Our teaching methods for cracking it were developed through exhaustive analysis of all available GREs and careful research into the methods by which standardized tests are constructed. Our focus is on the basic concepts that will enable you to attack any problem, strip it down to its essential components, and solve it in as little time as possible.

THINK LIKE THE TEST-WRITERS

You might be surprised to learn that the GRE isn't written by distinguished professors, renowned scholars, or graduate-school admissions officers. For the most part, it's written by ordinary ETS employees, sometimes with freelance help from local graduate students. There's no reason to be intimidated by these people.

As you become more familiar with the test, you will also develop a sense of "the ETS mentality." This is a predictable kind of thinking that influences nearly every part of nearly every ETS exam. By learning to recognize the ETS mentality, you'll earn points even when you aren't sure why an answer is correct. You'll inevitably do better on the test by learning to think like the people who wrote it.

THE ONLY "CORRECT" ANSWER IS THE ONE THAT EARNS YOU POINTS

The instructions on the GRE tell you to select the "best" answer to each question. ETS calls them "best" answers, or the "credited" responses, instead of "correct" answers to protect itself from the complaints of test-takers who might be tempted to quarrel with ETS's judgment. Remember, you have to choose from the choices ETS gives you, and sometimes, especially on the Verbal section, you might not LOVE any of them. But your job is to find the one answer for which ETS gives credit.

CRACKING THE SYSTEM

"Cracking the system" is our term for getting inside the minds of the people who write these tests. The emphasis on earning points rather than on finding the "correct" answer may strike you as somewhat cynical, but it is crucial to doing well on the GRE. After all, the GRE leaves you no room to make explanations or justifications for your responses.

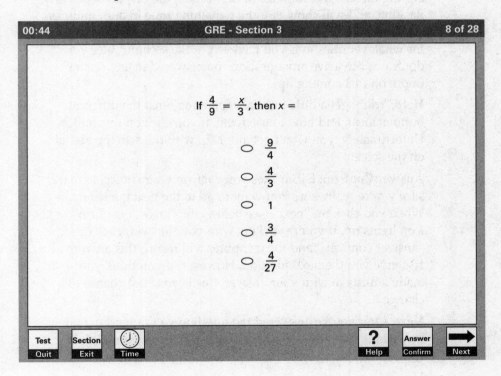

This is NOT a test of intelligence!

You'll do better on the GRE by putting aside your feelings about *real* education and surrendering yourself to the strange logic of the standardized test.

COMPUTER-ADAPTIVE TESTING

Okay, let's start talking strategy for the Verbal and Quantitative sections (the essay section is a completely different animal, which we'll deal with later). Come back to this chapter a few days before test day to review it.

WHAT THE VERBAL AND QUANTITATIVE QUESTIONS LOOK LIKE

When there's a question on the screen, it will look like this:

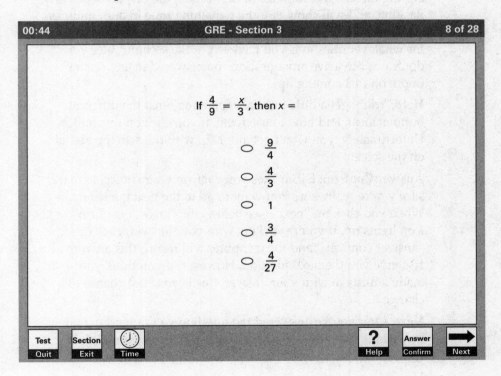

The problem you're working on will be in the middle of the screen. The answer choices will have little bubbles next to them. To choose an answer, you click on the bubble that corresponds to the choice you have selected.

A readout of the time remaining in the section will be displayed in the upper left corner (if you want it to be displayed); the number of questions you've done and the total number of questions in the section will be displayed in the upper right corner. The bottom of the screen will contain the following buttons, from left to right:

Test Quit: You can end the test at any moment by clicking on this button. However, unless you become violently ill, we do not recommend that you ever do this. Even if you decide not to have this test scored (an option you get when you're done with the exam), you should finish the test. After all, it's great practice for when you finally want the test to count. Besides, you can't get a refund from ETS.

Section Exit: You'll be taken out of the section you're working on by clicking on this button. You should only click on this button when you're sure that you're done with a section. Once you exit, there's no turning back.

Time: You can make visible or hide the digital countdown by clicking on this button. Some people like to have it on the screen; others like to look at their watches instead. Whatever you decide, when time is almost up, the display will appear or reappear on the screen even if you've told it to go away earlier. During the last five minutes of the section, the display will start flashing, and will show you the remaining time in both minutes AND seconds. This is a good time to guess your favorite letter for whatever questions you have left in the section, since you don't want to leave any questions unanswered in any section (more on that coming up).

Help: You'll get a little tutorial explaining what the different buttons mean and how to use them, if you click on this button. Unfortunately, you won't get any help with the actual material on the screen!

Answer Confirm: ETS makes you confirm your choice, to make sure you're really sure you want to go to the next question. When you click on "next" (see below) the "answer confirm" icon lights up. If you're sticking with your answer, click on "answer confirm," and the computer will record this answer and give you the next question. However, if you think you made a mistake with your answer, this is your last chance to change it.

Next: After you've answered the question you're working on by clicking the bubble next to the answer choice you think is correct, click on this button.

The ETS Elf

Remember when you were a kid and you thought that people on TV were really in the television? Well, that's sort of what's happening with the GRE. It's like an irritating little ETS Elf is hanging out inside your computer, crafting your test as you go along. This is simplified, of course, but you'll see what we mean.

Say you're doing the first math question in the Math section. The ETS Elf is in the computer, waiting to see what you'll pick. He's starting you out with, say, a 500 as a score. You pick your answer; you got it right! The ETS Elf bumps your score up to, say, a 550, laughs maniacally, and throws you your next question— a harder math question. He waits to see what you'll pick . . . oops! You got it wrong. The ETS Elf knocks your score down to, say, a 510, and gives you a slightly easier problem next. Let's say you don't know what the answer to this one is, but you make an educated guess (we'll teach you how) and get it right. The ETS Elf raises your score to a 530, and gives you a slightly harder problem. And so on, and so forth.

So, when you get a correct answer, the ETS Elf "rewards" you with a harder question; when you get an incorrect answer, the ETS Elf "rewards" you with an easier question. Potentially, every tester can have a different test in terms of the questions that he or she sees. You won't know how you did on the prior question, so just focus on doing your best on each question.

Some Questions Are More Equal than Others

At the beginning of your test, your score moves up and down in larger increments (sometimes as much as 80 points) than it does at the end, when the ETS Elf has largely zeroed in on your score and is now merely refining it—trying to decide whether you deserve, say, a 630 or a 640.

This means that the ETS Elf gives varying weights to the questions. The questions are roughly divided into thirds, and the first third of the questions in any section is weighted the most. This means that **the first third of the questions in a section determines the bulk of your score**. The second third accounts for a lesser amount of the scaled score, and the third third counts for a relatively insignificant amount of your overall score. So, make sure you do your best on the first third of the questions in each section.

| You CAN improve your scores!

Answer Every Question

Again, be sure to be accurate on early questions. The ETS Elf doesn't let you go backward, so do not move on to the next question until you are sure about your answer (or about your guess). You'll be penalized for incorrect answers, but the penalty becomes less strict as you get deeper into each section. But get this: You will also be penalized for not giving an answer to every question in a section.

Basically, the ETS Elf will reduce your raw score by the percentage of unanswered questions in a section (e.g., a 30-question section with 6 questions left blank will mean a 20 percent reduction of your raw score). So, do not leave any question unanswered.

LET THE COMPUTER HELP YOU

During the last five minutes of a section, the time display on the computer screen will start flashing, showing you the remaining time in both minutes and seconds. Let this be your signal to start wrapping things up by guessing your favorite letter for whatever questions you have left in the section, since you don't want to leave any questions unanswered in any section. So, remember:

1. Don't rush

Instinct might suggest that if there's a penalty for blanks and a possibility for lost points due to incorrect answers, testers should work as quickly as possible, in order to leave enough time to work the final few questions. But the impulse to rush through the early questions is dangerous, as these questions are worth considerably more points than the later ones. To maximize your score, work slowly and carefully at the beginning of the section. **A high degree of accuracy in the first third to half of each section is the single most important factor in earning the highest possible scores on the GRE.**

2. Guess aggressively

Once you've worked carefully through the first third to half of the section, for the remainder of the test it is important to avoid getting bogged down in time-consuming questions. If you encounter a question that seems extremely difficult or time-consuming, eliminate answers that you know are wrong, and make an educated guess (you're about to learn more about this). This will allow you to get to subsequent questions, which may be more easily worked, with enough time to work them.

3. Respond to every question

During the last five minutes of the section, when the time display starts flashing, start guessing your favorite letter for whatever questions you have left in the section, since you don't want to leave any questions unanswered in any section.

WAIT A MINUTE

Remember: All the answers you need are on your screen.

Remember, the question you see on your screen at a particular time depends on how you answered the previous question. And the ETS Elf picks the next question based on how you just did on the previous one. This means you can never skip a question; otherwise, how would the Elf know what to give you next?

Since you have to answer every question, but may not know how to do every question, you're probably going to have to guess at least once, and maybe more times, on the test. But we're not talking about random guessing. After all, the right answer is on the screen.

CAN I HAVE PARTIAL CREDIT?

Remember when you were in high school, and even if you got a question wrong on a test, your teacher gave you partial credit? For example, you used the right formula on a math question, miscalculated and got the wrong result, but your teacher gave you some credit because you understood the concept?

Well, those days are over. ETS doesn't care how you got your answer; it only cares about whether or not you have clicked on the right answer choice. You might as well benefit from this by getting questions right without really knowing how to do them. And you do that with the Process of Elimination, or POE. POE is your new way of life. Learn it. Live it. Love it.

THE AMAZING POWER OF POE—PROCESS OF ELIMINATION

One fabulous thing about the GRE is that the "best" answer is always on the screen; you don't have to come up with it out of thin air. However, because there are roughly four times as many wrong answers as there are right answers, it's often easier to identify wrong answers than to identify the right one.

POE is your new way of life.

THE IMPORTANCE OF WRONG ANSWERS

By using POE, you will be able to improve your score on the GRE by looking for wrong answers instead of right ones on questions you find to be difficult. Why? Because, once you've found the wrong ones, picking the right one can be a piece of cake.

Wrong answers on standardized multiple-choice tests are known in the testing industry as "distractors." They are called distractors because their purpose is to distract testers away from correct choices on questions they don't understand. This keeps them from earning points accidentally, by picking the right answer for the wrong reasons.

This simple fact will be an enormous help to you. By learning to recognize these distractors, you will greatly improve your score.

IMPROVE YOUR ODDS INDIRECTLY

Every time you are able to eliminate an incorrect choice on a GRE question, you improve your odds of finding the best answer. The more incorrect choices you eliminate, the better your odds.

For this reason, some of our test-taking strategies are aimed at helping you to arrive at ETS's answer indirectly. Doing this will make you much more successful at avoiding the traps laid in your path by the test-writers. This is because most of the traps are designed to catch unwary test-takers who try to approach the problems directly.

POE AND GUESSING

If you guessed blindly on a five-choice GRE problem, you would have one chance in five of picking ETS's answer. Eliminate one incorrect choice, and your chances improve to one in four. Eliminate three, and you have a 50/50 chance of earning points by guessing. Get the picture? You must answer each question to get to the next one, so you'll have to guess sometimes. Why not improve your odds?

Guess, but guess intelligently.

USE THAT PAPER!

For POE to work, it's crucial that you keep track of what choices you're eliminating. By crossing out a clearly incorrect choice, you permanently eliminate it from consideration. If you don't cross it out, you'll keep considering it. Crossing out incorrect choices can make it much easier to find the "credited response," because there will be fewer places where it can hide. But how can you cross anything out on a computer screen?

By using your scratch paper! Even though on the GRE, the answer choices have empty bubbles next to them, you're going to pretend that they are labeled A, B, C, D, and E (and so are we, throughout this book). Use the time during your tutorial (which you'll learn about on the next page) to write down the letters A, B, C, D, E on your scratch paper.

A B C D E	A B C D E	A B C D E	A B C D E
A B C D E	A B C D E	A B C D E	A B C D E

Carve up at least a couple of pages (front and back) like this. This will give you a bunch of distinct work areas per page, and is especially helpful for the math section; you don't want to get confused when your work from one question runs into your work from a previous question.

Do this and you can physically cross off choices that you're eliminating. Do it every time you do any GRE question, in this book or anywhere else. Get used to not writing near the question, since you won't be able to on test day.

MORE ABOUT SCRATCH PAPER

You'll get about six sheets of scratch paper on test day, and although that may be more than enough, it couldn't hurt to have more. You don't want to run out during a section, right? So, why not ask for extra paper before the test starts? Some test centers don't like to give out extra sheets until the initial six are used up, but it doesn't hurt to ask.

PACE YOURSELF

Remember, you don't get points for speed; the only thing that matters is accuracy. Take as much time as necessary to work through each problem carefully (as long as you leave some time at the end of the section to complete the rest of it).

If you miss the question that you're looking at on the screen at any given time, you will need to get at least the next two right just to get your score back up to where it was before (roughly). But if you're making careless errors, you won't even realize you're missing questions. Not using POE is like being careless. So keep track of the choices you've eliminated.

Always cross off wrong answer choices on your scratch paper.

DOUBLE-CHECK

Get in the habit of double-checking all of your answers before you choose them. Remember, there is no skipping a question and coming back to it later. Once you confirm your answer, that question is out of your life forever. Again, that means that you can't afford to make any careless errors. You must make educated guesses by eliminating as many wrong answers as you can and making sure your thought process and calculations are sound. And don't worry—you're about to get some help in that department.

AT THE TESTING CENTER

Don't be surprised if you're the only one taking the GRE, or indeed, any test, at your testing center. You'll be asked for two forms of identification; one must be a photo ID. Then an employee will take a digital photograph of you (even worse than your driver's license picture!) before taking you to the computer station where you will take the test. You get a desk, a computer, a keyboard, a mouse, about six pieces of scratch paper, and a few pencils. Some test centers will even offer you earplugs. Before the test begins, make sure your desk is sturdy and you have enough light, and don't be afraid to speak up if you want to move.

If there are other people in the room, they might not be taking the GRE. They could be taking a nursing test, or a licensing exam for architects. They may not even be starting their exams at the same time. Therefore, you should pay no attention to when other people finish sections or take breaks—it has no relation to how you're doing.

The testing center employee will get you set up at your computer, but from then on, the computer itself will act as your proctor. It will tell you how much time you have left in a section, when time is up, and when to move on to the next section.

If you need more scratch paper, or have a question, the test center employees will be available because they will be monitoring the testing room for security purposes with closed-circuit television. But don't worry, you won't even notice.

THE TUTORIAL

Before the actual test begins, you'll get an interactive tutorial on how to take the test, computer-wise. Even a computer novice should have no problem with this extremely simple interface. You'll learn how to use the mouse, select an answer, move on to the next question, see how much time you have left in a section, and even stop the test if you need to (but you won't need to). Take as much time as you need to practice each of these functions and get comfortable with your surroundings, the computer and mouse, and the test directions; there is no time limit on the tutorial.

Use the time you have during the tutorial to set up your scratch paper, jot down the step-by-step strategies for each section of the test, and note any math formulas or vocabulary words you always have trouble remembering. You can do whatever you want with this paper and this time, so use them both wisely.

Remember, you can ask for extra paper too. Take as much as you can get. If you have to request more scratch paper during the test, try to do so between the timed sections. But talk to the proctor at the test center before the test begins to make whatever arrangements are necessary to ensure that you will have plenty of scratch paper.

LET IT GO

When you begin a new section, focus on that section and put the last one behind you. Don't think about that pesky antonym from an earlier section while a geometry question is on your screen now. You can't go back, and besides, your impression of how you did on a section is probably much worse than reality.

THIS IS THE END

When you're done with the test, the computer will ask you (twice) if you want this test to count. If you say "no," the computer will not record your score, no schools will ever see it, and neither will you. You can't look at your score and THEN decide whether you want to keep it or not. And you can't change your mind later. If you say you want the test to count, the computer will give you your score right there on the screen. A few weeks later, you'll receive your verified score in the mail (but no copy of the test you took!), along with your Analytical Writing section score, and you can't change your mind and cancel them.

TEST DAY TIPS

- Dress in layers, so that you'll be comfortable regardless of whether the room is cool or warm.

- Don't bother bringing a calculator; you're not allowed to use one.

- Be sure to have breakfast, or lunch, depending on the time for which your test is scheduled (but don't eat anything, you know, "weird"). And take it easy on the liquids and the caffeine.

- Do a few GRE practice problems beforehand to warm up your brain. Don't try to tackle difficult new questions, but review a few questions that you've done before to help you review the problem-solving strategies for each section of the GRE. This will also help you put your "game-face" on and get you into test mode.

- Make sure to bring two forms of identification, one with a recent photograph, to the test center. Acceptable forms of identification include your driver's license, photo-bearing employee ID cards, and valid passports.

- If you registered by mail, you must also bring the authorization voucher sent to you by ETS.

The Week Before the Test

A week before the test is not the time for any major life changes. This is NOT the week to quit smoking, start smoking, quit drinking coffee, start drinking coffee, start a relationship, end a relationship, or quit a job. Business as usual, okay?

Remember: Stay Current

The information in this book is accurate right now and will be updated yearly. But remember, the publishing business is such that if the test changed tomorrow (which it won't), the book might be a little behind. But the websites won't be. So, before you take your GRE, check out www.gre.org or www.PrincetonReview.com to see if there is any last minute GRE news.

PART II

How to Crack the Verbal Section

3

The Geography of the Verbal Section

WHAT'S IN THE VERBAL SECTION

Every GRE contains a scored verbal section, which lasts 30 minutes and contains 30 questions, in no particular order, broken down as follows:

- Six to eight Analogies
- Five to seven Sentence Completions
- Eight to ten Antonyms
- Two to four Reading Comprehension passages, with a total of six to ten questions

Most of the time, the Verbal section starts with a few Antonyms. Analogies and Antonyms are classified by ETS as "vocabulary" problems, and Sentence Completions and Reading Comprehension are classified as "reading" problems. You might not see Reading Comp until question eight or twelve. Generally, the higher you're scoring, the more "vocabulary" questions you'll see. Vocabulary is a big part of all these question types, but so is strategy.

ON THE SCREEN

All Verbal questions are multiple-choice questions with five answer choices. The Reading Comprehension passages will appear on split screens, usually with a scroll bar. Make sure you scroll down as far as you can, to guarantee that you are seeing the entire passage.

POE

There is never a "right" answer to a Verbal question. ETS calls the correct answer the "credited response," or "best" answer. Think of the best answer as the one that is the least bad. So, if you can recognize the bad answers and eliminate them, you can zero in on the best answer. That's how Process of Elimination (POE) works. However, if you're not sure what a word in an answer choice means, *don't eliminate it*. It might be the best answer. Only eliminate answers you *know* are wrong.

POE is your new way of life.

SCRATCH PAPER

You're going to learn strategies for all four types of Verbal questions. So the first thing you should do during the tutorial on the actual GRE is write down all the strategies on your scratch paper, so you never have to think, "What should I do next?"

You may be tempted to do the verbal questions in your head. Don't. Use your scratch paper, not only for jotting down strategy, but also for POE. Always write down A, B, C, D, E on your scratch paper so you can physically cross out choices you're eliminating.

THE IMPORTANCE OF VOCABULARY

Because of its heavy emphasis on the GRE, you need to work on your vocabulary right away. Most people seem to find that increasing their Verbal scores is more difficult than increasing their Math scores. The reason for this is that vocabulary places something of a ceiling on your score. The better your vocabulary, the higher your ceiling and the higher your possible scores.

The best way to build a good vocabulary is to read a wide variety of good books over the course of a lifetime. Since you don't have a lifetime to prepare for the GRE, you should turn ahead to page 80, the GRE Hit Parade. It contains a relatively short vocabulary list of the words that are most frequently tested on the GRE. It also contains some solid vocabulary-building advice. Skim through it right now and plan a vocabulary-building program for yourself. You should work on your vocabulary a little bit every day while you work through the rest of the book.

Using your newly strengthened vocabulary as a foundation, you will be able to take full advantage of the powerful problem-solving techniques we describe in the next four chapters. Our techniques will enable you to get as much mileage as possible from the words you do know. But the more words you know, the better.

> Start working on your vocabulary now.

THREE KINDS OF WORDS

Think of vocabulary words in terms of these three categories:

- **Words you know**—These are words you can define accurately. If you can't give a definition of a word that's pretty close to what a dictionary would say, then it's not a word you know.

- **Words you sort of know**—These are words you've seen or heard before, or maybe even used yourself, but can't define accurately. You may have a sense of how these words are used, but beware! Day-to-day usage is often different from the dictionary meanings of words, and *the only meanings that count on the GRE are those given in the dictionary*. You have to treat these words very differently from the words you can define. After you encounter a word you sort of know in this book, be sure to look it up in the dictionary and make it a word you know from then on.

- **Words you've never seen**—You can expect to see some words in this book you've never seen before. After you encounter a word like this, *go to the dictionary and look it up!* If it's been on one GRE, there's a good bet it will show up again. If you've never seen one of the words in an answer choice, *don't eliminate that choice*. Focus on the answer choices for which you can define the words.

4

Analogies

WHAT YOU WILL SEE

The Verbal section of your GRE will contain eight to ten Analogies.

ETS's DIRECTIONS

ALWAYS write A, B, C, D, E on your scratch paper to represent the answer choices.

Take a minute to read the following set of directions. These are the directions exactly as they will appear on your GRE. You shouldn't even glance at them when you take the test. If you do, you will waste time and lose points. Read them now and you'll never have to read them again:

> Directions: In each of the following questions, a related pair of words or phrases is followed by five pairs of words or phrases. Select the pair that best expresses a relationship similar to that expressed in the original pair.

WHAT IS AN ANALOGY?

An analogy tests your ability to recognize pairs of words that have similar relationships. Your job is to figure out the relationship between the original pair of words, we'll call them the "stem words," and find an answer choice in which the words have the same relationship.

Let's look at an example:

FRICTION : ABRASION ::

- ◯ sterility : cleanliness
- ◯ dam : flood
- ◯ laceration : wound
- ◯ heat : evaporation
- ◯ literacy : ignorance

THE BASIC TECHNIQUE

In this example, we know from the directions that a related pair of words or phrases is followed by five pairs of words or phrases. So ETS considers the words "friction" and "abrasion" to be related in some way. What's the relationship? If you can define both of the stem words, your first step in solving a GRE Analogy is to make a simple sentence that shows the relationship between the stem words. We would say, "Friction causes abrasion." We wouldn't say, "Abrasive substances can sometimes simulate a feeling of friction." Get it? Don't tell a story. Just define one word in terms of the other. In other words, make a "defining" sentence.

PROCESS OF ELIMINATION

The best answer to an Analogy will be the pair of words in an answer choice that has the same relationship as the original pair. So use Process of Elimination. The words have to fit exactly in the sentence you made for the original pair of words. If you know the words in the answer choice and they don't fit into the sentence, eliminate that choice. Be sure to cross off answer choices on your scratch paper! If you're not sure you can define the words in an answer choice, don't eliminate that choice!

Let's look at our example:

Do you know the DICTIONARY DEFINITION of the word?

FRICTION : ABRASION ::

- ○ sterility : cleanliness
- ○ dam : flood
- ○ laceration : wound
- ○ heat : evaporation
- ○ literacy : ignorance

(A) Does "sterility cause cleanliness"? No. So cross off choice (A) on your scratch paper.

(B) Does a "dam cause a flood"? No. Eliminate this choice.

(C) Does a "laceration cause a wound"? Nope. Get rid of this choice.

(D) Does "heat cause evaporation"? Maybe. Let's keep this choice and look at the last choice.

(E) Does "literacy cause ignorance"? No way.

So, by Process of Elimination, the best choice to this analogy must be (D), "heat : evaporation."

DEFINE ONE OF THE WORDS IN TERMS OF THE OTHER WORD

Always try to make your sentence define one of the words in terms of the other. Try to keep it short and simple. Let's try another example:

LISTLESS : EXCITE ::

- ○ stuffy : brag
- ○ skeptical : convince
- ○ industrious : produce
- ○ scholarly : instruct
- ○ impenetrable : ignore

Here's how to crack it

We could express the relationship between the stem words in several different ways. We could say, "Someone listless is difficult to excite," or we could put it, "Listless means difficult to excite." It doesn't matter which we choose. We don't need to find the *perfect* sentence. **All that matters is that you find a sentence that expresses the relationship between the stem words.**

Let's go through the answer choices.

(A) Does "stuffy" mean difficult to "brag"? No. So cross off this choice.

(B) Does "skeptical" mean difficult to "convince"? Yes, but don't stop here. You should check every answer choice.

(C) Does "industrious" mean difficult to "produce"? No. So we can eliminate this choice.

(D) Does "scholarly" mean difficult to "instruct"? No. Eliminate.

(E) Does "impenetrable" mean difficult to "ignore"? No. So this choice doesn't work either.

The best answer is (B). Notice how the words in choice (B) fit *exactly* into our sentence.

Do You Have to Make a Sentence From Left to Right?

No. Sometimes it's easier to define the second word in terms of the first. Do it! Just be sure to plug in the answer choices in the same order that you used to make your sentence.

Write it Down!

This can't be stressed enough. If you try to make your sentence "in your head," you might forget it after you try a few answer choices. Then you would have to go back to the stem words and start all over. Even worse, if you try to "remember" your sentence, you might change it to agree with one of the answer choices. That defeats the whole purpose of Process of Elimination!

So remember, always write your sentence on your scratch paper. If you make your sentence from right to left, draw an arrow indicating this for that question to remind you to plug in the answer choices from right to left.

COMMON GRE RELATIONSHIPS

Certain relationships show up frequently on the GRE. If you are very familiar with these relationships, it will be easier for you to make good sentences for the stem words on many Analogies questions. Try the following drill to learn some common relationships:

Drill

Make a sentence for each of the following pair of stem words. You don't have to make your sentence from left to right. Go in the direction that makes the most definitive sentence. (Check your work on page 40.)

STEM WORDS	YOUR SENTENCE
ORGAN : KIDNEY	_____
CENTRIFUGE : SEPARATE	_____
LASSITUDE : ENERGY	_____
FERVOR : ZEALOT	_____
EULOGY : PRAISE	_____
FRUIT: APPLE	_____
MISER : THRIFT	_____
COMPLIANT : SERVILE	_____
LUBRICANT : ABRASION	_____
INEVITABLE : CHANCE	_____

Now try another example:

ETERNAL : END ::

- ⬭ precursory : beginning
- ⬭ grammatical : sentence
- ⬭ implausible : credibility
- ⬭ invaluable : worth
- ⬭ frenetic : movement

Here's how to crack it

This is a very common relationship on the GRE. "Eternal means without end," would be the perfect sentence.

(A) Does "precursory" mean without "beginning"? If you're not sure, keep this choice. By the way, take a minute to look up the word "precursor"; it's on the Hit Parade.

(B) Does "grammatical" mean without "sentence"? No, so you can definitely cross off this choice.

(C) Does "implausible" mean without "credibility"? Yes. So let's keep this choice and consider the others.

(D) Does "invaluable" mean without "worth"? No, just the opposite. Eliminate this one.

(E) Does "frenetic" mean without "movement"? No. So this choice doesn't work.

The best answer is (C). Notice how the words in choice (C) fit *exactly* into our sentence.

Do you know the DICTIONARY DEFINITIONS of the words in the answer choices?

GET MORE SPECIFIC

What happens when more than one answer choice fits your first sentence? Did you make a mistake? No, you might just need to get more specific. Your first sentence should be simple and definitive. Use it to eliminate as many answer choices as you can, and then add information to your first sentence to make it more specific.

DOLPHIN : MAMMAL ::

- ○ larva : insect
- ○ penguin : bird
- ○ sonnet : stanza
- ○ computer : machine
- ○ peninsula : island

If you can't define a word, DON'T eliminate it.

Here's how to crack it

This is another very common relationship on the GRE. "A dolphin is a type of mammal," would be the right sentence with which to begin.

(A) Is a "larva" a type of "insect"? Well, strictly speaking, no. But as always, if you're not sure, keep this choice.

(B) Is a "penguin" a type of "bird"? Definitely; let's keep this choice.

(C) Is a "sonnet" a type of "stanza"? No, so we can get rid of this one.

(D) Is a "computer" a type of "machine"? Yes, so let's keep this one, too.

(E) Is a "peninsula" a type of "island"? No. So this choice doesn't work.

Now, we're left with a few choices that all seem okay. How can we make our original sentence more specific to weed out the wrong answers? A dolphin is *what type* of mammal? A dolphin is a type of mammal that lives in the water. Is a larva a type of insect that lives in the water? No. Ditch it! Is a penguin a type of bird that lives in the water? Close enough. Is a computer a type of machine that lives in the water? Not by a long shot. The best answer is (B).

PARTS OF SPEECH

If the first stem word is a verb and the second is an adjective, the first word in each answer choice will be a verb and the second will be an adjective. ETS never violates this principle. Use it to your advantage.

You may sometimes have trouble determining the part of speech of one of the words in the stem. If this happens, look at the answer choices. ETS uses one of the choices to "establish the parts of speech" when one of the stem words is ambiguous. In other words, if you aren't sure about the words in the stem, check the words in the choices. The parts of speech should be clear from at least one of the choices.

Always determine the parts of speech before you make your sentence for the stem words.

Try this example:

GREEN : EXPERIENCE ::

- ○ ungainly : grace
- ○ rank : knowledge
- ○ indolent : laziness
- ○ impassioned : ardor
- ○ dispirited : despondence

Here's how to crack it

Notice not only that "green" is an adjective, which you can see from the first answer choice, but also that a secondary meaning is being tested. The first meaning we think of is the color green. But what does it mean if a *person* is "green"? Here, green means "lacking experience."

(A) Does "ungainly" mean lacking "grace"? If you're not sure, keep this choice.

(B) Does "rank" mean lacking "knowledge"? No, so you can definitely cross off this choice.

(C) Does "indolent" mean lacking "laziness"? If you're not sure, keep this choice.

(D) Does "impassioned" mean lacking "ardor"? If you're not sure, keep this choice. But really, it means just the opposite. (If you know these words, you can eliminate this choice—so study the Hit Parade!)

(E) Does "dispirited" mean lacking "despondence"? If you're not sure, keep this choice.

Here's where the vocabulary kicks in. If you know that "green" means lacking "experience," and "ungainly" means lacking "grace," that's what you should guess. We'll discuss guessing in greater detail below. The best answer to this one is (A).

> WHAT IF I DON'T KNOW SOME OF THE WORDS IN THE ANSWER CHOICES?

Use Process of Elimination. Assuming you know both words in the stem, you can still ask yourself whether *any* word could create a relationship in the choice identical to the relationship in the stem. If not, you can eliminate that choice.

Eliminate the answer choices that contain words that you can define and that you know can't be correct. But if you're not sure of the meaning of one of the words in an answer choice, don't eliminate that choice! Then see what you have left.

Example:

DRAWL : SPEAK ::

○ spurt : expel
○ foster : develop
○ scintillate : flash
○ pare : trim
○ saunter : walk

Here's how to crack it

Our sentence defining the relationship between the stem words would be "To drawl means to speak slowly."

(A) Does "spurt" mean to "expel" slowly? No, so eliminate this one. Think about it for a second. Could any word mean to "expel" slowly? It's not likely, since "expel" means to force out.

Always eliminate UNRELATED answer choices.

(B) Does "foster" mean to "develop" slowly? No, so you can definitely cross off this choice.

(C) Does "scintillate" mean to "flash" slowly? If you're not sure, keep this choice.

(D) Does "pare" mean to "trim" slowly? No, so you can eliminate this choice.

(E) Does "saunter" mean to "walk" slowly? If you're not sure, keep this choice.

Now that we're down to two choices, perhaps you know that "saunter" does mean to walk slowly, and it fits our sentence exactly, so it must be the best answer choice. Great. But also, could any word mean "to flash slowly"? No; to flash means to occur or emerge suddenly like a flame. (By the way, look up the word "scintillate.")

WHAT IF I DON'T KNOW ONE OF THE STEM WORDS?

Don't give up if you don't know the stem words!

Now you have a good understanding of the sort of relationship that must exist between stem words and correct answer choices in GRE Analogies. Now we're going to show you how to use the same concept to eliminate incorrect answer choices *even if you don't know the meaning of either of the words in the stem.*

REALLY?

How can it be possible to eliminate choices if you don't know the words in the stem? Think about it. Since you know that the stem words must have a relationship, and since the correct answer choice must have a relationship similar to that for the stem words, then the correct answer choice must also have a relationship between the two words. So if the words in an answer choice do NOT have a relationship, that choice cannot be correct! **An answer choice containing two words that aren't related can NEVER be the best answer.**

IMMEDIATELY ELIMINATE NON-RELATIONSHIPS

Try the example below. Notice that we've left out the words in the stem. Eliminate all the answer choices that do not have relationships. That usually won't be enough to narrow it down to only one answer choice, but don't worry, you'll soon see what to do *after* you've eliminated non-relationships.

Example:

XXXXX : XXXXX ::

○ precipitous : mountain
○ judicious : system
○ dispersive : discharge
○ strident : sound
○ epidemic : disease

Here's how to crack it

(A) Are "precipitous" and "mountain" related? No. Precipitous means like a precipice, or extremely steep. Is a mountain necessarily precipitous? No. Eliminate this choice; it can't be the best answer choice.

(B) Are "judicious" and "system" related? No. Judicious means having good judgment, and it's a quality of a person, not a system. Eliminate this choice.

(C) Is there a relationship between "dispersive" and "discharge"? No. Dispersive just means tending to disperse. Is a discharge necessarily dispersive? Nope. Cross out this choice.

(D) Is there a relationship between "strident" and "sound"? Perhaps you're not sure what the dictionary definition of "strident" is, so keep this choice.

(E) Is there a relationship between "epidemic" and "disease"? Sure. A disease can be described as epidemic if it spreads to a lot of people. There's definitely a relationship, so this answer stays.

So even without knowing anything about the stem words in this analogy, we've gotten it down to two possible choices. There's another technique you should use right about now.

Eliminate unrelated pairs.

WORKING BACKWARD

Once you've eliminated answer choices that don't have relationships, you may have two or three choices that do have relationships. Don't forget that the relationship between the stem words must be exactly the same relationship as the one between the words in the correct answer. So, make a sentence for the words in each related answer choice and work backward to the stem words. Would the stem words fit exactly in the sentence you make for the answer choice? If not, the relationship for that answer choice can't be the same as the one for the stem words. Eliminate that choice.

Now let's take another look at the problem we were just doing, as it would appear on the GRE with the stem words. Remember, we've already eliminated the first three choices.

NOISOME : ODOR ::

- ○ precipitous : mountain
- ○ judicious : system
- ○ dispersive : discharge
- ○ strident : sound
- ○ epidemic : disease

Here's how to crack it

(D) What's the relationship between "strident" and "sound"? If you're not sure, just start with choice (E) instead. But if you can define "strident," then your sentence for this answer choice would be "strident means having a harsh or unpleasant sound." Could "noisome" mean having an unpleasant "odor"? That's certainly possible. Let's go to choice (E). Notice that since all the first words of the other pairs are adjectives, "epidemic" is being used as an adjective, too, and not a noun. A sentence using "epidemic" as an adjective with the word "disease" might be, "An epidemic disease is one that spreads rapidly." Could a noisome odor be one that spreads rapidly? What do you really think? Between these two choices, which one is more likely? Noisome does mean having a bad odor, so the best choice is (D).

Here's another example of how first eliminating unrelated pairs, and then working backward, can enable you to zero in on ETS's answer:

LAMENTATION : REMORSE ::

- ◯ reassurance : interactions
- ◯ elegy : sorrow
- ◯ instigation : responses
- ◯ acknowledgment : ideas
- ◯ ornateness : filigree

Here's how to crack it

Let's approach this assuming that you can't exactly define "lamentation."

(A) Is there a relationship between "reassurance" and "interactions"? No. You could tell a convoluted story linking these two words, but we're not going to do that! This can't be the best answer choice.

(B) Is there a relationship between "elegy" and "sorrow"? Maybe you're not exactly sure what "elegy" means at this moment (it's on the Hit Parade, so get to work learning those words). So keep this choice.

(C) Is there a relationship between "instigation" and "responses"? No. Again, you could tell a creative story linking these two words, but ... get rid of it!

(D) Is there a relationship between "acknowledgment" and "ideas"? No. This can't be the best answer choice.

(E) Is there a relationship between "ornateness" and "filigree"? A bit of a stretch, but perhaps. So let's work backward. What would your sentence be? "Filigree" adds "ornateness" to something. Could "remorse" add "lamentation" to something? It's not likely that remorse adds anything to something.

So, Process of Elimination tells us that the best answer must be choice (B). Notice that when we made our sentence from right to left for answer choice (E), we tried the stem words from right to left in the same sentence. Remember that the best answer choice has to have a relationship just like the one between the stem words. So the stem words have to fit exactly into the sentence you make for the answer choice you're considering.

DON'T ELIMINATE WORDS YOU ONLY "SORT OF KNOW"

You can't be certain that two words are unrelated if you are not really sure what one of them means. Hence, don't eliminate any words you only "think" you know.

Here's another example:

SUPPLICANT : BESEECHING ::
- minister : tortured
- coquette : flirtatious
- benefactor : cordial
- lawyer : articulate
- thief : violent

If you only "sort of know" the meaning of a word, DON'T ELIMINATE IT!

Here's how to crack it

Once again, we're assuming that we don't know the meaning of one or both of the words in the stem. Let's eliminate non-related answer choices and work backward.

(A) Is there a relationship between "minister" and "tortured"? Nope. This can't be the best answer choice.

(B) Is there a relationship between "coquette" and "flirtatious"? Maybe, or maybe you're not sure. Keep this choice.

(C) Is there a relationship between "benefactor" and "cordial"? Maybe, or maybe you're not sure. Keep this choice.

(D) Is there a relationship between "lawyer" and "articulate"? No. Cross off this choice.

(E) Is there a relationship between "thief" and "violent"? No. Get rid of this choice.

Now that you're down to only two choices, use whatever you know about the words in those two choices. Focus on the choice for which you have a better sense of the words' meanings. In this case, how would you define a "benefactor"? If you know that a "benefactor" would be defined in terms of providing financial assistance, rather than in terms of some attitude, then you can eliminate (C). The connection between "benefactor" and "cordial" just isn't clear. Looks like the answer is (B).

If you've eliminated all the answer choices with words that you know or sort of know, and you're left with a couple of choices with words that you've never seen before, just guess and move on. Your GRE score is going to be much higher if you are guessing between two choices than it would be if you hadn't eliminated those other three choices by using our techniques.

WON'T IT TAKE HOURS TO APPLY ALL THESE TECHNIQUES?

No. With a little practice, you'll make them your automatic way to solve GRE Analogies. In fact, they'll save you time by making you much more efficient in your approach to the more difficult questions. Get to work learning the Hit Parade now!

ANSWER KEY—ANALOGIES DRILL

STEM WORDS	YOUR SENTENCE
ORGAN : KIDNEY	The kidney **is a type of** organ.
CENTRIFUGE : SEPARATE	The **function of** a centrifuge **is to** separate.
LASSITUDE : ENERGY	Lassitude **means a lack of** energy.
FERVOR : ZEALOT	A zealot **is characterized by** fervor.
EULOGY : PRAISE	A eulogy **is a speech of** praise.
FRUIT : APPLE	An apple **is a type of** fruit.
MISER : THRIFT	A miser **uses excessive** thrift.
COMPLIANT : SERVILE	Servile **means excessively** compliant.
LUBRICANT : ABRASION	The **function of** a lubricant **is to prevent** abrasion.
INEVITABLE : CHANCE	Inevitable **means without** chance.

Have you been studying your vocabulary words?

5

Sentence Completions

WHAT YOU WILL SEE

The Verbal section of your GRE will contain five to seven Sentence Completions.

ETS's Directions

Read and learn the following set of directions. These are the directions as they will appear on your GRE. You shouldn't even glance at them when you take the test. Here are the directions:

> Directions: Each sentence below has one or two blanks, each blank indicating that something has been omitted. Beneath the sentence are five words or sets of words. Choose the word or set of words for each blank that best fits the meaning of the sentence as a whole.

OUR APPROACH TO SENTENCE COMPLETIONS

Our techniques for cracking Sentence Completions take advantage of the way that these questions are designed: All are based on POE. Sometimes you will be able to use POE to eliminate all four incorrect choices. On every Sentence Completion, you should be able to eliminate at least a few choices.

"I Already Know How to Do These"

Sentence completions look very familiar—you've known them since kindergarten as *fill in the blanks*—but beware! The way ETS designs these problems is very different from the way that your elementary school or high school teachers made up vocabulary quizzes. GRE Sentence Completions are more than just a vocabulary test. These questions test your problem-solving skills as well as your vocabulary.

HOW ETS WRITES SENTENCE COMPLETION QUESTIONS

Let's pretend a test writer has a rough idea for a question:

These are like those old fill-in-the-blank questions from grade school.

Museums are good places for students of _____.

- ○ art
- ○ science
- ○ religion
- ○ dichotomy
- ○ democracy

Here's how to crack it

As it's written, this question is unanswerable. Almost any choice could be defended (okay, probably not "dichotomy"). ETS couldn't use this question on a real test.

To make this into a real GRE question, we'd have to change the sentence so that only one of the answer choices can be defended.

Here's another try:

> Museums, which house many paintings and sculptures, are good places for students of _____.
>
> ○ art
> ○ science
> ○ religion
> ○ dichotomy
> ○ democracy

Here's how to crack it

Now there's only one justifiable answer: choice (A). The clause added to the original sentence makes this obvious. This clause—containing the words *paintings and sculptures*—is "the clue." The finished question is very easy. Every sentence completion has a clue.

How could this problem become more difficult? With a harder "clue"—by throwing in some moderately difficult vocabulary words:

> Museums, which house many elaborate talismans, are good places for students of _____.
>
> ○ art
> ○ science
> ○ religion
> ○ dichotomy
> ○ democracy

Here's how to crack it

The answer is choice (C). To find it, you need to know that *talismans* are religious amulets or charms.

Here's another try:

> Museums, because they house not just paintings, but paintings that depict human anatomy with great accuracy, are good places for students of _____.
>
> ○ art
> ○ science
> ○ religion
> ○ dichotomy
> ○ democracy

Always write A, B, C, D, E on your scratch paper to represent the answer choices.

Here's how to crack it

Here, the answer is (B). Even though you would never think of museums that house paintings as good places for students of science, you can't choose your answer according to what *you* would say. The best answer must be based on the clue in the sentence—regardless of how weird it might be in "real life." And this time, the clue is about anatomy, so the answer is "science."

Let's try another:

> Museums, because they house paintings and sculptures selected to reflect the tastes of the broadest possible segment of the population, are good places for students of _____.
>
> ○ art
> ○ science
> ○ religion
> ○ dichotomy
> ○ democracy

Here's how to crack it

Here the answer is (E). The average person doesn't pick it, because *democracy* is a word not usually associated with *museums*. The average person doesn't take the trouble to decipher the clue, but instead reacts according to what would be true in real life. Most people have heard of art museums and science museums, and as a result, they are strongly attracted to both of those choices.

THE CLUE—LOOK BEFORE YOU LEAP

Find the clue(s) for the blank(s).

Many testers read Sentence Completions quickly, then go immediately to the choices and begin plugging them into the blank(s). Don't do it.

By finding the clue, we can figure out in advance what the word in the blank has to mean. If you take the time to understand what the sentence is really about, you'll have a much easier time finding ETS's answer among the choices.

COVER THE ANSWER CHOICES ON THE SCREEN

Always physically cover the answer choices, read through the entire sentence, then find the clue and write down your own words for the blank on your scratch paper *before* you look at the answer choices.

Here's an example of what we mean. Here's a Sentence Completion without answer choices:

> Popular songs often _____ the history of a society in that their subjects are frequently the events that have influenced and steered the society.

Here's how to crack it

What does the blank in the sentence refer to? It's about "popular songs" and the "history of a society." Is the GRE a test of what you know about popular songs? Although you may wish it were, ask yourself what you know about popular songs *from the rest of the sentence*. We know that "their subjects are frequently the events that have influenced and steered the society."

So what would be a good word for the blank? The word in the blank has to mean something like "describe," because the clue in the sentence tells us that the subjects of popular songs are frequently the events that have influenced and steered the society. So you'd write "describe" on your scratch paper (and A, B, C, D, E, of course!).

Now that we've figured out what the word in the blank has to mean, let's uncover the answer choices.

> Popular songs often _____ the history of a society in that their subjects are frequently the events that have influenced and steered the society.
>
> ○ confuse
> ○ renounce
> ○ recount
> ○ foresee
> ○ confront

Don't look at the answer choices until you've written something down on your scratch paper.

Here's how to crack it

(A) Does *confuse* mean describe? Nope. Eliminate this choice.

(B) Does *renounce* mean describe? No. Cross off this one.

(C) Does *recount* mean describe? Maybe. Let's keep this one.

(D) Does *foresee* mean describe? No, so this can't be the best answer.

(E) Does *confront* mean describe? Well, compare this with (C). Which of these comes closest to just meaning "describe"? You can also go back to the sentence. Is there any clue for a confrontational relationship of popular songs to the history of society? No. By using POE, we found out that the best answer must be (C).

FINDING YOUR OWN WORDS

After you've identified the clue in the sentence, don't try to think of a "GRE word" for the blank(s)—after all, "describe" is a pretty bland word, but it did the trick just now. You should try to get the proper meaning of the words that go in the blanks, but you shouldn't worry about finding the exact word that ETS will use in the best answer choice. It's perfectly fine to use a phrase to express the meaning that you know would fit. Often you can use a part of the clue from the sentence itself.

SENTENCE COMPLETION DRILL PART 1

In each of the following sentences, find the clue and underline it. Then, see if you can anticipate ETS's answer. Write a word or phrase near the blank. It doesn't matter if your guesses are awkward or wordy. All you need to do is express the right idea.

Although a few of the plot twists in her novel were unexpected, overall, the major events depicted in the work were _____ enough.

A recent poll shows that, while 81 percent of college students are eligible for some form of financial aid, only 63 percent of these students are _____ such aid.

A business concerned about its efficiency should pay attention to the actions of its staff, because the mistakes of each of its employees often _____ the effectiveness of the organization of which they are a part.

Langston Hughes's creative works were the highlight, not the _____, of his writings; he was also a prolific writer of nonfiction and political commentary.

SENTENCE COMPLETION DRILL PART 2

Now that you've anticipated ETS's answers, look at the same four questions again, this time with the answer choices provided. Use the words you wrote above to eliminate answer choices. Answers can be found on page 53.

Although a few of the plot twists in her novel were unexpected, overall, the major events depicted in the work were _____ enough.

- ◯ lively
- ◯ well developed
- ◯ predictable
- ◯ complex
- ◯ creative

A recent poll shows that, while 81 percent of college students are eligible for some form of financial aid, only 63 percent of these students are _____ such aid.

- ◯ complaining about
- ◯ recipients of
- ◯ dissatisfied with
- ◯ paying for
- ◯ turned down for

A business concerned about its efficiency should pay attention to the actions of its staff, because the mistakes of each of its employees often _____ the effectiveness of the organization of which they are a part.

- ◯ remake
- ◯ provoke
- ◯ celebrate
- ◯ undermine
- ◯ control

Langston Hughes's creative works were the highlight, not the _____, of his writings; he was also a prolific writer of nonfiction and political commentary.

- ◯ peculiarity
- ◯ product
- ◯ initiator
- ◯ average
- ◯ entirety

TRIGGER WORDS

Besides the clue, certain words signal changes in the meaning or direction of a sentence. We call them trigger words. They provide important structural indicators of the meaning of the sentence, and they are often the key to figuring out which words will best fill in the blanks in a Sentence Completion.

Here are some of the most important Sentence Completion trigger words and punctuation:

<table>
<tr><td>• but</td><td>• while</td><td>• thus</td></tr>
<tr><td>• although</td><td>• however</td><td>• similarly</td></tr>
<tr><td>• unless</td><td>• unfortunately</td><td>• and</td></tr>
<tr><td>• rather</td><td>• in contrast</td><td>• therefore</td></tr>
<tr><td>• yet</td><td>• despite</td><td>• heretofore</td></tr>
<tr><td>• previously</td><td></td><td>• ; (semicolon) and : (colon)</td></tr>
</table>

> Trigger words help you to find the relationship between the two blanks. Are they the same or opposites?

Notice that words like "thus" and "and" indicate that one part of the sentence is similar in meaning to the other, whereas words like "but" and "however" indicate an opposite direction. Paying attention to trigger words is crucial to understanding the meaning of the sentence. Here's an example of a Sentence Completion question in which finding ETS's answer depends on understanding the function of a trigger word:

> In American film, some character actors have found it _____ to gain widespread recognition, although within the smaller community of actors, directors, and producers they are highly regarded.
>
> ○ difficult
> ○ acceptable
> ○ unsatisfactory
> ○ relatively simple
> ○ discouraging

Here's how to crack it

What does the blank refer to? The blank is describing how some actors have found gaining widespread recognition. What's the clue in the sentence that tells us how these actors have found it? We know that "within the smaller community of actors, directors, and producers they are highly regarded." So, have these actors found it easy or hard to gain recognition?

Did you notice the trigger word *although*? This indicates a contrast in the meaning of the sentence. So *although* these actors are highly regarded in the smaller community, they have found it hard to gain widespread recognition. Write the word *hard* on your scratch paper, then uncover the answer choices and use the Process of Elimination.

(A) Does *difficult* mean *hard*? Yes. This looks good, but be sure to check every answer choice.

(B) Does *acceptable* mean *hard*? No. Eliminate this choice.

(C) Does *unsatisfactory* mean *hard*? No. Eliminate this choice.

(D) Does *relatively simple* mean *hard*? No. Eliminate this choice.

(E) Does *discouraging* mean *hard*? No. Eliminate this choice.

So the best answer is (A).

POSITIVE/NEGATIVE

You should always try to come up with your own word for each blank. In some cases, however, you may think of *several* words that could go in the blanks, or you might have a "feeling" instead of a word. Rather than spend a lot of time trying to find the "perfect" word, just ask yourself whether the missing word will be a "good" word (one with positive connotations) or a "bad" word (one with negative connotations). Then write a + or a – symbol on your scratch paper.

Here's an example:

If you can't come up with exact words, write positive or negative for the blank(s) on your scratch paper.

> Despite the fact that over time the originally antagonistic response to his sculpture had lessened, to this day, hardly any individuals _____ his art.
>
> ○ applaud
> ○ castigate
> ○ evaluate
> ○ denounce
> ○ ignore

Here's how to crack it

What's the blank describing? How individuals react to the artist's work. What's the clue in the sentence? We know that "the originally antagonistic response to his sculpture had lessened." So how are people now responding? Again, notice how the trigger word in this sentence helps you decide what the word in the blank has to mean. The word "despite" indicates that even though the originally antagonistic response had lessened, hardly any individuals responded *positively* to his art. Write a + sign on your scratch paper before you uncover the answer choices.

(A) Is *applaud* a positive word? Sure, let's keep it and go to the other choices.

(B) Is *castigate* a positive word? Perhaps, or maybe you're not sure, so keep it and consider the other choices. (It's on the Hit Parade, so you should know this word before you take the GRE!)

(C) Is *evaluate* a positive word? No, so eliminate this choice.

(D) Is *denounce* a positive word? No, so cross off this choice.

(E) Is *ignore* a positive word? No, so get rid of this choice.

Now that you're down to two choices, what do you do? Well, you know that *applaud* is a positive word, and you know that the word in the blank has to be a positive word; if you're not sure whether *castigate* is a positive word, then guess (A). In fact, (A) is the best answer choice. Do you see how important it is to figure out what the blank has to mean *before* you go to the answer choices?

TWO BLANKS: ELIMINATE CHOICES ONE BLANK AT A TIME

Use POE. On two-blank sentences, eliminate entire answer choices using one blank at a time.

Many Sentence Completions will have two blanks rather than just one. This doesn't mean that two-blank Sentence Completions are more difficult to solve than one-blank Sentence Completions. **Two-blank Sentence Completions are easier than one-blank Sentence Completions if you work on only one blank at a time.**

You'll do much better if you concentrate on just one of the blanks at a time. A two-blank answer choice can be the best only if it works for *both* of the blanks; if you can determine that one of the words in the choice doesn't work in its blank, you can eliminate that choice without checking the other word. Which blank should you concentrate on? The one for which you have a better clue. Often, this will be the second blank.

Once you've decided which blank you have a better clue for, and have written down a word for it, go to the answer choices and look *only* at the ones provided for that blank. Then eliminate any choice that doesn't work for that blank.

Here's an example of how you can crack a two-blank Sentence Completion by tackling it one blank at a time:

> In contrast to physicists who base their research on scientific theory, he modeled his procedure on rigorous _____; so despite the fact that his method was less sophisticated, his results were _____ sound.
>
> ○ fiction . . methodologically
> ○ abstraction . . arguably
> ○ intuition . . scientifically
> ○ observation . . factually
> ○ speculation . . implicitly

Here's how to crack it

What is the first blank describing? It's talking about how the physicist modeled his procedure. What clue does the sentence give us for how his procedure was modeled? You know that it was modeled "in contrast to physicists who base their research on scientific theory." So, the word for the first blank has to mean something that's the opposite of *theory*. Go to the first words in the answer choices.

(A) Is *fiction* the opposite of *theory*? No. We're still talking about a physicist, after all. So we can eliminate this entire choice.

(B) Is *abstraction* the opposite of *theory*? No, it's the same. So we can eliminate this whole answer choice.

(C) Is *intuition* the opposite of *theory*? No. Again, the sentence is still talking about a scientist. So we can eliminate this entire choice.

(D) Is *observation* the opposite of *theory*? Sure. Let's keep this one.

(E) Is *speculation* the opposite of *theory*? No, it's very similar. We can get rid of this answer choice too.

Have you been learning your GRE vocabulary?

Wow, the only answer left is (D)! You won't *always* be able to eliminate all four wrong answer choices using just one blank, the way we could on this example, so *always be sure to check that the second word works in the other blank.*

MORE ON TWO-BLANK QUESTIONS

Looking for positive and negative words is especially useful on two-blank Sentence Completions. Trigger words and punctuation are also especially important on questions with two blanks.

Trigger words like *although* and *but* show that the relationship between the two blanks involves an opposition (–/+ or +/–); trigger words like *and* and *thus* (and punctuation like semicolons and colons) show that the relationship between the two blanks involves a similarity (–/– or +/+). Using this information, you can confidently eliminate any choice with a different arrangement. This is a useful POE technique even when you have your own words for the blanks. Cross out choices that don't fit the pattern.

Try this example:

> Although he asserted his theology was derived from _____ school of thought, it actually utilizes conventions from many religions and so it rightfully could be described as having _____ origins.
>
> ○ a particular . . diverse
> ○ a cogent . . multitalented
> ○ a prominent . . coherent
> ○ an influential . . reductive
> ○ a single . . consonant

Here's how to crack it

What are the two blanks describing? His theology. What clue does the sentence provide? We know that "it actually utilizes conventions from many religions." So the word for the second blank has to mean something like "composed of many parts." What about the first blank? Notice the trigger word *although* at the beginning of the sentence. From this trigger word, we know that the words for the two blanks will be opposites. Let's eliminate answer choices on the basis of the second blank first.

(A) Does *diverse* mean "composed of many parts"? [...] try to eliminate other choices.

(B) Does *multitalented* mean "composed of many [...] in. And remember, the blanks are talking abo[...]

(C) Does *coherent* mean "composed of many parts[...]

(D) Does *reductive* mean "composed of many part[...] nate this whole answer choice.

(E) Does *consonant* mean "composed of many pa[...] don't eliminate it.

Now that we're down to three choices, let's look at [...] the two words in the remaining answer choices. Remember, we've determined that the two words should be nearly *opposite* in meaning.

(A) Is *a particular* the opposite of *diverse*? Yes. This choice is looking good.

(B) Is *a cogent* the opposite of *multitalented*? If you aren't sure, then you can't eliminate this choice.

(E) Is *a single* the opposite of *consonant*? Well, if you don't know exactly what *consonant* means, it's tough to say. But once again, you do know that the best answer must be two words that are opposites, and you know that *diverse* works well in the second blank, so you should guess (A). In fact, that's the best answer choice.

Let's try another example:

> The notion that socialism inhibits individual expression is supported by historical studies that have shown that individualism has _____ only in societies where socialist programs have been _____.
>
> ⬭ diminished . . debated
> ⬭ thrived . . abandoned
> ⬭ grown . . fostered
> ⬭ triumphed . . improved
> ⬭ wallowed . . restrained

Here's how to crack it

What's the clue in this sentence? Remember not to use your own knowledge to fill in the blanks. The sentence tells us, "The notion that socialism inhibits individual expression is supported by historical studies . . . . " Now, what's the relationship between the blanks? In this case, we know from the clue that the words for the two blanks are going to be opposites. It could be that the word for the first blank is positive and the one for the second blank is negative, or vice versa. No problem. Just eliminate all the answer choices for which the two words are *not opposites*.

(A) Is *diminished* the opposite of *debated*? No, so eliminate this choice.

(B) Is *thrived* the opposite of *abandoned*? Maybe. Let's keep this choice and consider the rest of the choices.

(C) Is *grown* the opposite of *fostered*? No. So eliminate this choice.

(D) Is *triumphed* the opposite of *improved*? No. So eliminate this choice.

(E) Is *wallowed* the opposite of *restrained*? Well, maybe you're not sure exactly what *wallowed* means. Again, concentrate on the information that you know for sure.

We know from the clue that socialism inhibits individualism. So would individualism *thrive* when socialism is *abandoned*? Sure. Choice (B) is the best answer.

ANSWER KEY—SENTENCE COMPLETION DRILL PART 2

1. C
2. B
3. D
4. E

6
Antonyms

WHAT YOU WILL SEE

The Verbal section of your GRE will contain at least eight to ten Antonyms. They usually start off the section. The first five questions in the Verbal section tend to mix Antonyms and Analogies, but you will almost always see an Antonym first.

ETS's DIRECTIONS

Take a minute to read the following set of directions. These are the directions as they will appear on your GRE. Read them now and you'll never have to read them again:

> Directions: Each question below consists of a word printed in capital letters, followed by five words or phrases. Choose the word or phrase that is most nearly opposite in meaning to the word in capital letters.
>
> Since some of the questions require you to distinguish fine shades of meaning, be sure to consider all the choices before deciding which one is best.

YES, THERE REALLY ARE TECHNIQUES

You CAN improve your scores!

You may think that doing well on Antonyms all comes down to vocabulary; that is, if you have a big vocabulary, you'll do well on Antonyms, and if you have a tiny vocabulary, you'll have trouble. And, for the most part, you're right. The best way to improve your Antonym score *is* to improve your GRE vocabulary. So if you haven't begun studying our GRE Hit Parade (see chapter 8), definitely start now.

But even though a big vocabulary makes Antonyms easier to crack, we do have techniques that can enable you to squeeze the maximum number of points out of any vocabulary. These techniques are based on our new friend, POE.

APPROACHING ANTONYMS

Remember, there are three types of words on the GRE:

- Words you know
- Words you sort of know
- Words you have never seen

Your approach to Antonyms will vary depending on the type of word that you are dealing with. Since you are studying the Hit Parade, you may find that you can now define some more words.

But you have to be extremely honest with yourself! It's better to be conservative, and to admit that you only "sort of" know a word, than to think you can define a word when you really can't.

WHEN YOU CAN DEFINE THE STEM WORD

When you are absolutely sure that you know what the stem word means, don't just jump at the first choice that looks right. Even ETS warns you in the directions to check all of the answer choices. Avoid careless errors by using the following steps:

- As usual, write down A, B, C, D, E on your scratch paper.
- Cover the answer choices on the screen.
- Write down your own simple opposite for the stem word.
- Uncover the answers and use POE.
  - At first, eliminate the answer choices that are nowhere near your own opposite for the stem word.
  - Next, make opposites for the choices that remain and work backward to the stem word.

Try this example:

BELITTLE:

- ○ lessen
- ○ intensify
- ○ compliment
- ○ begrudge
- ○ fawn

Improving your vocabulary is the single most important thing you can do to improve your Verbal score.

Here's how to crack it

We can define *belittle*, right? It means something like "to put down." So our own opposite would be a word such as "praise."

(A) Does *lessen* mean "praise"? No. Cross out (A) on your scratch paper.

(B) Does *intensify* mean "praise"? No. Cross out (B) on your scratch paper.

(C) Does *compliment* mean "praise"? Yes. Keep it.

(D) Does *begrudge* mean "praise"? No. Cross out (D) on your scratch paper.

(E) Does *fawn* mean "praise"? Well, it's close. Let's make an opposite for *fawn* just to be sure. *Fawn* means to flatter excessively. The opposite would be to ignore. So it's not quite right.

The best answer is (C).

Let's do another one:

PRIM:

- ⃝ enormous
- ⃝ unsuitable
- ⃝ arid
- ⃝ healthy
- ⃝ slight

Here's how to crack it

Let's assume we can define *prim*. It means something like "proper," so our own word for the opposite would be something like "improper."

(A) Does *enormous* mean "improper"? No, so cross out (A) on your scratch paper.

(B) Does *unsuitable* mean "improper"? Yes, so hang on to this one.

(C) Does *arid* mean "improper"? No, so cross out (C) on your scratch paper.

(D) Does *healthy* mean "improper"? No, so cross out (D) on your scratch paper.

(E) Does *slight* mean "improper"? No, so cross out (E) on your scratch paper.

The answer is (B).

So, when you know all of the words in the problem, it's pretty easy to eliminate the wrong answers, but what do you do if you don't?

<aside>Do you really know the definition of the word? Or do you only "sort of know" it?</aside>

WHEN YOU "SORT OF KNOW" THE STEM WORD

What do you do when you come across a word that you can correctly use in a sentence, but for which you can't quite come up with a Webster-perfect definition? Let's take a look.

POSITIVE/NEGATIVE

Sometimes you can't define a stem word, but you do know whether it has a positive or negative connotation. If the stem word has a positive connotation, its antonym has to be negative, so you can eliminate positive answer choices. If the stem word is negative, eliminate negative choices.

Write a + sign down on your scratch paper if the stem word is positive, and a – sign if the stem word is negative. Then write down + or – next to the A, B, C, D, E you've already written down, depending on whether the corresponding word is positive or negative. Don't forget that you're looking for the *opposite* of the stem.

Try using positive/negative on this example:

DEBILITATE:

- ⃝ discharge
- ⃝ strengthen
- ⃝ undermine
- ⃝ squelch
- ⃝ delete

Here's how to crack it

Let's say we're not entirely sure what *debilitate* means, but we know it's a negative word. Since *debilitate* is negative, the antonym must be positive, so we can eliminate negative answer choices. That gets rid of (C), (D), and (E). Right now, we're left with (A) and (B).

WORKING BACKWARD FROM THE ANSWER CHOICES

Instead of taking a guess here, let's take each remaining answer choice and turn it into its opposite. Then we can compare it with the word in capital letters. That way, we can see if one of those opposites could mean the same thing as "debilitate." Doing this can sometimes trigger an accurate definition of the word.

(A) *Discharge* means to let out. Could *debilitate* mean to keep in? Not really.

(B) Could *debilitate* mean to weaken? That's what it means. The ETS answer is (B).

Let's try it again:

> MALADROIT:
> - ○ ill-willed
> - ○ dexterous
> - ○ cowardly
> - ○ enduring
> - ○ sluggish

Here's how to crack it

Let's assume you aren't sure what *maladroit* means, but you "sort of know" that it's a negative word. That eliminates (A), (C), and (E). Not bad at all. Now work backward by turning each remaining choice into its opposite and see what you have:

(B) clumsy

(D) short-lived

After you turn each word into its opposite, compare it to the capitalized word and determine whether it could mean the same thing.

> Could *maladroit* mean *clumsy*?

> Could *maladroit* mean *short-lived*?

If no choice presents itself yet, eliminate the least likely choices, one at a time, and try to zero in on ETS's answer. Spending a few extra seconds on the question often makes something click in your mind. This may help reveal what ETS is up to. The answer to this question is (B). Look it up.

Down to two choices? Make opposites for the choices and work backward.

ELIMINATE CHOICES THAT DON'T HAVE OPPOSITES

What's the opposite of *chair*? What's the opposite of *flower*? What's the opposite of *philosophy*?

These words have no clear opposites. If they were choices on an Antonym question on the GRE, you could cross them out automatically, even if you didn't know the meaning of the word in capital letters. Why? Because if a choice *has no* opposite, the stem word can't possibly *be* its opposite.

Here's an example:

CARNAL:

- ○ sensual
- ○ aural
- ○ oral
- ○ unusual
- ○ spiritual

Here's how to crack it

Have you been learning your vocabulary words?

Let's assume we don't know the meaning of *carnal*. Work through the choices, turning each into its opposite:

(A) There's no clear opposite. Cross it out.

(B) If you don't know this word, *don't* cross it out!

(C) There's no clear opposite. Cross it out.

(D) usual

(E) earthly

Doing this improves our guessing odds to one in three. Not bad. Our chances of finding ETS's answer now depend on whether narrowing down our choices has made anything click in our minds. By the way, the answer is (E); *carnal* means *earthly*.

WORD ASSOCIATION

Sometimes you're not sure what the stem word means, but you've heard it used with another word or phrase. Use that knowledge to help you eliminate incorrect answer choices and maybe jog your memory of a word's meaning.

ALLEVIATE:

- ○ alienate
- ○ worsen
- ○ revitalize
- ○ aerate
- ○ elevate

Here's how to crack it

You're not exactly sure what *alleviate* means. However, you've probably heard it used in the phrase "alleviate pain." Make opposites for the answer choices and plug them into your phrase.

(A) Does "welcome pain" make any sense? Not really.

(B) Does "improve pain" make any sense? Sort of.

(C) Does "debilitate pain" make any sense? Not really.

(D) Does "suffocate pain" make any sense? Not really.

(E) Does "lower pain" make any sense? Maybe.

You've narrowed it down, and maybe by now you realize (B) looks good. This technique won't necessarily eliminate all of the incorrect answer choices, but it can help you narrow them down.

COMBINE TECHNIQUES

Don't be afraid to combine all of these techniques. Sometimes you can eliminate a couple of choices by using positive/negative, then use word association on the choices that remain. Don't forget to work backward when you are down to two choices.

SECONDARY MEANINGS

ETS likes to use the secondary meanings of words—in other words, a meaning of a word that doesn't come to your mind right away. (Isn't that just like them?)

Try this example:

CATHOLIC:
- ⊖ uncharitable
- ⊖ reticent
- ⊖ specialized
- ⊖ irreverent
- ⊖ reckless

Here's how to crack it

What's the first meaning you think of? The religion? What's the opposite? It doesn't have one.

CHECK THE PARTS OF SPEECH

You can determine the parts of speech in the same way you would on Analogy questions. To figure out whether the stem word is a noun, a verb, or an adjective, just check the answer choices. You can see from (A) in the example above that the stem word *catholic* is an adjective, because *uncharitable* is an adjective. Let's work backward with the answer choices:

(A) Could *catholic* mean "charitable"? Sounds like a trap. ETS wants you to think about religion here, but don't fall for it.

(B) Could *catholic* mean "talkative"? Not likely.

(C) Could *catholic* mean "generalized"? Maybe.

(D) Could *catholic* mean "reverent"? Sounds like a trap. Again, don't fall for it.

(E) Could *catholic* mean "careful"? Maybe.

Well, we've eliminated three choices, so it's time to guess. Not bad for not knowing the stem word. The answer is (C). *Catholic* means generalized or universal.

Check parts of speech if you think the word seems "easy."

IF YOU'VE NEVER SEEN THE WORD BEFORE

Go for the extremes. "Extreme" words are more likely to be correct than moderate words. Look at the following example. What is the most extreme answer choice? Is it correct?

Start working on your vocabulary now!

AMENABLE:
- ⬭ intrinsic
- ⬭ progressive
- ⬭ enthusiastic
- ⬭ tenuous
- ⬭ obstinate

Here's how to crack it

The most extreme answer choices are *enthusiastic* and *obstinate*. The best thing to do in this situation is to just guess one of these two choices. The answer is (E). *Amenable* means open to different possibilities, and *obstinate* means stubborn. Remember, an educated guess is better than a random guess, especially since you can't skip any questions.

7
Reading
Comprehension

WHAT YOU WILL SEE

The Verbal section of your GRE will contain two to four reading passages and a total of six to ten questions. You probably won't see any Reading Comps until around questions eight to twelve.

THE DIRECTIONS

These are the directions as they will appear on your GRE:

> <u>Directions</u>: Each passage in this group is followed by questions based on its content. After reading a passage, choose the best answer to each question. Answer all questions following a passage on the basis of what is stated or implied in that passage.

Here are *our* directions:

> <u>Directions</u>: This is not really a test of reading, nor is it a test of comprehension. It's a treasure hunt! The answers are in the passage.

This is not a test of intelligence!

TYPES OF PASSAGES

There are two basic types of GRE reading passages: science and non-science. The science passages may be either specific or general. Knowing a little about the types will help you anticipate the main ideas.

Specific science passages deal with the "hard facts" of science. They are almost always objective or neutral in tone. The terminology may be complex, but the main idea or theme will not be. Don't be thrown into confusion by big words. If you don't understand them, neither does anyone else. If you focus on the main idea, you won't have to worry about the jargon.

General science passages deal with the history of a scientific discovery, the development of a scientific procedure or method, why science fails or succeeds in explaining certain phenomena, and similar "soft" themes. The authors of these passages often have a more definite point of view than do the authors of the specific science passages; that is, the tone may not be neutral or objective, and the author may be expressing an opinion. The main theme will be whatever point or argument the author is trying to argue.

Non-science passages will be about either humanities or social studies topics. Humanities passages typically take a specific point of view, or compare several views. The language may be abstract and dense. Social science passages usually introduce an era or event by focusing on a specific problem, topic, person, or group of persons. The tone is likely to be partisan and opinionated, although some social science passages take the form of a neutral discussion of facts.

SAMPLE PASSAGE

In the discussion that follows, we will refer again and again to the sample passage below.

Within the atmosphere are small amounts of a number of important gases, popularly called "greenhouse gases," because they alter the flow of life- and heat-energy through the atmosphere,
5 much as does the glass shell of a greenhouse. Their effect on incoming solar energy is minimal, but collectively they act as an insulating blanket around the planet. They do this by absorbing and returning to the Earth's surface much of its
10 outgoing heat, trapping it within the lower atmosphere. A greenhouse effect is natural and essential to a livable climate on Earth.

Greenhouse gas concentrations, however, are being drastically affected by human activities.
15 One of the most important gases, carbon dioxide, is an important nutrient for plants, but it is potentially dangerous to our climate if its quantity is enormously augmented. Its concentration has increased from about 280
20 parts per million in 1850 to about 350 today, mainly because of a large increase in fossil fuel burning, forest removal, and agriculture. Other gases, such as nitrous oxide, methane, and surface ozone, although they are less abundant,
25 are also increasing rapidly and are potentially dangerous. Man-made chlorofluorocarbons (CFCs) are used as, among other things, coolants in refrigerators and air conditioners. The most common industrially produced CFCs,
30 although measured in parts per trillion, are among the most potent and the most rapidly increasing greenhouse gases in existence. One free chlorine atom, produced in the stratosphere by the effects of ultraviolet light on CFCs, can
35 eliminate 100,000 molecules of ozone.

The result? Increased concentration of greenhouse gases enhance the global greenhouse effect, trapping more heat near the Earth's surface. A warmer atmosphere can hold
40 more water vapor, which is itself a powerful greenhouse gas, and amplify the warming. On the other hand, the increase in airborne moisture may mean more clouds, which would cut off sunlight and limit or modulate warming.

45 On the basis of climate models, some scientists predict a potential increase in global

Reading these passages is like going on a treasure hunt.

surface temperature of between 1.5°C and 4.5°C in the next fifty years. This may not seem like much, but 4.5°C equals the total temperature
50 rise since the peak of the last ice age 18,000 years ago, and the increase will be even higher in some regions. The average could be slightly lower in the tropics, but at least doubled at high latitude—mainly because of the disappearance
55 of ice and snow. Snow-free land surfaces absorb more of the Sun's rays than snow-covered surfaces, so warming by the Sun will increase as the duration and area of snow cover diminishes. Moreover, the increases in temperature can be
60 quite large where there is relatively low energy from the Sun because of the very shallow, strong temperature inversions typical of the Arctic cold season. Reduced ice cover on the polar seas will also increase the heat transfer
65 from water to the overlying air.

Don't read for "comprehension." Read to find the answers.

Don't Try to Read Every Word

Most test-takers read much too slowly and carefully on Reading Comp, trying to memorize all the details crammed into the passage. When they reach the end of the passage, they often realize that they have no idea what they have just read. They've wasted a lot of time and gotten nothing out of it. You'll know better.

On the GRE, you read for one reason only: *to earn points*. The questions test only a tiny fraction of the boring, hard-to-remember details that are packed into each passage. So don't try to read and remember everything in the passage.

Don't read every word of the passage. Just spend a minute or two noting what the general topic of the passage is on your scratch paper, and if the passage is organized in a specific way. In other words, case the joint—get familiar with the passage. Quickly.

Approaching the Passage

The main idea of the passage is what the passage is *about*. The main idea may be presented immediately, in the very first sentence. Or it may be presented gradually, in the first sentences of the paragraphs. Or the main idea may come last, as a conclusion to or summary of the details or arguments that have been presented.

Just focus on the first sentence and last sentence of each paragraph. Don't try to memorize what you are reading, or learn any of the supporting details. All you should be aiming for is a general sense of the overall passage, which can be reduced to a few simple words that you can easily jot down. Remember, the passage isn't going anywhere. It will be on the screen until you answer the question. You don't have to memorize anything.

Ready to try it?

Let's try this technique on the sample passage we gave you earlier.

From the first sentence of the first paragraph you find out that the passage is about so-called "greenhouse gases." And from the last sentence of the paragraph you see that the passage is going to discuss "the greenhouse effect."

Now let's look at the second paragraph. The first sentence talks about how greenhouse gases are affected by human activities. The last sentence is some detail about CFCs. Even though we really don't know anything about CFCs or ozone, we still can tell that they are affected by human activity.

Let's go to the third paragraph. The first sentence of the third paragraph says that the result of the CFC/ozone thing is an enhanced greenhouse effect, trapping more heat near the Earth's surface. The last sentence says "on the other hand," (a trigger phrase; remember Sentence Completions?) there might be more clouds cutting off sunlight.

> Concentrate on the main idea of the passage, not the details.

On to the last paragraph. The first sentence mentions that "some scientists predict a potential increase in global surface temperature . . . " The last sentence is about reduced ice cover on the polar seas also increasing the heat transfer from water to air. Now, try to summarize the main idea of the passage. On your scratch paper, write:

possible causes and results of the greenhouse effect

That's what the whole passage is about. If we *didn't* read about something in those topic sentences of each paragraph, it definitely is *not* the main idea. Now that we've dealt with the passage, let's move on to the questions, which will pop up one at a time on your screen.

THE QUESTIONS

There are two types of questions: specific and general. Most of the questions you will see will be specific.

- **Specific questions** concern specific *details* in the passage. You should go back to the passage to find exactly what the passage said for each specific detail question. If you don't find it immediately, skim quickly to the next place the detail is discussed.

- **General questions** ask about the main idea, the theme, or the tone of the passage *as a whole*.

SPECIFIC QUESTIONS

Most specific questions have what we call a "lead" word or phrase. These are words or phrases that will be easy to skim for in the passage. Here's how it works:

- Identify the lead word or phrase in the question. It will be the most descriptive word in the question. For example, in the question, "According to the passage, mayonnaise was invented because . . . ," the lead word is *mayonnaise*.

- Quickly skim the passage to find that word or phrase.
- Scroll so that the lead words are in the middle of the screen. This should put the part of the passage that must be paraphrased to answer the question right next to the answer choices.
- If this doesn't do it, look for the next occurrence of the lead words and repeat the process.
- Read the question again and answer it in your own words, based on the information you found in the passage.
- Use POE.

THE ANSWER CHOICES (POE)

Use that paper!

The following techniques will help you use POE to eliminate incorrect answer choices and zero in on ETS's answer.

USE COMMON SENSE, BUT NOT OUTSIDE KNOWLEDGE

ETS takes its reading passages from textbooks, collections of essays, works of scholarship, and other sources of serious reading matter. You won't find a passage arguing that literature is stupid, or that history doesn't matter. As a result, you will often be able to eliminate answer choices simply because the facts or opinions they represent couldn't possibly be found in ETS reading passages.

However, be careful not to answer questions based on the fact that you did your undergraduate thesis on the topic at hand. This is a treasure hunt; in other words: **The answers are in the passage.**

AVOID EXTREME STATEMENTS

ETS doesn't want to spend all its time defending its answer choices. If even one percent of the people taking the GRE decided to quibble with an answer, ETS would be deluged with angry phone calls. To keep this from happening, ETS constructs correct answer choices that cannot be disputed.

What makes a choice indisputable? Take a look at the following example:

(A) Ella Fitzgerald had many fans.
(B) Everyone loved Ella Fitzgerald.

Which choice is indisputable? Choice (A). Choice (B) contains the highly disputable word *everyone*. Did *everyone* really love Ella Fitzgerald? Every person on the face of the Earth? Choice (A) is complaint-proof; (B) isn't.

The more extreme a choice is, the less likely it is to be ETS's answer.

Certain words make choices extreme and, therefore, easy to dispute. Here are a few of these extreme words:

- must
- the first
- each
- every
- all
- the best
- only
- totally
- always
- no

You shouldn't automatically eliminate a choice containing one of these words, but you should turn your attention to it immediately and attack it vigorously. If you can find even one exception, you can eliminate that choice.

Other words make choices moderate, more mushy, and, therefore, hard to dispute. Here are a few of these words:

- may
- can
- some
- many
- sometimes
- often

AVOID DIRECT REPETITIONS

You should be very wary of choices that exactly reproduce a lot of the jargon from the passage. The best answer will almost always be a paraphrase, not a direct repetition. Of course, there will often have to be *some* words from the passage in the answer. But the more closely a choice resembles a substantial part of the passage, the less likely the choice is to be the best answer.

ALWAYS write A, B, C, D, E on your scratch paper to represent the answer choices.

CRACKING THE QUESTION

When it's time to attack a question, remember these steps:
1. Read the question and make sure you understand what it's asking.
2. Go back to the passage and read more in depth where you need to.
3. Paraphrase the answer in your own words.
4. Use POE on the answer choices.

Let's go back to the sample passage on page 65, and try a question:

> It can be inferred from the passage that an increase in the levels of greenhouse gases in the atmosphere could result in
>
> ○ a moderation of the changes in global temperature
> ○ a reduction in ultraviolet radiation at the Earth's surface
> ○ a long-term increase in the turbulence of weather patterns
> ○ increased snow cover in higher latitudes
> ○ corresponding increases in stratospheric ozone levels

Here's how to crack it

This is a typical specific question. What are the lead words? We need to go back to the passage to find out what "could result" when there's "an increase in the levels of greenhouse gases in the atmosphere." Again, don't try to answer this question using your memory, or using what you may know about the topic apart from the passage.

The third paragraph says that "increased concentration of greenhouse gases enhance the global greenhouse effect, trapping more heat near the Earth's surface. A warmer atmosphere can hold more water vapor . . . and amplify the warming. On the other hand, the increase in airborne moisture may mean more clouds, which would cut off sunlight and limit or modulate warming." So, in our own words, the increased greenhouse effect might make the Earth both warmer and cooler. Now, let's use POE on the answer choices.

Remember: All the answers you need are on the screen.

(A) Well, this choice has something to do with the Earth's temperature, so let's keep it.

(B) You may be tempted to keep this answer choice, because the paragraph says that increased greenhouse gases could "cut off sunlight." But there is nothing about "ultraviolet radiation" in that paragraph, and there's nothing about the effects on *temperature* in this choice. And since this isn't testing your scientific knowledge, you're not expected to bring in any outside information about sunlight and ultraviolet radiation. So eliminate this choice.

(C) There's nothing in this choice about temperature, and there's nothing in the paragraph about the "turbulence of weather patterns." Eliminate this choice.

(D) There is nothing in the third paragraph about snow cover, and there's nothing in this answer choice about temperature. If you're not sure, go to the fourth paragraph, where it says that snow-cover will diminish. Eliminate this choice.

(E) Ozone isn't mentioned in the third paragraph. We're looking for something to do with temperature. Eliminate.

The best answer is (A). Notice that it's a paraphrase, not a direct repetition, of what is stated in the passage.

Let's try another question.

The author refers to the last ice age primarily in order to

○ dramatize the effect that reduced ice cover has on atmospheric temperatures

○ show that temperatures in the tropics and polar regions are becoming more uniform

○ illustrate the decrease in global levels of ice and snow

○ trace the decline in surface ozone levels over an extended period

○ emphasize the significance of an apparently minor climatic change

Here's how to crack it

Use the lead words to go back to the right paragraph in the passage. You're looking for something about "the last ice age." It's in the fourth paragraph, the one with more details about the greenhouse effect. In the first sentence of that paragraph, it says that some scientists predict a warming of between 1.5 and 4.5°C in the next fifty years. Then it says, "This may not seem like much, but 4.5°C equals the total temperature rise since the peak of the last ice age 18,000 years ago, and the increase will be even higher in some regions."

So the author refers to the last ice age in order to, in our own words, show that a 4.5 degree change in global surface temperature can have major consequences. In any case, it's again got something to do with changes in the Earth's *temperature*, so that if an answer choice doesn't mention temperature, it can't be the best answer choice.

(A) "Reduced ice cover" is in the wrong part of the paragraph, so eliminate it.

(B) This mentions temperature, so let's keep it and try to get rid of some other choices.

(C) Nothing in this choice mentions temperature, so get rid of it.

(D) Nothing about temperature here either, so this choice is gone.

(E) This looks good. It's about what we said in our own words.

But let's go back to the passage to make sure that (B) is wrong. In the fourth paragraph it says, "The average could be slightly lower in the tropics, but at least doubled at high latitude." So we know that temperatures in the tropics and polar regions are *not* becoming more uniform.

The best answer is (E).

Let's try another question.

> Put your finger on the place in the passage where you found the answer to the question. Answer the question in your own words before you go on to the answer choices.

The passage indicates that a reduction in the amount of ice on the surface of the polar seas would result in

○ a decrease in the frequency of Arctic temperature inversions

○ increased transfer of heat from the sea to the polar atmosphere

○ increased absorption of solar energy by polar land surfaces

○ rapid reversal of the warming caused by greenhouse gases

○ decreased heat transfer, which would cool the polar atmosphere

Here's how to crack it

This is another specific question with lead words. The lead words are "a reduction in the amount of ice on the surface of the polar seas." After answering the last question, we know that we're going to go back to the fourth paragraph again.

The last sentence says, "Reduced ice cover on the polar seas will also increase the heat transfer from water to the overlying air." So the answer to the question will be a paraphrase of that sentence.

Let's use POE.

(A) You should be very suspicious of direct repetitions in answer choices like this one. The passage mentions "temperature inversions" of the typical Arctic cold season, but the question we're trying to answer is about what would happen after a reduction in the amount of ice on the surface of polar seas. Get rid of this choice.

(B) This looks like a good paraphrase of the last sentence.

(C) Use common sense! The question is about what would happen after a reduction in the amount of ice on the surface of polar seas. Eliminate.

(D) Again, use common sense. This choice would go against the main idea of the whole passage. It's also very extreme wording. Eliminate.

(E) No, the passage says that reduced ice cover will increase the heat transfer. The best answer is (B). Eliminate.

LINE REFERENCE QUESTIONS

These questions ask you to interpret the meaning of a certain word or phrase in the context of the passage. You will usually be referred to a specific line number in the text. These questions can be phrased in a number of ways:

> The "great orchestra" (line 29) is used as a metaphor for . . .

> The author uses the term "indigenous labor" (line 40) to mean . . .

> The author quotes Stephen Hawking (line 13) in order to . . .

Do you really think ETS is going to tell you exactly where an answer is? No way. Therefore, you will generally *not* find ETS's answer in the exact line referred to.

Read at least the five lines before the line reference, and the five lines after it as well.

Here's the best way to do these questions: Scroll so that the line referred to is in the middle of the screen. This should put the part of the passage that must be paraphrased to answer the question right next to the answer choices.

MAIN IDEA QUESTIONS

A main idea question asks you to find the main idea of the passage. It can be phrased in several different ways:

> The author's main purpose is . . .

> The main idea of the passage is . . .

> Which of the following is the best title for the passage?

> Which of the following questions does the passage answer?

A word about answer choices: All of these are *general* questions; therefore, they will almost always have *general* answers. That means that you can eliminate any choice that is too specific. The main idea of a passage will never be something that couldn't possibly be accomplished in a few short paragraphs. (The author's purpose in writing a 250-word essay could never be "to explain the origin of the universe.")

> Be skeptical of answer choices that are too EXTREME.

The incorrect choices on a question like this will probably be statements that are partly true, or are true of part of the passage, but not of the whole thing. Refer back to the sample passage on page 65 for the following question:

> The author is primarily concerned with
>
> ○ explaining the effects that ultraviolet light might have on terrestrial life
> ○ illustrating the effects of greenhouse gases on solar radiation
> ○ discussing the possible effects of increased levels of greenhouse gases
> ○ exploding theories about the causes of global warming
> ○ challenging hypotheses about the effects of temperature on the atmosphere

Here's how to crack it

This is a general question. It's asking for the "primary purpose" of the passage—in other words, the main idea. We said that the passage is about the possible causes and effects of the greenhouse effect. Let's use POE.

Down to two choices? Go back to the place in the passage where you found the answer to the question.

(A) This choice doesn't even mention the greenhouse effect, so it can't be the best answer. Eliminate it.

(B) This mentions greenhouse gases, so let's keep it and check the other choices.

(C) This also mentions greenhouse gases, so let's keep this one, too. We'll consider the other choices before we come back to the ones we've kept.

(D) Nothing about greenhouse gases in this. And what are "exploding theories"? Get rid of this one.

(E) What about the greenhouse effect? Also, there was no "challenging" involved.

Now that we've eliminated three choices, let's go back to (B) and (C). Is there anything about "solar radiation" in our notes? No. So that can't be the primary concern of the passage. Choice (C) is right in line with what we wrote down as the main idea. It's the best choice.

You must be absolutely certain to cross out incorrect choices (of course you'll write A, B, C, D, E down on your scratch paper for this purpose) as you eliminate them. The key to doing well on Reading Comp is to narrow the field as rapidly as possible. Small differences between a couple of choices are easier to see once you've swept away the clutter.

QUESTIONS ABOUT TONE, ATTITUDE, OR STYLE

The second type of general question asks you to identify the author's tone, style, or overall point of view. Is the author being critical, neutral, or sympathetic? Is the passage subjective or objective? Like main idea questions, these questions can be phrased in several ways:

The author's tone is best described as . . .

The author views his subject with . . .

The author's presentation is best characterized as . . .

The passage is most likely from . . .

The author most likely thinks the reader is . . .

These questions are usually easy to spot, because the answers seldom contain many words. In fact, each choice may be just a single word. These questions are also usually easy to answer, because ETS writes them in very predictable ways. Here are the main things for you to remember:

- ETS is politically correct. Any negative or politically *incorrect* choices can quickly be eliminated.

- ETS has respect for the authors and the subjects of these Reading Comp passages. If an answer choice says that the purpose of a passage is "to demonstrate the intellectual dishonesty of our founding fathers," you can safely eliminate it without so much as glancing at the passage.

- You can eliminate any choice that is too negative or too extreme. ETS's reading passages don't have strong emotions. ETS is a middle-of-the-road, responsible establishment—i.e., boring. The tone of a passage will never be scathing. An author's style would never be violent. An author will never be irrational.

Least/Except/Not Questions

Lots of careless errors are made on these questions. In order for you to avoid making them, you need to keep reminding yourself that ETS's answer will be the choice that is *wrong*. Here are some of the ways these questions are phrased:

For the latest on the GRE, check www.PrincetonReview.com or www.gre.org.

> Which of the following statements would the author be LEAST likely to agree with?

> According to the passage, all of the following are true EXCEPT . . .

> Which of the following does NOT support the defense?

The best answer will be the wrong answer, the crazy choice that normally would be the first choice to eliminate.

For EXCEPT questions, look for "correct" answers (there should be four of them)—and eliminate them. That is, refer back to the passage with each remaining choice and see if the passage supports it. If it does, it's not good. You're looking for the one choice that doesn't make sense.

I, II, III Questions

These time-consuming questions, in which you are asked to deal with three statements identified with Roman numerals, are a good place to use POE. Start with the shortest of the Roman-numeral statements and go back to the passage to find out if it's true or false.

When you find a false statement, be sure to eliminate all appropriate answer choices on your scratch paper that include the Roman numeral for that statement. When you find a true statement, cross out any answer choice that does not include its Roman numeral on your scratch paper. Don't do more work than you have to.

Let's try an example from our sample passage on page 65.

The discussion of water vapor in the passage suggests which of the following conclusions?

I. Water vapor in the atmosphere helps to create an insulating layer that traps heat in the atmosphere.

II. Water vapor in the upper levels of the atmosphere can have a significant effect on ozone levels.

III. Water vapor in the atmosphere could act to decrease as well as increase global temperatures.

○ I only
○ III only
○ I and II only
○ I and III only
○ I, II, and III

Here's how to crack it

Notice that this is another specific question with lead words. Let's go back to the passage to find out what it said about "water vapor." Water vapor is mentioned in the third paragraph. There it says, "A warmer atmosphere can hold more water vapor, which is itself a powerful greenhouse gas, and amplify the warming." Let's use this information to cancel some of the answer choices.

Roman numeral I seems like a good paraphrase of the sentence in the passage, so this Roman numeral must be part of the best answer, and we can eliminate all the choices that don't include it—eliminate (B).

There was nothing in the passage connecting water vapor and ozone levels. Eliminate all the choices that contain Roman numeral II. That gets rid of (C) and (E).

Now let's consider Roman numeral III. Go back to the third paragraph again. Read the last sentence of that paragraph. Remember what we learned when we answered the second question, that the greenhouse effect might have both warming and cooling effects on temperature. So if water vapor is itself a greenhouse gas, then it could have both of these effects as well. The best answer is (D).

8

Vocabulary for the GRE

VOCAB, VOCAB, VOCAB

The techniques for cracking the Verbal section on the GRE are very effective, but how helpful they are to you will depend on the quality of your vocabulary. Again, our techniques can help you get maximum possible mileage out of the words you do know. The more words you know, the more help the techniques can be.

THE HIT PARADE

The Princeton Review has compiled a vocabulary list that contains the most frequently tested words on the GRE. We made this list, which we call the Hit Parade, by analyzing released GREs with our computers. Keep in mind that Hit Parade words make very good guesses on questions where you don't know what else to pick.

GET TO WORK!

Learning the GRE Hit Parade may be the single most important thing you do to prepare for the GRE. Learning these words will give you a solid background in the vocabulary most likely to appear on your test. It will also give you a better idea of the kinds of words that crop up again and again on the GRE. Learning the Hit Parade will give you a feel for the level of vocabulary that ETS likes to test. Then it will be easier to spot other possible GRE words in your everyday life.

Each word on the Hit Parade is followed by the part of speech and a brief definition. Most of the words on the list have other meanings as well, but the definitions we have given are the ones you are most likely to find on the GRE.

LEARNING NEW WORDS

How will you remember all these words? By developing a standard routine for learning new words. Here are some tips:

- When you come across a word you don't know, look it up. If you don't have a dictionary handy, write down the new word and look it up later. If you have somehow managed to make it through college without owning a dictionary, go buy one right now.

- When you look up the word, say it out loud, being careful to pronounce it correctly. Saying the word to yourself isn't enough. You'll remember it better if you make a little noise.

- When you look up your word in the dictionary, don't assume that the first definition is the one that applies. The first definition may be an archaic one, or one that applies only in a particular context. Scan through all the definitions, looking for the one that fits the context in which you found your word.

- Now that you've learned the dictionary's definition of your new word, restate it in your own words. You'll find it much easier to remember a word's meaning if you make it your own. You'll have to be certain, of course, that your definition is consistent with the one in the dictionary.

Improving your vocabulary is the single most important thing you can do to improve your Verbal score.

- Mnemonics—Use your imagination to create a mental image to fix the new word in your mind. For example, if you're trying to remember the word "dogmatic," which means stubborn, picture in your mind a stubborn dog who keeps pulling you toward a tree he wants to sniff even though you don't want him to go there. The crazier the image, the better.

- Keep a vocabulary notebook. Simply having a notebook with you will remind you to be on the lookout for new words, and using it will help you to remember the ones you encounter. Writing something down makes it easier to memorize. Jot down the word when you find it, note its pronunciation and definition (in your own words) when you look it up, and jot down your mnemonic or mental image. You might also copy the sentence in which you originally found the word, to remind yourself of how the word looks in context.

- Do the same thing with flash cards. Write the word on one side and the pronunciation, meaning, and perhaps a mental image on the other. Stick five or six of your flash cards in your pocket every morning and use them when you can.

- Use your new word every chance you get. Make it part of your life. Insert it into your speech at every opportunity. A powerful vocabulary requires lots of exercise.

Learn new words little by little; don't try to learn a ton at once!

THE GRE HIT PARADE

Start working on your vocabulary now!

abate	verb	to lessen in intensity or degree
aberrant	adjective	deviating from the norm
abscond	verb	to depart clandestinely; to steal away and hide
accolade	noun	an expression of praise
acerbic	adjective	having a sour or bitter taste or character
acumen	noun	quick, keen, or accurate knowledge or insight
adulation	noun	excessive praise; intense adoration
adulterate	verb	to reduce purity by combining with inferior ingredients
aesthetic	adjective	dealing with, appreciative of, or responsive to art or the beautiful
aggrandize	verb	to increase in intensity, power, or prestige
alacrity	noun	eager and enthusiastic willingness
alchemy	noun	a medieval science aimed at the transmutation of metals, especially base metals, into gold
amalgamate	verb	to combine several elements into a whole
ameliorate	verb	to make better or more tolerable
amenable	adjective	agreeable; responsive to suggestion
anachronism	noun	something or someone out of place in terms of its historical or chronological context
anomaly	noun	deviation from the normal order, form, or rule; abnormality
approbation	noun	an expression of approval or praise
archaic	adjective	outdated; associated with an earlier, perhaps more primitive, time
arduous	adjective	strenuous, taxing, requiring significant effort
ascetic	noun	one who practices rigid self-denial, especially as an act of religious devotion

assuage	verb	to ease or lessen; to appease or pacify
astringent	adjective	having a tightening effect on living tissue; harsh; severe
audacious	adjective	daring and fearless; recklessly bold
austere	adjective	without adornment; bare; severely simple; ascetic
avarice	noun	greed, especially for wealth
aver	verb	to state as a fact; to confirm or support
axiom/axiomatic	noun/adjective	a universally recognized principle; taken as a given; possessing self-evident truth
bolster	verb	to provide support or reinforcement
bombast/bombastic	noun/adjective	self-evident or pompous writing or speech; pompous; grandiloquent
bucolic	adjective	rustic and pastoral; characteristic of rural areas and their inhabitants
burgeon	verb	to grow rapidly; to flourish
cacophony	noun	harsh, jarring, discordant sound; dissonance
canon	noun	an established set of principles or code of laws, often religious in nature
canonical	adjective	following or in agreement with orthodox requirements
capricious	adjective	inclined to change one's mind impulsively; erratic; unpredictable
castigation	noun	severe criticism or punishment
catalyst	noun	a substance that accelerates the rate of a chemical reaction without itself changing; a person or thing that causes change
caustic	adjective	burning or stinging; causing corrosion
censure	verb	to criticize severely; to officially rebuke

chary	adjective	wary; cautious
chicanery	noun	trickery or subterfuge
cogent	adjective	appealing forcibly to the mind or reason; convincing
complaisance	noun	the willingness to comply with the wishes of others
connoisseur	noun	an informed and astute judge in matters of taste; expert
contentious	adjective	argumentative; quarrelsome; causing controversy or disagreement
contrite	adjective	regretful; penitent; seeking forgiveness
convention	noun	a generally agreed-upon practice or attitude
convoluted	adjective	complex or complicated
credulous	adjective	tending to believe too readily; gullible
culpable	adjective	deserving blame
cynicism	noun	an attitude or quality of belief that all people are motivated by selfishness
dearth	noun	smallness of quantity or number; scarcity; a lack
decorum	noun	polite or appropriate conduct or behavior
demur	verb	to question or oppose
derision	noun	scorn, ridicule, contemptuous treatment
desiccate	verb	to dry out or dehydrate; to make dry or dull
diatribe	noun	a harsh denunciation
didactic	adjective	intended to teach or instruct
dilettante	noun	one with an amateurish or superficial interest in the arts or a branch of knowledge
disabuse	verb	to undeceive; to set right
discordant	adjective	conflicting; dissonant or harsh in sound

discretion	noun	cautious reserve in speech; ability to make responsible decisions
disinterested	adjective	indifferent; free from self-interest
disparage	verb	to slight or belittle
disparate	adjective	fundamentally distinct or dissimilar
dissemble	verb	to disguise or conceal; to mislead
divulge	verb	to disclose something secret
dogmatic	adjective	stubbornly opinionated
ebullience	noun	the quality of lively or enthusiastic expression of thoughts and feelings
eccentric	adjective	departing from norms or conventions
eclectic	adjective	composed of elements drawn from various sources
effrontery	noun	extreme boldness; presumptuousness
elegy	noun	a mournful poem, especially one lamenting the dead
eloquent	adjective	well-spoken; expressive; articulate
emollient	adjective	soothing, especially to the skin; making less harsh; mollifying
empirical	adjective	based on observation or experiment
endemic	adjective	characteristic of or often found in a particular locality, region, or people
enervate	verb	to weaken; to reduce in vitality
enigmatic	adjective	mysterious; obscure; difficult to understand
ennui	noun	dissatisfaction and restlessness resulting from boredom or apathy
ephemeral	adjective	brief; fleeting
equivocate	verb	to use ambiguous language with a deceptive intent
erudite	adjective	very learned; scholarly
esoteric	adjective	intended for or understood by a small, specific group
eulogy	noun	a speech honoring the dead

evanescent	adjective	tending to disappear like vapor; vanishing
exacerbate	verb	to make worse or more severe
exculpate	verb	exonerate; to clear of blame
exigent	adjective	urgent; pressing; requiring immediate action or attention
exonerate	verb	to remove blame
extemporaneous	adjective	improvised; done without preparation
facetious	adjective	playful; humorous
fallacy	noun	an invalid or incorrect notion; a mistaken belief
fawn	verb	to flatter or praise excessively
fervent	adjective	greatly emotional or zealous
filibuster	noun	intentional obstruction, especially using prolonged speechmaking to delay legislative action
flout	verb	to demonstrate contempt for, as in a rule or convention
fortuitous	adjective	happening by fortunate accident or chance
fulminate	verb	to loudly attack or denounce
furtive	adjective	marked by stealth; covert; surreptitious
garrulous	adjective	pointlessly talkative, talking too much
germane	adjective	relevant to the subject at hand; appropriate in subject matter
glib	adjective	marked by ease or informality; nonchalant; lacking in depth; superficial
grandiloquence	noun	pompous speech or expression
gregarious	adjective	sociable; outgoing; enjoying the company of other people
hackneyed	adjective	rendered trite or commonplace by frequent usage
halcyon	adjective	calm and peaceful

harangue	verb	to deliver a pompous speech or tirade
hedonism	noun	devotion to pleasurable pursuits, especially to the pleasures of the senses
hegemony	noun	the consistent dominance of one state or ideology over others
heretical	adjective	violating accepted dogma or convention
hubris	noun	arrogant presumption or pride
hyperbole	noun	an exaggerated statement, often used as a figure of speech
iconoclast	noun	one who attacks or undermines traditional conventions or institutions
idolatrous	adjective	given to intense or excessive devotion to something
imminent	adjective	about to happen; impending
immutable	adjective	not capable of change
impassive	adjective	revealing no emotion
impecunious	adjective	lacking funds; without money
imperturbable	adjective	marked by extreme calm, impassivity, and steadiness
impetuous	adjective	hastily or rashly energetic; impulsive and vehement
implacable	adjective	not capable of being appeased or significantly changed
impunity	noun	immunity from punishment or penalty
inchoate	adjective	in an initial stage; not fully formed
incipient	adjective	beginning to come into being or to become apparent
indifferent	adjective	having no interest or concern; showing no bias or prejudice
inert	adjective	unmoving; lethargic; sluggish
infelicitous	adjective	unfortunate; inappropriate
ingenuous	adjective	artless; frank and candid; lacking in sophistication

inimical	adjective	damaging; harmful; malevolent
innocuous	adjective	harmless; causing no damage
insipid	adjective	without taste or flavor; lacking in spirit; bland
intractable	adjective	not easily managed or directed; stubborn, obstinate
intransigent	adjective	refusing to compromise
intrepid	adjective	steadfast and courageous
inured	adjective	accustomed to accepting something undesirable
inveigle	verb	to obtain by deception or flattery
irascible	adjective	easily angered; prone to temperamental outbursts
laconic	adjective	using few words; terse
laud	verb	to praise highly
loquacious	adjective	extremely talkative
lucid	adjective	clear; easily understood
luminous	adjective	characterized by brightness and the emission of light
magnanimity	noun	the quality of being generously noble in mind and heart, especially in forgiving
malevolent	adjective	having or showing often vicious ill will, spite, or hatred
malleable	adjective	capable of being shaped or formed; tractable; pliable
martial	adjective	associated with war and the armed forces
maverick	noun	an independent individual who does not go along with a group or party
mendacity	noun	the condition of being untruthful; dishonesty
mercurial	adjective	characterized by rapid and unpredictable change in mood
meticulous	adjective	characterized by extreme care and precision; attentive to detail
misanthrope	noun	one who hates all other humans

mitigate	verb	to make or become less severe or intense; to moderate
mollify	verb	to calm or soothe; to reduce in emotional intensity
morose	adjective	sad; sullen; melancholy
mundane	adjective	of the world; typical of or concerned with the ordinary
nascent	adjective	coming into being; in early developmental stages
nebulous	adjective	vague; cloudy; lacking clearly defined form
neologism	noun	a new word, expression, or usage; the creation or use of new words or senses
neophyte	noun	a recent convert; a beginner; novice
noxious	adjective	harmful; injurious
obdurate	adjective	unyielding; hardhearted; intractable
obfuscate	verb	to deliberately obscure; to make confusing
obsequious	adjective	exhibiting a fawning attentiveness
obstinate	adjective	stubborn; hardheaded; uncompromising
obtuse	adjective	lacking sharpness of intellect; not clear or precise in thought or expression
obviate	verb	to anticipate and make unnecessary
occlude	verb	to obstruct or block
odious	adjective	evoking intense aversion or dislike
onerous	adjective	troubling; burdensome
opaque	adjective	impenetrable by light; not reflecting light
opprobrium	noun	disgrace; contempt; scorn
oscillation	noun	the act or state of swinging back and forth with a steady, uninterrupted rhythm
ostentatious	adjective	characterized by or given to pretentiousness

Try using these vocabulary words in your everyday conversations.

paean	noun	a song or hymn of praise and thanksgiving
parody	noun	a humorous imitation intended for ridicule or comic effect, especially in literature and art
pedagogy	noun	the art or profession of training, teaching, or instructing
pedantic	adjective	the parading of learning; excessive attention to minutiae and formal rules
penurious	adjective	penny-pinching; excessively thrifty; ungenerous
penury	noun	poverty; destitution
perennial	adjective	recurrent through the year or many years; happening repeatedly
perfidy	noun	intentional breach of faith; treachery
perfunctory	adjective	cursory; done without care or interest
pernicious	adjective	extremely harmful; potentially causing death
perspicacious	adjective	acutely perceptive; having keen discernment
peruse	verb	to examine with great care
pervade	verb	to permeate throughout
pervasive	adjective	having the tendency to permeate or spread throughout
phlegmatic	adjective	calm; sluggish; unemotional
pine	verb	to yearn intensely; to languish; to lose vigor
pious	adjective	extremely reverent or devout; showing strong religious devotion
pirate	verb	to illegally use or reproduce
pith/pithy	noun/adjective	the essential or central part; precise and brief
placate	verb	to appease; to calm by making concessions
platitude	noun	a superficial remark, especially one offered as meaningful

plethora	noun	an overabundance; a surplus
plummet	verb	to plunge or drop straight down
polemical	adjective	controversial; argumentative
pragmatic	adjective	practical rather than idealistic
prattle	verb	to babble meaninglessly; to talk in an empty and idle manner
precipitate	verb/adjective	to cause or to happen before anticipated or required; acting with excessive haste or impulse
precursor	noun	one that indicates or announces someone or something to come
predilection	noun	a disposition in favor of something; preference
preen	verb	to dress up; to primp; to groom oneself with elaborate care
prescience	noun	foreknowledge of events; knowing of events prior to their occurring
presumptuous	adjective	overstepping due bounds (as of propriety or courtesy); taking liberties
prevaricate	verb	to deliberately avoid the truth; to mislead
pristine	adjective	pure; uncorrupted; clean
probity	noun	adherence to highest principles; uprightness
proclivity	noun	a natural predisposition or inclination
prodigal	adjective	recklessly wasteful; extravagant; profuse; lavish
prodigious	adjective	abundant in size, force, or extent; extraordinary
profligate	adjective	excessively wasteful; recklessly extravagant
profuse	adjective	given or coming forth abundantly; extravagant
proliferate	verb	to grow or increase swiftly and abundantly
prolific	adjective	producing large volumes or amounts; productive

propensity	noun	a natural inclination or tendency; penchant
prosaic	adjective	dull; unimaginative
pungent	adjective	characterized by a strong, sharp smell or taste
putrefy	verb	to rot; to decay and give off a foul odor
quaff	verb	to drink deeply
qualm	noun	misgiving; reservation; cause for hesitancy
querulous	adjective	prone to complaining or grumbling; quarrelsome
query	noun	question; inquiry; doubt in the mind; reservation
quiescence	noun	stillness; motionlessness; quality of being at rest
quixotic	adjective	foolishly impractical; marked by lofty romantic ideals
quotidian	adjective	occurring or recurring daily; commonplace
rancorous	adjective	characterized by bitter, long-lasting resentment
rarefy	verb	to make or become thin, less dense; to refine
recalcitrant	adjective	obstinately defiant of authority; difficult to manage
recant	verb	to retract, especially a previously held belief
recondite	adjective	hidden; concealed; difficult to understand; obscure
redoubtable	adjective	awe-inspiring; worthy of honor
refulgent	adjective	radiant; shiny; brilliant
refute	verb	to disprove; to successfully argue against
relegate	verb	to forcibly assign, especially to a lower place or position
renege	verb	to fail to honor a commitment; to go back on a promise
repudiate	verb	to refuse to have anything to do with; disown

rescind	verb	to invalidate; to repeal; to retract
reticent	adjective	quiet; reserved; reluctant to express thoughts and feelings
reverent	adjective	marked by, feeling, or expressing profound awe and respect
rhetoric	noun	the art or study of effective use of language for communication and persuasion
salubrious	adjective	promoting health or well-being
sanction	noun	authoritative permission or approval; a penalty intended to enforce compliance
satire	noun	a literary work that ridicules or criticizes a human vice through humor or derision
sedulous	adjective	diligent; persistent; hardworking
shard	noun	a piece of broken pottery or glass
solicitous	adjective	concerned and attentive; eager
solvent	adjective	able to meet financial obligations; able to dissolve another substance
soporific	adjective	causing drowsiness; tending to induce sleep
sordid	adjective	characterized by filth, grime, or squalor; foul
sparse	adjective	thin; not dense; arranged at widely spaced intervals
specious	adjective	seeming true, but actually being fallacious; misleadingly attractive
spendthrift	noun	one who spends money wastefully
sporadic	adjective	occurring only occasionally, or in scattered instances
spurious	adjective	lacking authenticity or validity; false; counterfeit
squalid	adjective	sordid; wretched and dirty as from neglect
squander	verb	to waste by spending or using irresponsibly
static	adjective	not moving, active, or in motion; at rest

stoic	adjective	indifferent to or unaffected by pleasure or pain; steadfast
stupefy	verb	to stun, baffle, or amaze
stymie	verb	to block; thwart
subpoena	noun	a court order requiring appearance and/or testimony
subtle	adjective	not obvious; elusive; difficult to discern
succinct	adjective	brief; concise
superfluous	adjective	exceeding what is sufficient or necessary
supplant	verb	to take the place of; supersede
surfeit	verb	excess; overindulgence
synthesis	noun	the combination of parts to make a whole
tacit	adjective	implied; not explicitly stated
tenacity	noun	the quality of adherence or persistence to something valued
tenuous	adjective	having little substance or strength; flimsy; weak
terse	adjective	brief and concise in wording
tirade	noun	a long and extremely critical speech; a harsh denunciation
torpid	adjective	lethargic; sluggish; dormant
torque	noun	a force that causes rotation
tortuous	adjective	winding; twisting; excessively complicated
tout	verb	to publicly praise or promote
transient	adjective	fleeting; passing quickly; brief
trenchant	adjective	sharply perceptive; keen; penetrating
truculent	adjective	fierce and cruel; eager to fight
ubiquitous	adjective	existing everywhere at the same time; constantly encountered; widespread
unfeigned	adjective	genuine; not false or hypocritical
untenable	adjective	indefensible; not viable; uninhabitable

urbane	adjective	sophisticated; refined; elegant
vacillate	verb	to waver indecisively between one course of action or opinion and another
variegated	adjective	multicolored; characterized by a variety of patches of different color
veracity	noun	truthfulness; honesty
vexation	noun	annoyance; irritation
vigilant	adjective	alertly watchful
vilify	verb	to defame; to characterize harshly
virulent	adjective	extremely harmful or poisonous; bitterly hostile or antagonistic
viscous	adjective	thick; sticky
vituperate	verb	to use harsh, condemnatory language; to abuse or censure severely or abusively; berate
volatile	adjective	readily changing to a vapor; changeable; fickle; explosive
voracious	adjective	having an insatiable appetite for an activity or pursuit; ravenous
waver	verb	to move to and fro; to sway; to be unsettled in opinion
zealous	adjective	fervent; ardent; impassioned

Improving your vocabulary is the single most important thing you can do to improve your Verbal score.

PART III

How to Crack
the Math Section

9

The Geography of the Math Section

WHAT'S IN THE MATH SECTION

Every GRE contains a scored "Quantitative Ability," or Math, section. This section will last 45 minutes and contain 28 questions in two different question formats, which pop up in no particular order:

- 13 to 15 four-choice Quantitative Comparison questions
- 12 to 16 five-choice Problem Solving questions, including 4 to 6 chart questions (with 2 to 3 charts)

JUNIOR HIGH SCHOOL?

The GRE mostly tests how much you remember from the math courses you took in seventh, eighth, and ninth grade. Why is a passing knowledge of eighth-grade algebra important for a future Ph.D. in English literature? Don't ask us. Apparently ETS thinks there's a connection.

But here's some good news: GRE math is easier than SAT math. Why? Because many people study little or no math in college. If the GRE tested "college-level" math, everyone but math majors would bomb.

If you're willing to do a little work, this is good news for you. By brushing up on the modest amount of math you need to know for the test, you can significantly increase your GRE Math score. All you have to do is shake off the rust.

IT'S REALLY A READING TEST

In constructing the Math section, ETS is limited to the math that nearly everyone has studied: arithmetic, basic algebra, basic geometry, and elementary statistics. There's no calculus (or even precalculus), no trigonometry, and no major-league algebra or geometry. Because of these limitations, ETS has to resort to traps in order to create hard problems. Even the most difficult GRE math problems are typically based on relatively simple principles. What makes the problems difficult is that these simple principles are disguised. So this is more of a reading test than a math test. Read carefully, and you will prevail.

> Practice doing simple math with your pencil in real life. Don't use a calculator!

MAXIMIZE YOUR SCORE

You will score higher if you spend your time working slowly and carefully at the beginning of the section. Remember, the questions you answer at the beginning of each section of the GRE have a much greater impact on your final score than do the questions you answer at the end.

SCRATCH PAPER

Your use of scratch paper is crucial on the Math section. Don't try to do any calculations in your head. Write it all down so you don't make careless errors. The first thing you should do for *every* question is write down A, B, C, D, E on your scratch paper (or A, B, C, D if it's a Quantitative Comparison).

READ AND COPY CAREFULLY

You can do all the calculations right and still get a question wrong. How? What if you solve for x but the question was, "What is the value of $x + 4$?" Ugh. Always *reread* the question. Take your time and don't be careless. The problem will stay on the screen as long as you want it to, so reread the question and double-check your work before answering it.

Or how about this: The radius of the circle is 5, but when you copied the picture onto your scratch paper, you accidentally made it 6. Ugh! Many of the mistakes you will make at first probably stem from copying information down incorrectly. Learn from your mistakes! You have to be extra careful when copying down information.

ON THE SCREEN

GRE Math questions come in two flavors, which are both multiple choice. The first question type is the five-choice Problem Solving question (which is in the same format as the Verbal questions). These questions are usually pretty straightforward. You're given a problem, offered five solutions, and asked to pick one. The second type is the Quantitative Comparison, or "Quant Comp" problem, which will be explained in detail below.

CHART QUESTIONS

A subset of the five-choice Problem Solving question type is the chart question, which comes with, yes, charts, graphs, or tables that you have to interpret. There are usually two or three questions per chart or set of charts. Like the Reading Comprehension questions, chart questions appear on split screens. Be sure to click on the scroll bar and scroll down as far as you can; there may be additional charts underneath the top one, and you certainly want to make sure you've seen all the charts. You generally don't have to do all the calculations to answer chart questions, because the answer choices are often far enough apart that you can approximate. Because chart questions generally focus on percentages, they'll be discussed in depth in the percentages section of the Variables and Equations chapter.

CRACKING QUANT COMP QUESTIONS

Quant Comp questions ask you to compare a quantity in Column A to a quantity in Column B. They have four answer choices instead of five, and the answer choices are *always* the same. Here they are:

- ◯ the quantity in Column A is always greater
- ◯ the quantity in Column B is always greater
- ◯ the quantities are always equal
- ◯ it cannot be determined from the information given

Your job is to *compare* the quantities in the columns, and choose one of these answers.

The content of the Quant Comp problems is drawn from the same basic arithmetic, algebra, and geometry concepts that are used on the GRE math problems in other formats. So, to solve these problems, you'll apply the same techniques that you use on the other GRE Math questions. But Quant Comps also have a few special rules you need to remember.

THERE IS NO "E"

With only four choices on Quant Comp questions, your odds of guessing are even better—a blind guess is one out of four, which is better than one out of five. When using your scratch paper to eliminate answer choices, be sure to write down only A,B, C, D, instead of A, B, C, D, E.

IF A QUANT COMP CONTAINS ONLY NUMBERS, THE ANSWER CAN'T BE "D"

Any problem containing only numbers and no variables *must* have a single solution. Therefore, on such problems choice (D) can be eliminated immediately — after all, the solution *can* be determined. For example, if you're being asked to compare 3/2 and 3/4, you know that the answer can be determined, so the answer cannot be (D).

IT'S NOT WHAT IT *IS;* IT'S WHICH IS *BIGGER*

You don't always have to calculate the exact values in both columns before you compare. After all, your mission here is simply to compare the two columns. It's often helpful to treat the two columns as if they were two sides of an equation. Anything you can do to both sides of an equation, you can also do to the expressions in both columns. You can add the same number to both sides; you can multiply both sides by the same positive number; you can simplify a single side by multiplying it by some form of one. But there's one exception: Don't multiply or divide both sides by a negative number.

If you *can* simplify the terms of a Quant Comp, you should *always* do so. As is so often true on the GRE, finding the answer is frequently a matter of simplifying, reducing, factoring, or unfactoring.

Here's a quick example:

Column A	Column B
$\dfrac{1}{16}+\dfrac{1}{7}+\dfrac{1}{4}$	$\dfrac{1}{4}+\dfrac{1}{16}+\dfrac{1}{6}$

- ○ the quantity in Column A is always greater
- ○ the quantity in Column B is always greater
- ○ the quantities are always equal
- ○ it cannot be determined from the information given

Don't do any calculating! Remember, it's not what's *in* each column — it's which column is *bigger*! The first thing you should do is eliminate (D). After all, there are only numbers here, so there is definitely a solution. After that, get rid of numbers that are common to both columns (think of this as simplifying). Both columns contain a $\frac{1}{16}$ and a $\frac{1}{4}$, so they can't possibly make a difference to the outcome. With them eliminated, you are merely comparing the $\frac{1}{7}$ in Column A to the $\frac{1}{6}$ in Column B. Now we can eliminate (C) as well — after all, there is no way that $\frac{1}{7}$ is ever equal to $\frac{1}{6}$. So, we're down to two choices, (A) and (B). If you don't remember how to compare fractions, don't worry — it's covered in the Numbers chapter. But in case you can't wait, the answer to this question is (B).

MORE TIPS FOR A HIGHER GRE MATH SCORE

On all question types, be sure to use Process of Elimination whenever you can. When you read a math problem, don't forget to read the answer choices *before* you start to solve the problem, because they are a part of the problem and can help guide you. Often, you will be able to eliminate a couple of answer choices before you begin to calculate the exact answer. *Physically* eliminate them on your scratch paper.

YOU KNOW MORE THAN YOU THINK

Say you were asked to find 30 percent of 50. Don't do any math yet. Now, let's say that you glance at the answer choices and you see these:

- ◯ 5
- ◯ 15
- ◯ 30
- ◯ 80
- ◯ 150

Think about it. Whatever 30 percent of 50 is, it must be less than 50, right? So any answer choice greater than 50 can't be right. That means you should eliminate both 80 and 150 before you even do any calculations! That is known as . . .

BALLPARKING

Ballparking will help you eliminate answer choices and increase your odds of zeroing in on the correct answer. Remember to eliminate any answer choice that is "out of the ballpark."

Ballparking answers will help you eliminate choices.

How to Study

Make sure you learn the content of each chapter cold before you go on to the next one. Don't try to cram everything in all at once. It's much better to do a small amount of studying each day over a longer period. You will master both the math concepts and the techniques if you focus on a little bit at a time.

Practice, Practice

Since most of us don't do much math in "real life," you can start by *not avoiding* math as you normally would. Balance your checkbook—without a calculator! Make sure your check is added correctly at a restaurant, and figure out the exact percentage you want to leave for a tip. The more you practice simple adding, subtracting, multiplying, and dividing on a day-to-day basis, the more your arithmetic skills will improve for the GRE.

After you work through this book, be sure to practice on our online tests and real GREs. Practice will rapidly sharpen your test-taking skills. Unless you trust our techniques, you may be reluctant to use them fully and automatically on a real administration of the GRE. The best way to develop that trust is to practice before you get to the real test.

10
Numbers

GRE MATH VOCABULARY

Quick—what's an integer? Is 0 even or odd? How many even prime numbers are there?

Even though all of the math terms we will review are very simple, that doesn't mean they're not important. Every GRE Math question uses these simple rules and definitions. You absolutely need to know this math "vocabulary." Don't worry, we will only cover the math terms that you *must* know for the GRE.

Learn this math vocabulary!

INTEGERS

The integers are the "big places" on the number line: –6, –5, –4, –3, –2, –1, 0, 1, 2, 3, 4, 5, 6.

Remember, fractions are NOT integers.

Notice that fractions, such as $\frac{1}{2}$, are not integers.

Remember that the number zero is an integer! Positive integers get bigger as they move away from 0 (6 is bigger than 5); negative integers get smaller as they move away from zero (–6 is smaller than –5).

CONSECUTIVE INTEGERS

Consecutive integers are integers listed in order of increasing value without any integers missing in between, such as:

- 0, 1, 2, 3, 4, 5
- –6, –5, –4, –3, –2, –1, 0
- –3, –2, –1, 0, 1, 2, 3

By the way, no numbers other than integers can be consecutive. However, you can list integers by type. In other words, if you were asked to list a group of consecutive even integers, you could put down: 2, 4, 6, 8, 10.

ZERO

Zero is a special little number. It is an integer, but it is neither positive nor negative. However:

- 0 is even.
- The sum of 0 and any other number is that other number.
- The product of 0 and any other number is 0.

DIGITS

There are 10 digits: 0, 1, 2, 3, 4, 5, 6, 7, 8, 9.

Simple, right? Just think of them as the numbers on your phone dial. All integers are made up of digits. For example, the integer 10,897 has 5 digits: 1, 0, 8, 9, 7. So, it's a 5-digit integer. Each of its digits has its own name:

- 7 is the units digit.
- 9 is the tens digit.
- 8 is the hundreds digit.
- 0 is the thousands digit.
- 1 is the ten thousands digit.

POSITIVE OR NEGATIVE

Numbers can be positive (+) or negative (–). For the GRE, you'll need to remember what happens when you multiply positive and negative numbers:

- pos × pos = pos   2 × 2 = 4
- neg × neg = pos   –2 × –2 = 4
- pos × neg = neg   2 × –2 = –4

EVEN OR ODD

An even number is any integer that can be divided evenly by 2; an odd number is any integer that can't.

- Here are some even integers: –4, –2, 0, 2, 4, 6, 8, 10.
- Here are some odd integers: –3, –1, 1, 3, 5, 7, 9, 11.

Keep in mind

- Zero is even.
- Fractions are neither even nor odd.
- Any integer is even if its units digit is even; any integer is odd if its units digit is odd.
- The results of adding and multiplying odd and even integers:
  - even + even = even
  - odd + odd = even
  - even + odd = odd
  - even × even = even
  - odd × odd = odd
  - even × odd = even

Be careful: Don't confuse odd and even with positive and negative.

PRIME NUMBERS

A prime number is a number that is divisible only by itself and 1. Here are *all* the prime numbers less than 30: 2, 3, 5, 7, 11, 13, 17, 19, 23, 29.

- 0 is not a prime number.
- 1 is not a prime number.
- 2 is the only even prime number.

DIVISIBILITY

Here are some rules for divisibility:

- An integer is divisible by 2 if its units digit is divisible by 2. For example, we know just by glancing that 598,447,896 is divisible by 2, because the units digit, 6, is divisible evenly by 2.
- An integer is divisible by 3 if the sum of its digits is divisible by 3. For example, we know that 2,145 is divisible by 3, because 2 + 1 + 4 + 5 = 12, and 12 is divisible by 3.
- An integer is divisible by 4 if its last two digits form a number divisible by 4. For example, 712 is divisible by 4 because 12 is divisible by 4.
- An integer is divisible by 5 if its units digit is either 0 or 5.

- An integer is divisible by 6 if it's divisible by *both* 2 *and* 3.
- An integer is divisible by 9 if the sum of its digits is divisible by 9.
- An integer is divisible by 10 if its units digit is 0.

Remainders

The remainder is the number left over when one integer cannot be divided evenly by another. The remainder is always an integer. (Remember grade school math class? It's the number that came after the big "R.")

For example, 4 divided by 2 is 2; there is nothing left over, so there's no remainder. In other words, 4 is divisible by 2. You could also say that the remainder is 0.

Five divided by 2 is 2 with 1 left over; 1 is the remainder. Six divided by 7 is 0 with 6 left over; 6 is the remainder.

You CAN improve your scores!

Factors

A number a is a factor of another number b if b can be divided by a without leaving a remainder. 1, 2, 3, 4, 6, and 12 are all factors of 12. Write down the factors systematically in pairs of numbers that when multiplied together make 12, starting with 1 and the number itself:

There are only a few factors of any number; there are many multiples of any number.

- 1 and 12
- 2 and 6
- 3 and 4

If you always start with 1 and the number itself and work your way up, you'll remember them all.

Multiples

A multiple of a number is that number multiplied by an integer other than 0. –20, –10, 10, 20, 30, 40, 50, 60 are all multiples of 10 (10×-2, 10×-1, 10×1, 10×2, 10×3, 10×4, 10×5, 10×6).

MORE MATH VOCABULARY

Like we said, the Math section is almost as much of a vocabulary test as the Verbal section. Below, you'll find some standard terms that you should commit to memory before you do any practice problems:

Term	Meaning
sum	the result of addition
difference	the result of subtraction
product	the result of multiplication
quotient	the result of division
numerator	the top number in a fraction
denominator	the bottom number in a fraction

ORDER OF OPERATIONS

Many problems require you to perform more than one operation to find ETS's answer. It is absolutely necessary that you perform these operations in *exactly* the right order. In many cases, the correct order will be apparent from the way the problem is written. In cases where the correct order is not apparent, you need only remember the following mnemonic:

Please Excuse My Dear Aunt Sally, or **PEMDAS**.

PEMDAS stands for Parentheses, Exponents, Multiplication, Division, Addition, Subtraction. This is the order in which the operations are to be performed. (Exponents are numbers raised to a power; don't worry, we'll review them soon.)

Here's an example:

$$11 - (7 - 6) - (4 + 3) - 2 =$$

Here's how to crack it

Start with the parentheses. The expression inside the first pair of parentheses, $7 - 6$, equals 1. The expression inside the second pair equals 7. We can now rewrite the problem like this:

$$11 - 1 - 7 - 2 =$$
$$10 - 7 - 2 =$$
$$3 - 2 =$$
$$= 1$$

FRACTIONS

Remember elementary school? A fraction is another way of writing a division problem. For example, the fraction $\frac{2}{3}$ is just another way of writing $2 \div 3$.

A fraction is shorthand for division.

REDUCING FRACTIONS

To reduce a fraction, simply express the numerator and denominator as the products of their factors. Then cross out, or "cancel," factors that are common to both. Here's an example:

$$\frac{16}{20} = \frac{2 \times 2 \times 2 \times 2}{2 \times 2 \times 5} = \frac{\cancel{2} \times \cancel{2} \times 2 \times 2}{\cancel{2} \times \cancel{2} \times 5} = \frac{2 \times 2}{5} = \frac{4}{5}$$

You can achieve the same result by dividing numerator and denominator by the factors that are common to both. In the example you just saw, 4 is a factor of both the numerator and the denominator. That is, both the numerator and the denominator can be divided evenly (without remainder) by 4. Doing this yields the much more manageable fraction $\frac{4}{5}$.

When you confront GRE math problems involving big fractions, always reduce them before doing anything else.

Remember, **you cannot reduce across an equal sign (=), a plus sign (+), or a minus sign (−).**

MULTIPLYING FRACTIONS

There's nothing tricky about multiplying fractions. Just work straight across. All you have to do is place the product of the numerators over the product of the denominators. But see whether you can reduce before you multiply; then you'll be multiplying smaller numbers. Here's an example:

$$\frac{4}{5} \times \frac{10}{12} =$$

$$\frac{\overset{1}{\cancel{4}}}{\cancel{5}} \times \frac{\overset{2}{\cancel{10}}}{\cancel{12}} =$$

$$\frac{1}{1} \times \frac{2}{3} = \frac{2}{3}$$

When one fraction is multiplied by another fraction, the product is *smaller* than either of the original fractions. What happens when you multiply $\frac{1}{2}$ by $\frac{1}{2}$? You get $\frac{1}{4}$, which is smaller than $\frac{1}{2}$.

DIVIDING FRACTIONS

Dividing fractions is just like multiplying fractions, with one crucial difference: You have to turn the second fraction upside down (that is, put its denominator over its numerator), then reduce before you multiply. Remember the word "reciprocal"? Here's an example:

$$\frac{2}{3} \div \frac{4}{5} =$$

$$\frac{2}{3} \times \frac{5}{4} =$$

$$\frac{\overset{1}{\cancel{2}}}{3} \times \frac{5}{\underset{2}{\cancel{4}}} =$$

$$\frac{1}{3} \times \frac{5}{2} = \frac{5}{6}$$

ETS sometimes gives you problems involving fractions whose numerators or denominators are themselves fractions. These problems look intimidating, but if you're careful, then you won't have any trouble with them. All you have to do is remember what we said about a fraction being shorthand for division.

Always rewrite the expression horizontally. Here's an example:

$$\frac{7}{\frac{1}{4}} = 7 \div \frac{1}{4} = \frac{7}{1} \times \frac{4}{1} = \frac{28}{1} = 28$$

ADDING AND SUBTRACTING FRACTIONS

Adding and subtracting fractions that have the same (common) denominator is easy—just add up the numerators and put the sum over that common denominator. Here's an example:

$$\frac{1}{10} + \frac{2}{10} + \frac{4}{10} =$$
$$\frac{1+2+4}{10} = \frac{7}{10}$$

When you're asked to add or subtract fractions with *different* denominators, you need to fiddle around with them so that they end up with a *common* denominator. To do this, all you need to do is multiply the dominators of the two fractions and use a technique we call **the Bowtie**:

$$\frac{2}{3} + \frac{3}{4} =$$

$$\overset{8}{\underset{3}{\frac{2}{3}}} \times \overset{9}{\underset{4}{\frac{3}{4}}} = \frac{8}{12} \Big| \frac{9}{12} = \frac{8}{12} + \frac{9}{12} = \frac{17}{12}$$

In other words, multiply the denominators together to get the new denominator, and multiply diagonally up (as shown) to get the new numerators. Then just add or subtract. Using the Bowtie on these fractions doesn't change the values of the terms, but it does put them in a form that's easier to handle.

COMPARING FRACTIONS

The GRE often presents you with math problems in which you are asked to compare two fractions and decide which is larger. These problems are a snap if you use the Bowtie. You can ignore the denominator and simply find which fraction would have a larger numerator if they had a common denominator. Just multiply the denominator of each fraction by the numerator of the other. Then compare your two products.

$$\frac{3}{7} \qquad \frac{7}{12}$$

$$\overset{36}{\underset{7}{\frac{3}{7}}} \times \overset{49}{\underset{12}{\frac{7}{12}}}$$

> To add, subtract, or compare fractions, use the BOWTIE.

Multiplying the first denominator by the second numerator gives us 49; be sure to write 49 above $\frac{7}{12}$ on your scratch paper. Multiplying the second denominator by the first numerator gives us 36; write that above $\frac{3}{7}$ on your scratch paper. Since 49 is bigger than 36, $\frac{7}{12}$ is bigger than $\frac{3}{7}$.

When using the Bowtie, always work from bottom to top, in the direction of the arrows, as in the problem we just solved. Working in the other direction will give you the wrong answer!

Comparing more than two fractions

You will sometimes be asked to compare more than two fractions. On such problems, don't waste time trying to find a common denominator for all of them. Simply use the Bowtie to compare two of the fractions at a time. Here's an example:

$$\frac{3}{7} \quad \frac{4}{8} \quad \frac{7}{11}$$

Here's how to crack it

ETS loves to compare fractions, especially in Quantitative Comparison questions.

Compare the first two fractions and eliminate the smaller one on your scratch paper (read the question carefully!); compare the remaining fraction with the next in line and eliminate the smaller one; and so on. In this case, $\frac{7}{11}$ wins.

$$\overset{24}{}\quad\overset{28}{}$$
$$\frac{3}{7}\diagdown\diagup\frac{4}{8}$$

$$\overset{44}{}\quad\overset{56}{}$$
$$\frac{4}{8}\diagup\diagdown\frac{7}{11}$$

CONVERTING MIXED NUMBERS INTO FRACTIONS

A **mixed number** is a number that is represented as an integer and a fraction, like this: $2\frac{2}{3}$. In most cases on the GRE, you should get rid of mixed fractions by converting them to fractions. How do you do this? By multiplying the denominator by the integer, adding the numerator, and putting the whole thing over the denominator. In other words $\frac{3\times 2+2}{3}$ or $\frac{8}{3}$.

The result, $\frac{8}{3}$, is equivalent to $2\frac{2}{3}$. The only difference is that $\frac{8}{3}$ is easier to work with in math problems. Also, answer choices are usually in this form.

Be careful

The most common source of errors on GRE fraction problems is carelessness. You'll see problems in which finding ETS's answer will require you to perform several of the steps or operations we've described. Remember that the goal of all these steps and operations is to *simplify* the fractions. **Always write down every step! Use that scratch paper!**

DECIMALS

Decimals are just fractions in a different form. Basically, decimals and fractions are two different ways of expressing the same thing. Every decimal can be written as a fraction; every fraction can be written as a decimal. For example, the decimal .35 can be written as the fraction $\frac{35}{100}$. These two expressions, .35 and $\frac{35}{100}$, have exactly the same value.

To turn a fraction into its decimal equivalent, all you have to do is divide the numerator by the denominator. Here, for example, is how you would find the decimal equivalent of $\frac{3}{4}$:

$$\frac{3}{4} = 3 \div 4 = 4\overline{)3.00} = 0.75$$

The long division shows:

$$
\begin{array}{r}
0.75 \\
4\overline{)3.00} \\
2.8 \\
\hline
20 \\
20 \\
\hline
0
\end{array}
$$

ADDING AND SUBTRACTING DECIMALS

Simply line up the decimal points and proceed as you would if the decimal points weren't there. If the decimal points are missing from the numbers you need to add or subtract, put them in. You can make all your numbers line up evenly by adding zeros to the right of the ones that need them. Here, for example, is how you would add the decimals 23.4, 76, 234.567, and 0.87:

$$
\begin{array}{r}
23.400 \\
76.000 \\
234.567 \\
+ \quad 0.870 \\
\hline
334.837
\end{array}
$$

Subtraction works the same way:

$$
\begin{array}{r}
16.55 \\
- \quad 4.30 \\
\hline
12.25
\end{array}
$$

Don't forget about decimal points when working with decimals.

NUMBERS ■ 111

MULTIPLYING DECIMALS

The only tricky part is remembering where to put the decimal point. Handle the multiplication as you would with integers. Then position the decimal point according to this simple two-step rule:

Use that paper!

1. Count the total number of digits to the right of the decimal points in the numbers you are multiplying. If you are multiplying 2.341 and 7.8, for example, you have a total of four digits to the right of the decimal points.

2. Place the decimal point in your solution so that you have the same number of digits to the right of it. Here's what you get when you multiply the numbers above:

$$\begin{array}{r} 2.341 \\ \times\ \ 7.8 \\ \hline 18.2598 \end{array}$$

Except for placing the decimal point, we did exactly what we would have done if we had been multiplying 2,341 and 78:

$$\begin{array}{r} 2{,}341 \\ \times\ \ \ 78 \\ \hline 182{,}598 \end{array}$$

DIVIDING DECIMALS

Before you can divide decimals, you have to convert the divisor into an integer. (Vocab review: In the division problem $10 \div 2 = 5$, the 10 is the dividend, the 2 is the divisor, and the 5 is the quotient.) Just set up the division as a fraction. All you have to do is move the decimal point all the way to the right. You must then move the decimal point in the dividend the same number of spaces to the right. Here's an example:

$$20 \div 1.2$$

Here's how to crack it

First, set up the division problem as a fraction:

$$\frac{20}{1.2}$$

Now start moving decimal points. The divisor, 1.2, has one digit to the right of the decimal point. To turn 1.2 into an integer, therefore, we need to move the decimal point one space to the right. Doing so turns 1.2 into 12.

Because we've moved the decimal point in the divisor one place, we also need to move the decimal point in the dividend one place. This turns 20 into 200. Here's what we're left with:

$$\frac{200}{12}$$

Now all we would have to do to find our answer is complete the division: 200 divided by 12 is 16.66 repeating.

COMPARING DECIMALS

Which is larger: 0.00099 or 0.001? ETS loves this sort of problem. You'll never go wrong, though, if you:

- Line up the numbers on their decimal points.
- Fill in the missing zeroes.

Here's how to answer the question we just asked. First, line up the two numbers on their decimal points:

$$0.00099$$
$$0.001$$

Now fill in the missing zeros:

$$0.00099$$
$$0.00100$$

Can you tell which number is larger? Of course you can. 0.00100 is larger than 0.00099, because 100 is larger than 99.

Convert decimals to fractions

Fractions are safer and easier to work with than decimals. When you're trying to solve a decimal problem, convert the decimals to fractions. If the answer choices are decimals, convert back to decimals when you finish the work.

> Decimals are DANGEROUS.
> Fractions are safer.

EXPONENTS AND SQUARE ROOTS

WHAT ARE EXPONENTS?

Exponents are a sort of mathematical shorthand. Instead of writing (2)(2)(2)(2) we can write 2^4. The little 4 is called an exponent and the big 2 is called a base. The following is all you need to remember about exponents: **When in doubt, expand it out!**

Multiplication with exponents

It's easy to multiply two or more numbers with the same base. All you have to do is add up the exponents. For example:

$$2^2 \times 2^4 =$$
$$2^{2+4} = 2^6$$

You can see this when you expand it out, which is just as good a way to solve the problem:

$$2^2 \times 2^4 =$$
$$2 \times 2 \times 2 \times 2 \times 2 \times 2 = 2^6$$

Be careful, though. This rule does *not* apply to addition. $2^2 + 2^4$ *does not equal* 2^6. There's no quick and easy method of adding numbers with exponents. But you'll never have to do it on the GRE.

Division with exponents

Dividing two or more numbers with the same base is easy, too. All you have to do is subtract the exponents. For example:

$$2^6 \div 2^2 = 2^{6-2} = 2^4$$

You can see this easily when you expand it out.

$$2^6 \div 2^2 = \frac{2 \times 2 \times 2 \times 2 \times 2 \times 2}{2 \times 2} = 2 \times 2 \times 2 \times 2 = 2^4$$

If you EXPAND IT OUT, you'll never be in doubt.

Once again, don't assume this same shortcut applies to subtraction of numbers with exponents. It doesn't. But again, you won't have to worry about it on the GRE.

Another time you might need to divide with exponents is when you see a negative exponent. You just put 1 over it and get rid of the negative. For example:

$$3^{-2}$$

should be rewritten as

$$\frac{1}{3^2}$$

That gives us

$$\frac{1}{9}$$

Please excuse . . .

Remember PEMDAS? Pay close attention when there are exponents inside and outside the parentheses. You can simply multiply the exponents. Here's an example:

$$(4^5)^2 =$$
$$4^{5 \times 2} =$$
$$4^{10}$$

Don't be shy about expanding these out on your scratch paper. It doesn't take too much time, and it's better to be correct than to be quick.

$$(4^5)^2 =$$
$$(4 \times 4 \times 4 \times 4 \times 4)(4 \times 4 \times 4 \times 4 \times 4) = 4^{10}$$

IF YOU ALWAYS EXPAND IT OUT, YOU'LL NEVER BE IN DOUBT

When solving problems involving exponents, it's extremely important to pay careful attention to terms within parentheses. When an exponent appears on the outside of a parenthetical expression, expanding it out is the best way to ensure that you don't make a careless mistake. For example, $(3x)^2 = (3x)(3x) = 9x^2$, not $3x^2$.

The same is true of fractions within parentheses: $\left(\frac{3}{2}\right)^2 = \left(\frac{3}{2}\right)\left(\frac{3}{2}\right) = \frac{9}{4}$.

The Peculiar Behavior of Exponents

- Raising a number greater than 1 to a power greater than 1 results in a *bigger* number. For example, $2^2 = 4$.

- Raising a fraction between 0 and 1 to a power greater than 1 results in a *smaller* number. For example, $\left(\frac{1}{2}\right)^2 = \frac{1}{4}$.

- A negative number raised to an even power becomes *positive*. For example, $(-2)^2 = 4$ because $(-2)(-2) = 4$.

- A negative number raised to an odd power remains *negative*. For example, $(-2)^3 = -8$ because $(-2)(-2)(-2) = -8$.

- A number raised to a negative power is equal to 1 over the number raised to the positive version of that power. For example, $2^{-2} = \frac{1}{2^2} = \frac{1}{4}$.

- A number raised to the 0 power is ALWAYS 1, no matter what the number is. For example, $1{,}000^0 = 1$.

- A number raised to the first power is ALWAYS the number itself. For example, $1{,}000^1 = 1{,}000$.

Here's an example:

$$\text{If } a \neq 0, \text{ then } \frac{\left(a^6\right)^2}{a \cdot a^2} =$$

- ○ a^5
- ○ a^6
- ○ a^7
- ○ a^8
- ○ a^9

Always cross off wrong answer choices on your scratch paper.

Here's how to crack it

In the numerator, we have $(a^6)^2$, which is a^{12}. In the denominator, we have $a \times a^2$, which is a^3. So, $a^{12} \div a^3 = a^9$. That's choice (E).

Let's try another—this time, a Quant Comp.

Column A	Column B
27^4	9^6

- ○ the quantity in Column A is always greater
- ○ the quantity in Column B is always greater
- ○ the quantities are always equal
- ○ it cannot be determined from the information given

Here's how to crack it

Looks scary, huh? But remember what you learned about Quant Comp problems in the Math introduction. Your job is to *compare*, not calculate. First of all, eliminate (D)—when there are only numbers being compared, the answer *can* be determined. Now, as written, we can't compare these exponents yet—they don't have the same base. But we can fix that. Both 27 and 9 are powers of 3. So, let's change them both into powers of 3. 27 is $3 \times 3 \times 3$, so 27^4 is $(3 \times 3 \times 3)^4$. This equals $(3 \times 3 \times 3)(3 \times 3 \times 3)(3 \times 3 \times 3)(3 \times 3 \times 3)$, also known as 3^{12}. That takes care of Column A. In Column B, 9 is 3×3, so 9^6 is $(3 \times 3)^6$. This equals $(3 \times 3)(3 \times 3)(3 \times 3)(3 \times 3)(3 \times 3)(3 \times 3)$, also know as 3^{12}. So, we have 3^{12} in Column A and 3^{12} in Column B. They're equal, and the answer is (C).

WHAT IS A SQUARE ROOT?

The sign $\sqrt{}$ indicates the square root of a number. For example, $\sqrt{2}$ means that something squared equals 2.

If $x^2 = 16$, then $x = \pm 4$. You must be especially careful to remember this on Quantitative Comparison questions. But when ETS asks you for the value $\sqrt{16}$, or the square root of any number, you are being asked for the *positive* root only. Although squaring –5 will result in 25, just as squaring 5 will, when ETS asks for $\sqrt{25}$, the only answer it's looking for is +5.

PLAYING WITH SQUARE ROOTS

ALWAYS write down A, B, C, D for Quant Comps.

You multiply and divide square roots just like you would any other number:

$$\sqrt{3} \times \sqrt{12} = \sqrt{36} = 6$$

$$\sqrt{\frac{16}{4}} = \frac{\sqrt{16}}{\sqrt{4}} = \frac{4}{2} = 2$$

However, you can't add or subtract them unless the roots are the same:

So $\sqrt{2} + \sqrt{2} = 2\sqrt{2}$. (Just pretend there's an invisible 1 in front of the root sign.)

But $\sqrt{2} + \sqrt{3}$ does *not* equal $\sqrt{5}$!

Here's an example:

$$z^2 = 144$$

Column A	Column B
z	$\sqrt{144}$

You can multiply and divide any square roots, but you can only add or subtract roots when they are the same.

- ⭕ the quantity in Column A is always greater
- ⭕ the quantity in Column B is always greater
- ⭕ the quantities are always equal
- ⭕ it cannot be determined from the information given

Here's how to crack it

You want to pick (C), don't you? After all, if z^2 is 144, the square root of 144 must be z, right? Not so fast. If $z^2 = 144$, then z could be either 12 or –12. But when the radical sign ($\sqrt{}$) is used, only the positive root is being referred to. Therefore, Column A is 12 or –12, but Column B is 12. And that gives us (D) as the answer.

LEARN THESE FOUR VALUES

To use our techniques, you'll need to memorize the following values. You should be able to recite them without hesitation.

$$\sqrt{1} = 1$$
$$\sqrt{2} = 1.4$$
$$\sqrt{3} = 1.7$$
$$\sqrt{4} = 2$$

You'll see them again when we discuss geometry.

A FEW LAWS

ASSOCIATIVE LAW

There are actually two associative laws—one for addition and one for multiplication. For the sake of simplicity, we've lumped them together.

Don't worry about the word "associative." Here's all you need to know: *When you are adding a series of numbers or multiplying a series of numbers, you can regroup the numbers in any way you'd like.* Here are some examples:

$$4 + (5 + 8) = (4 + 5) + 8 = (4 + 8) + 5$$
$$(a + b) + (c + d) = a + (b + c + d)$$
$$4 \times (5 \times 8) = (4 \times 5) \times 8 = (4 \times 8) \times 5$$
$$(ab)(cd) = a(bcd)$$

Write everything down on scratch paper! Don't do anything in your head!

DISTRIBUTIVE LAW

This is often tested on the GRE. You must know it cold. Here's what it looks like:

$$a(b + c) = ab + ac$$
$$a(b - c) = ab - ac$$

For example:

$$12(66) + 12(24) =$$

Here's how to crack it

This is really just $ab + ac$. Using the distributive law, this must equal $12(66 + 24)$, or $12(90) = 1,080$.

FACTORING AND UNFACTORING

When you use the distributive law to rewrite the expression $xy + xz$ in the form $x(y + z)$, you are said to be *factoring* the original expression. That is, you take the factor common to both terms of the original expression x and "pull it out." This gives you a new, "factored" version of the expression you began with.

When you use the distributive law to rewrite the expression $x(y + z)$ in the form $xy + xz$, we say that you are *unfactoring* the original expression.

ETS is very predictable. Because of this, we can tell you that on any problem containing an expression that can be factored, you should always factor that expression. If, for example, you encounter a problem containing the expression $5x + 5y$, you should immediately factor it, to make the expression $5(x + y)$.

Similarly, whenever you find an expression that has been factored, you should immediately *un*factor it, by multiplying it out. In other words, if a problem contains the expression $5(x + y)$, you should unfactor it, yielding the expression $5x + 5y$.

Sometimes on a hard question you might see some ugly-looking thing like this that you have to simplify:

$$\frac{8^7 - 8^6}{7}$$

To simplify the numerator, you can factor out the biggest chunk that's common to both. In other words, the biggest thing that goes into both 8^7 and 8^6 is 8^6. So, you can "pull out" an 8^6, like so:

$$\frac{8^6(8^1 - 1)}{7}$$

This can be simplified even further:

$$\frac{8^6(7)}{7} = 8^6$$

You will learn more about factoring in the next chapter.

PROBABILITY

If you flip a coin, what's the probability that it will land heads up? One out of two, or $\frac{1}{2}$. What is the probability that it won't land heads up? One out of two, or $\frac{1}{2}$. If you flip a coin nine times, what's the probability that the coin will land on "heads" on the tenth flip? One out of two, or $\frac{1}{2}$. Previous flips do not affect anything.

Think of probability in terms of fractions:
- If it is impossible for something to happen, the probability of it happening is equal to 0.
- If something is certain to happen, the probability is equal to 1.
- If it is possible for something to happen, but not necessary, the probability is between 0 and 1, otherwise known as a fraction.

$$\text{probability} = \frac{\text{outcome you're looking for}}{\text{total outcomes}}$$

Let's see how it works:

> Fifteen marbles are placed in a bowl; some are red, and some are blue. If the number of red marbles is one more than the number of blue marbles, what is the probability that a marble taken from the bowl is blue?

○ $\frac{1}{15}$

○ $\frac{2}{15}$

○ $\frac{7}{15}$

○ $\frac{1}{2}$

○ $\frac{8}{15}$

Here's how to crack it

We have 15 marbles, and there's 1 more red than blue. That means there must be 8 red marbles and 7 blue marbles. Now we need the probability that we'd pick a blue marble. That would be 7 out of a possible 15. Express it as a fraction, and you get choice (C), $\frac{7}{15}$.

Let's try another one:

> In a bowl containing 10 marbles, 5 are yellow and 5 are green. If 2 marbles are picked from the bowl at random, what is the probability that they will <u>both</u> be green?

○ $\frac{1}{5}$

○ $\frac{2}{9}$

○ $\frac{1}{4}$

○ $\frac{1}{2}$

○ $\frac{15}{18}$

Here's how to crack it

Let's do this one draw at a time. On the first draw, the probability of drawing a green marble is 5 out of 10, or $\frac{1}{2}$—but now that marble is no longer in the bowl. So on the second draw, the probability of drawing a green marble is 4 (the number of remaining green marbles) out of 9 (the remaining marbles). Therefore, the probability of both is equal to $\frac{1}{2} \times \frac{4}{9}$, which is $\frac{4}{18}$, or $\frac{2}{9}$. That's choice (B). We don't care about the probability of *not* picking a green marble because that's not what the question is asking.

PERMUTATIONS AND COMBINATIONS

A permutation is an arrangement of things in a definite order. You may remember the word *factorial*. Four factorial, or 4!, equals $4 \times 3 \times 2 \times 1$, which is 24.

Suppose you were asked to figure out how many different ways you could arrange five statues on a shelf. All you have to do is multiply $5 \times 4 \times 3 \times 2 \times 1$, or 120. That's it.

Now, suppose there are five people running in a race. The winner of the race will get a gold medal, the person coming in second will get a silver medal, and the person coming in third will get a bronze medal. You're asked to figure out how how many orders of gold-silver-bronze winners there can be out of the five runners.

First, ask yourself, how many of these runners can come in first? Five. Once one of them comes in first, she's out of the picture, so how many can then come in second? Four. Once someone comes in second, she's out of the picture, so how many can then come in third? Three. Now, just multiply $5 \times 4 \times 3$, and you get 60. Bingo.

The difference between a permutation and a combination is that in a combination, order doesn't matter. For example, suppose you were asked to figure out how many different three-flavor combinations of ice cream flavors you could make out of the following five flavors: vanilla, chocolate, strawberry, butter pecan, and mocha. In this case, order doesn't matter, because vanilla-chocolate-strawberry is the same as chocolate-strawberry-vanilla. You can use brute force; in other words, write out every combination:

VCS   VCB   VCM   VSB   VSM   VBM   CSB   CSM   CBM   SBM

That's 10 combinations. Here's another way to look at it: Since the order in which you pick the ice cream flavors doesn't matter, you're really determining the number of groups of three you can make out of a possible five. Just take the three largest numbers (starting with 5) in descending order, multiply them, and then divide that product by the product of the three smallest numbers in ascending order. In other words, $\frac{5 \times 4 \times 3}{3 \times 2 \times 1}$. That's $\frac{60}{6}$, or 10. Bingo.

Or you might remember the following formula:

$$\frac{n!}{(n-r)!(r!)}$$

This is the formula if you have n things being used r at a time. Remember, that "!" sign means "factorial." In our ice cream example, we have 5 flavors being used 3 at a time. Let's plug that into the formula.

$$\frac{5!}{(5-3)!(3!)}$$

$$\frac{5 \times 4 \times 3 \times 2 \times 1}{(2 \times 1)(3 \times 2 \times 1)}$$

Don't forget to reduce:

$$\frac{5 \times 4}{2 \times 1} =$$

$$\frac{20}{2} =$$

$$= 10$$

Let's try an example:

Column A	Column B
12! ÷ 11!	$11^2 \times 10!$

⬭ the quantity in Column A is
   always greater
⬭ the quantity in Column B is
   always greater
⬭ the quantities are always equal
⬭ it cannot be determined from the
   information given

> POE is your new way of life.

Here's how to crack it

Remember, your job on a Quant Comp question is to *compare*, not calculate. Let's deal with Column A, and expand it out, just like we would if we were dealing with exponents:

$$\frac{12 \bullet 11 \bullet 10 \bullet 9 \bullet 8 \bullet 7 \bullet 6 \bullet 5 \bullet 4 \bullet 3 \bullet 2 \bullet 1}{11 \bullet 10 \bullet 9 \bullet 8 \bullet 7 \bullet 6 \bullet 5 \bullet 4 \bullet 3 \bullet 2 \bullet 1}$$

Always cross off wrong answer choices on your scratch paper.

We cancel out like terms, and we're left with 12. Now, to Column B. Take a look at what we have:

$$11 \bullet 11 \bullet 10 \bullet 9 \bullet 8 \bullet 7 \bullet 6 \bullet 5 \bullet 4 \bullet 3 \bullet 2 \bullet 1$$

Whatever this number is, don't you think it's going to be bigger than 12? Absolutely. So, the answer is (B).

Here's another one:

How many different ways can the multiples of 3 between 8 and 20 be ordered?

- ⬭ 4
- ⬭ 12
- ⬭ 24
- ⬭ 36
- ⬭ 48

Here's how to crack it

We know that order matters in the question—the question even uses the word "ordered." So this must be a permutation. What are the multiples of 3 between 8 and 20? They are 9, 12, 15, and 18. This question is really asking, "How many different ways can you order 4 things?" That's 4!, or $4 \times 3 \times 2 \times 1$, which is 24.

So, now you're back in shape, numbers-wise. It's time to move on to letters. Yep, there are letters in math, too.

11

Variables and Equations

DEALING WITH VARIABLES

So far, we've been playing with numbers. But many GRE math problems involve letters, or variables (such as n, x, or y). It's time to learn how to deal with those.

SOLVING FOR ONE VARIABLE

If you have one equation with one variable, you can solve it. Try to get the variable on one side of the equation, and the numbers on the other side. To do this, you can add, subtract, multiply, or divide both sides of the equation by the same number. Just remember that anything you do to one side of an equation, you must do to the other side. Be sure to write down every step. Let's look at a simple example:

$$3x - 4 = 5$$

Always write A, B, C, D, E on your scratch paper to represent the answer choices (or A, B, C, D if it's Quant Comp)

Here's how to crack it

You can get rid of negatives by adding something to both sides of the equation, just as you can get rid of positives by subtracting something from both sides of the equation.

$$
\begin{aligned}
3x - 4 &= 5 \\
+ 4 &= + 4 \\
3x &= 9
\end{aligned}
$$

You may already see that $x = 3$. But don't forget to write down that last step. Divide both sides of the equation by 3:

$$\frac{3x}{3} = \frac{9}{3}$$
$$x = 3$$

Let's try another one:

$$5x - 13 = 12 - 20x$$

Here's how to crack it

First of all, we want to get all the x values on the same side of the equation:

$$
\begin{aligned}
5x - 13 &= 12 - 20x \\
+20x &\qquad\quad + 20x \\
\hline
25x - 13 &= 12
\end{aligned}
$$

Now we can get rid of that negative 13:

$$
\begin{aligned}
25x - 13 &= 12 \\
+13 &\; +13 \\
\hline
25x &\quad = 25
\end{aligned}
$$

Now it might be pretty obvious that x is 1, but let's just finish it:

$$25x = 25$$
$$\frac{25x}{25} = \frac{25}{25}$$
$$x = 1$$

Let's try another one:

$$5x + \frac{3}{2} = 7x$$

Here's how to crack it

First multiply both sides by 2 to get rid of the fraction:

$$10x + 3 = 14x$$

Now get both x's on the same side:

$$
\begin{array}{rcl}
10x + 3 & = & 14x \\
-10x & & -10x \\
\hline
3 & = & 4x
\end{array}
$$

Now finish it up:

$$3 = 4x$$

$$\frac{3}{4} = \frac{4x}{4}$$

$$\frac{3}{4} = x$$

You must always do the same thing to both sides of an equation.

INEQUALITIES

In an equation, one side equals another. In an inequality, one expression does not equal another. The symbol for an equation is an equal sign. Here are the symbols for inequalities:

≠ is not equal to
> is greater than
< is less than
≥ is greater than or equal to
≤ is less than or equal to

You can manipulate any inequality in the same way you can an equation, with one important difference. When you multiply or divide both sides of an inequality by a negative number, the direction of the inequality symbol changes. That is, if $x > y$, then $-x < -y$.

To see what we mean, take a look at a simple inequality:

$$12 - 6x > 0$$

Here's how to crack it

You could manipulate this inequality without ever multiplying or dividing by a negative number. Just add $6x$ to both sides. The sign stays the same. Then divide both sides by positive 6. Again, the sign stays the same.

$$12 - 6x > 0$$

$$\underline{+6x > +6x}$$

$$12 > 6x$$

$$\frac{12}{6} > \frac{6x}{6}$$

$$2 > x$$

But suppose you subtract 12 from both sides at first:

$$12 - 6x > 0$$

$$\underline{-12 \quad\quad > -12}$$

$$-6x > -12$$

$$\frac{-6x}{-6} < \frac{-12}{-6}$$

$$x < 2$$

Notice that the sign flipped that time. But the answer is the same.

PLUGGING IN

When a problem has variables in the answer choices, PLUG IN!

Many GRE math problems have variables in the answer choices. ETS knows that most people try to do them algebraically. ETS also knows which algebraic mistakes most people will make, and what answers would result from those mistakes. That's how they design the wrong answers to these problems. (Remember distractors?) To avoid trap answers on these problems, the fastest and easiest way to find ETS's answer is by making up numbers and plugging them in. Plugging In makes word problems much less abstract, and much easier to solve. Here's what you do:

1. Pick a number for each variable in the problem and write it on your scratch paper.

2. Solve the problem using your numbers. Write down your numerical answer and circle it; that's your "target answer."

3. Write down the answer choices and plug your numbers in for each one to see which choice equals the target answer you found in step 2.

Here's an example:

$$3[3a + (5a + 7a)] - (5a + 7a) =$$

- ⬭ 9a
- ⬭ 12a
- ⬭ 15a
- ⬭ 33a
- ⬭ 47a

Here's how to crack it

All you have to do is come up with a number for the variable *a*. How about 2? Write down *a* = 2 on your scratch paper. Now the question says:

$$3\left[3(2)+\left(5(2)+7(2)\right)\right]-\left(5(2)+7(2)\right)=$$

Don't forget about PEMDAS.

$$3[6 + (10 + 14)] - (10 + 14) =$$
$$3[6 + 24] - 24 =$$
$$3(30) - 24 =$$
$$90 - 24 = 66$$

By Plugging In, we turned this algebra question into an arithmetic question, and we got 66. Circle the number 66 on your scratch paper, because that's your target answer. Now plug 2 in for the variable in all the answer choices until you get 66. You might see the right answer already, but let's just go through the motions.

- (A) 9(2) = 18—Nope.
- (B) 12(2) = 24—Nope.
- (C) 15(2) = 30—Nope.
- (D) 33(2) = 66—Bingo!
- (E) 47(2) = 94—Nope.

Even if you think you can do the algebra, plug in instead. Why? Because if you do the algebra wrong, you won't know it—one of ETS's wrong answers will be there waiting for you. But, if you plug in and you're wrong, you won't get an answer, and you'll know you're wrong, forcing you to try again. Plugging In is foolproof. Algebra isn't.

CAN I JUST PLUG IN ANYTHING?

You can plug in any numbers you like, as long as they're consistent with any restrictions stated in the problem, but it's faster if you use easy numbers. What makes a number easy? That depends on the problem. In most cases, smaller numbers are easier to work with than larger numbers. Usually, it's best to start small, with 3, for example. (Avoid 0 and 1; both 0 and 1 have special properties, which you'll hear more about later.) Do not plug in any numbers that show up a lot in the question or answer choices. Plug in numbers that make the arithmetic easy.

Try this one. Read through the whole question before you start to plug in numbers:

> The price of a certain stock increased 8 points, then decreased 13 points, and then increased 9 points. If the stock price before the changes was *x* points, which of the following was the stock price, in points, after the changes?
>
> ○ *x* − 5
> ○ *x* − 4
> ○ *x* + 4
> ○ *x* + 5
> ○ *x* + 8

Plug in numbers that will make the math EASY.

Here's how to crack it

Let's use an easy number like 10 for the variable (write down $x = 10$ on your scratch paper!). If the original price was 10, and then it increased 8 points, that's 18. Then it decreased 13 points, so now it's 5 (do everything out on the scratch paper—don't even add or subtract in your head). Then it increased 9 points, so now it's 14. So, it started at 10 and ended at 14. Circle 14 (our target answer) and plug in 10 for every x in the answer choices. Which one gives you 14?

    (A) $10 - 5 = 5$—Nope.
    (B) $10 - 4 = 6$—Nope.
    (C) $10 + 4 = 14$—Bingo!
    (D) $10 + 5 = 15$—Nope.
    (E) $10 + 8 = 18$—Nope.

Pretty easy, huh?

GOOD NUMBERS MAKE LIFE EASIER

Always PLUG IN when you see variables in the answer choices!

Small numbers aren't always best. In a problem involving percentages, for example, 10 and 100 are good numbers to use. In a problem involving minutes or seconds, 60 may be the easiest number to plug in. You should look for clues in the problem itself. Here's an example:

At the rate of $\dfrac{f}{3}$ feet per m minutes, how many feet can a bicycle travel in s seconds?

    ○ $\dfrac{fs}{60m}$

    ○ $\dfrac{60s}{fm}$

    ○ $\dfrac{fms}{180}$

    ○ $\dfrac{fm}{180s}$

    ○ $\dfrac{fs}{180m}$

Here's how to crack it

Don't forget to write everything down. Let's make $f = 12$ (because it's divisible by 3) and $m = 2$, so the bicycle is going 4 feet per 2 minutes. Since this question involves minutes and seconds, let's use a multiple of 60 for s. We don't want to use numbers that are in the answer choices (such as 60 or 180). What if we made it 120? After all, 120 seconds is the same as 2 minutes, and we already know it's 4 feet per 2 minutes. If s is 120, our target answer is 4. Circle it.

Now to the answers. Remember, $f = 12$, $m = 2$, $s = 120$, and the target is 4.

(A) $\dfrac{12(120)}{120} = 12$. Nope.

(B) $\dfrac{(60)120}{24} = 300$. Nope.

(C) $\dfrac{(12)(2)(120)}{180} = 16$. Nope.

(D) This will have a really big denominator. Nope.

(E) $\dfrac{(12)(120)}{180(2)} = \dfrac{144}{36} = \dfrac{12}{3} = 4$. Bingo!

See? No algebra, just multiplication and division. Checking all the choices is worth doing. It's fast and easy. If more than one answer choice works with the first numbers you plugged in, eliminate the choices that don't work, and plug in new numbers. Get a new target answer, and plug in your new numbers for the remaining answer choices. Then eliminate the answer choices that don't work with your new numbers.

DON'T LOOK A GIFT HORSE . . .

ETS will sometimes give you a value for one of the variables or terms in an expression and then ask you for the value of the entire expression. Nothing could be easier. Simply plug in the value that ETS gives you and see what you come up with. Here's an example:

Remember, the answer is on the screen!

If $x = 1$, then

$$\left(2 - \frac{1}{2-x}\right)\left(2 - \frac{1}{3-x}\right)\left(2 - \frac{1}{4-x}\right) =$$

○ $\dfrac{1}{6}$

○ $\dfrac{5}{6}$

○ $\dfrac{5}{2}$

○ $\dfrac{10}{3}$

○ $\dfrac{7}{2}$

Here's how to crack it

Forget about algebra, because you're actually being given a number to plug in. So, substitute 1 in for x, and you get this:

$$\left(2-\frac{1}{2-1}\right)\left(2-\frac{1}{3-1}\right)\left(2-\frac{1}{4-1}\right)=$$

$$(2-1)\left(2-\frac{1}{2}\right)\left(2-\frac{1}{3}\right)=$$

$$(1)\left(\frac{3}{2}\right)\left(\frac{5}{3}\right)=\frac{5}{2}$$

So, the answer is (C).

You should never, never, never try to solve problems like these by "solving for x" or "solving for y." Plugging In is much easier and faster, and you'll be less likely to make careless mistakes.

"MUST BE" PROBLEMS

Try to disprove answer choices on MUST BE problems. Plug in numbers, eliminate answer choices with those numbers, then plug in different numbers to eliminate any remaining choices.

These "algebraic reasoning" problems are much easier to solve by Plugging In than by "reasoning." On these, you will have to plug in more than once in order to find the correct answer.

Here's an example:

> If x is a positive integer, for which of the following equations must y be a negative integer?
>
> ○ $xy = 9$
> ○ $x + y = 7$
> ○ $x + 2y = 6$
> ○ $y - x = 4$
> ○ $-x - y = 3$

Here's how to crack it

We need a positive integer for x—how about 10? Plug that into the answer choices to see which one forces y to be negative.

(A) $10y = 9$. Nope. $y = \dfrac{9}{10}$, which isn't a negative integer. Eliminate this choice.

(B) $10 + y = 7$. Yes. $y = -3$. Keep it.

(C) $10 + 2y = 6$. That's $2y = -4$. $y = -2$, so let's keep it.

(D) $y - 10 = 4$. Nope. $y = 14$. Eliminate it.

(E) $-10 - y = 3$. That means $-y = 13$, or $y = -13$. Yes, keep it.

Okay, we eliminated (A) and (D). Now, because the question says "must be," we need to try another number in the choices we kept after the first round: (B), (C), and (E). Let's try plugging in the number 1:

(B) $1 + y = 7$. So $y = 6$. Eliminate it.

(C) $1 + 2y = 6$. That's $2y = 5$. y isn't an integer. Eliminate it.

(E) $-1 - y = 3$. That's $-y = 4$, or $y = -4$. Bingo.

Notice that on the "second round" of elimination we plugged in a "weird" number that we usually avoid. That's how we found what would always be true. That leads us to . . .

PLUGGING IN ON QUANT COMP

The easiest way to solve most Quant Comps involving variables is to plug in, just as you would on word problems. But because answer choice (D) is always an option, you always have to make sure it isn't the answer. So . . .

ALWAYS PLUG IN AT LEAST TWICE IN QUANT COMP

Plugging In on Quant Comp is just like Plugging In on "must be" problems. The reason for this is (D). On Quant Comps, it's not enough to determine whether one quantity is sometimes greater than, less than, or equal to the other; you have to determine whether it *always* is. If different numbers lead to different answers, then the correct answer is (D). Practice using this step-by-step procedure:

> On Quant Comp, plug in "normal numbers," and eliminate two choices. Then plug in "weird" numbers (zero, one, negatives, fractions, or big numbers) to try to disprove your first answer. If different numbers give you different answers, you've proved that the answer is D.

- Step 1: Write A, B, C, D on your scratch paper.

- Step 2: Plug in "normal" numbers like 2, 3, or 5.

- Step 3: Which column is bigger? Cross out the two choices that you've proved are wrong. Suppose the numbers you plugged in at first made Column A bigger; which answer choices cannot be correct? (B) and (C). Cross them out! (A) and (D) are still possible choices.

- Step 4: Now try to get a different answer! Plug in weird numbers such as 0, 1, negatives, fractions, or really big numbers. If you get a different result, then the answer is (D). If you keep getting the same result, that's your answer.

What makes certain numbers weird? They behave in unexpected ways when added, multiplied, or raised to powers. For example:

- 0 times any number is 0.

- 0^2 is 0.

- 1^2 is 1.

- $\left(\dfrac{1}{2}\right)^2$ is less than $\dfrac{1}{2}$.

- $(-2)(-2)$ is 4.

- A negative number squared is positive.

- Really big numbers (100, 1,000) can make a really big difference in your answer.

ZERO KILLS

One of the most important properties of zero is its ability to annihilate other numbers. Any number multiplied by 0 equals 0. This fact gives you an important piece of information. For example, if you are told that $ab = 0$, then you know without a doubt that either a or b or both must be equal to 0. You can plug in zero to make the arithmetic simple on Quant Comp questions. Keep this in mind.

LET'S DO IT

Okay, let's try a Quant Comp Plugging-In example:

Column A	Column B
	$y > 2$
$y - 6$	-3

○ the quantity in Column A is always greater
○ the quantity in Column B is always greater
○ the quantities are always equal
○ it cannot be determined from the information given

Here's how to crack it

See the variables? This is clearly a plug in problem. Let's start by plugging in 3 for y. That gives us –3 in both columns. So far the answer is (C). That means you can eliminate choices (A) and (B). But what if we plug in a different number for y? It has to be bigger than 2, so that rules out 0, 1, and negatives. But how about a much bigger number, like 100? That gives us 94 in Column A and –3 in Column B, which gives us (A). Since we got (C) with one number and (A) with another, the answer must be (D). Different numbers gave us different answers.

PLUGGING IN THE ANSWER CHOICES

You don't have to wait for variables to plug in. You get the answer choices, and you know one of them is correct. Why not plug *them* in? Simply try the number in an answer choice and see if it works. If it works, you have the right answer. If it doesn't work, you try another. There are only five choices on regular math problems. One of these choices has to be the right answer. You will often find this answer by trying just one or two of the choices; you will never have to try all five.

When plugging in the answer choices, it's usually a good idea to start in the middle and work your way out. As usual, we'll refer to the middle one as choice (C). Why work from the middle? Because GRE answer choices are almost always arranged in order of size. You may be able to tell not only that a particular choice is incorrect but also that it is too big or too small. Sometimes you can eliminate three choices just by trying one! Make sure you write down all the answer choices on your scratch paper so you can cross them out as you go.

Remember those "weird" numbers for the second round of Plugging In on Quant Comps: 0, 1, negatives, fractions, or really big numbers.

Here's an example:

> In a certain hardware store, 3 percent of the lawnmowers needed new labels. If the price per label was $4 and the total cost for new lawnmower labels was $96, how many lawnmowers are in the hardware store?
>
> ○ 1600
> ○ 800
> ○ 240
> ○ 120
> ○ 24

Are you tempted to do algebra? Are there numbers in the answer choices? Plug in the answer choices!

Here's how to crack it

The question is asking us for the number of lawnmowers in the hardware store, so let's plug in 240—answer choice (C). Now go back to the beginning of the question. Three percent of the lawnmowers need new labels, so that's 3 percent of 240, or 7.2. The price per label is $4 each, which would be 4 multiplied by 7.2, or $28.80. But the question says the total cost for new lawnmower labels is $96, not $28.80.

What we've learned by plugging in the middle choice is that (C) is not the answer, and that 240 is too small a number. Choices (D) or (E) are even smaller, so we can eliminate them. We know we need a bigger number, so let's try (B), 800.

Okay, now there are 800 lawnmowers, and 3 percent of them need new labels. That's 24 labels, and they cost $4 each. What's 4 multiplied by 24? Yes, it's 96. Everything in the question checks out, so (B) is our answer. Note that if (B) didn't work, we would automatically know that the answer is (A)—it would be the only choice left.

It might have been even easier to start with (B), or 800, since we needed to take a percentage of the number of lawnmowers, and it's really easy to find percentages of multiples of 100. You don't always have to start with (C); you can start with a value near the middle that's easy to work with.

Just make sure you write EVERYTHING down when doing these questions (and indeed, all math questions).

Here's another example:

A contest winner received $\frac{1}{4}$ of his winnings in cash, and received four prizes, each worth $\frac{1}{4}$ of the balance. If the cash and one of the prizes were worth a combined total of $35,000, what was the total value of his winnings?

○ $70,000
○ $75,000
○ $80,000
○ $95,000
○ $140,000

Here's how to crack it

When you're plugging in the answer choices, start with (C) (or the middle value).

Let's say the answer to the question (the total value of the winnings) is $80,000, or choice (C). Now go back to the beginning of the question. One-fourth of the winnings was in cash, so that's $20,000. The balance would be $60,000, and he got four prizes each worth $\frac{1}{4}$ of $60,000, or $15,000. Now, does the cash ($20,000) plus the value of one of the prizes ($15,000) equal $35,000, as the question requires? Yes, it does. We're done. The answer is (C). Plugging In is a fabulous technique for word problems that can really save you some time on the GRE.

Try this one:

The sum of x distinct integers greater than zero is less than 75. What is the greatest possible value of x?

○ 8
○ 9
○ 10
○ 11
○ 12

Here's how to crack it

Notice that this time the question is asking for the greatest value of x. The greatest number in the answer choices is 12, choice (E)—so that's where we'll start. Is the sum of 12 distinct integers greater than zero less than 75? Let's see:

$$1 + 2 + 3 + 4 + 5 + 6 + 7 + 8 + 9 + 10 + 11 + 12 = 78$$

So 12 is too big, but by just a little. That means the answer is 11, or (D). Didn't Plugging In make that easy?

FUNCTIONS AND FUNNY-LOOKING SYMBOLS

The GRE contains "function" problems, but they aren't like the functions that you may have learned in high school. GRE functions use funny-looking symbols, such as @, *, and #. Each symbol represents an arithmetic operation or a series of arithmetic operations. All you have to do is follow directions. Here's an example:

Column A   Column B

For any non-negative integer x, let $x* = x - 1$

$$\frac{15*}{3*} \qquad\qquad \left(\frac{15}{3}\right)*$$

○ the quantity in Column A is always greater
○ the quantity in Column B is always greater
○ the quantities are always equal
○ it cannot be determined from the information given

> With funny symbols, follow the directions. Just do it.

Here's how to crack it

Just follow the directions—15* = 15 – 1, or 14, and 3* = 3 – 1, or 2. So we get $\frac{14}{2}$, or 7, in Column A. Don't forget PEMDAS for Column B. First, $\frac{15}{3}$ is 5. Then, 5* = 5 – 1, or 4. So 7 in Column A and 4 in Column B means the answer is (A). Function questions aren't scary if you follow the directions. Be sure to write everything down on your scratch paper. By the way, these funny-looking symbols aren't always exponents, but you'll always be told what they mean in the question.

PERCENTAGES

You already know that a fraction is another way of representing division and that a decimal is the same thing as a fraction. Well, a percentage is also another way to represent division, and likewise, the same thing as a fraction or a decimal. A percentage is just a way of expressing a fraction whose denominator is 100.

Percent literally means "per 100" or "out of 100" or "divided by 100." If your best friend finds a dollar and gives you 50¢, your friend has given you 50¢ out of 100, or $\frac{50}{100}$ of a dollar, or 50% of a dollar.

You should memorize these percentage-decimal-fraction equivalents. Use these "friendly" fractions and percentages to eliminate answer choices that are way "out of the ballpark":

$$0.01 = \frac{1}{100} = 1\%$$

$$0.1 = \frac{1}{10} = 10\%$$

$$0.2 = \frac{1}{5} = 20\%$$

$$0.25 = \frac{1}{4} = 25\%$$

$$0.333... = \frac{1}{3} = 33\frac{1}{3}\%$$

$$0.4 = \frac{2}{5} = 40\%$$

$$0.5 = \frac{1}{2} = 50\%$$

$$0.6 = \frac{3}{5} = 60\%$$

$$0.666... = \frac{2}{3} = 66\frac{2}{3}\%$$

$$0.75 = \frac{3}{4} = 75\%$$

$$0.8 = \frac{4}{5} = 80\%$$

$$1.0 = \frac{1}{1} = 100\%$$

$$2.0 = \frac{2}{1} = 200\%$$

TRANSLATION

When you have to find exact percentages, it's much easier if you know how to "translate" word problems. Translating a problem lets you express it as an equation, instead of thinking about words. Here's a "dictionary" that will help:

Word	Equivalent Symbol
percent	/100
is	=
of, times, product	×
what (or any unknown value)	any variable (x, k, b)

Here's an example:

56 is what percent of 80?

- ○ 66%
- ○ 70%
- ○ 75%
- ○ 80%
- ○ 142%

Here's how to crack it

To find the exact percentage, let's translate the question and solve for the variable:

$$56 = \frac{x}{100}(80)$$

$$56 = \frac{80x}{100}$$

Don't forget to reduce:

$$56 = \frac{4x}{5}$$

Now multiply both sides of the equation by:

$$\left(\frac{5}{4}\right)\left(\frac{56}{1}\right) = \left(\frac{5}{4}\right)\left(\frac{4x}{5}\right)$$

$$(5)(14) = x$$

$$70 = x$$

> Don't forget to eliminate choices that are out of the ballpark!

That's answer choice (B). Did you notice (E)? Since 56 is less than 80, the answer would have to be less than 100%, so 142% is way too big and could have been eliminated from the get-go by Ballparking.

Let's try a Quant Comp example:

<u>Column A</u>   <u>Column B</u>

5 is r percent of 25

s is 25 percent of 60

r s

○ the quantity in Column A is always greater
○ the quantity in Column B is always greater
○ the quantities are always equal
○ it cannot be determined from the information given

Here's how to crack it

First, translate the first statement:

$$5 = \frac{r}{100}(25)$$

$$5 = \frac{25r}{100}$$

$$5 = \frac{r}{4}$$

$$(4)(5) = \left(\frac{r}{4}\right)(4)$$

$$20 = r$$

That takes care of Column A. Now translate the second statement:

$$s = \frac{25}{100}(60)$$

$$s = \frac{1}{4}(60)$$

$$s = 15$$

That takes care of Column B. The answer is (A).

CONVERTING FRACTIONS TO PERCENTAGES

Just translate the problem. Then solve for the variable. Here's an example:

Express $\frac{4}{5}$ as a percentage.

Here's how to crack it

$\frac{4}{5}$ is what percent?

$$\frac{4}{5} = \frac{x}{100}$$

$$\frac{400}{5} = x$$

$$80 = x$$

So $\frac{4}{5}$ is the same as 80%.

CONVERTING DECIMALS TO PERCENTAGES

Just move the decimal point two places to the right. This turns 0.8 into 80%, 0.25 into 25%, 0.5 into 50%, and 1 into 100%.

PERCENTAGE INCREASE/DECREASE

To find a percentage increase or decrease, first find the amount of increase or decrease, then ask yourself: "The amount of change is what percent of the original number?" Here's the formula:

$$\text{Amount change} = \frac{x}{100} \times \text{original number}$$

For example, if you had to find the percent decrease from 4 to 3, first figure out what the actual decrease is. The decrease from 4 to 3 is 1. So, $1 = \frac{x}{100}$ (4), since 4 is the original number. Now solve for x:

$$1 = \frac{4x}{100}$$
$$1 = \frac{x}{25}$$
$$25 = x$$

The percent decrease from 4 to 3 is 25%.

CHARTS

You'll probably be asked to solve a few percent problems about a chart. Every GRE Math section has a few questions based on a chart or graph (or on a group of charts or graphs). The most important thing that chart questions test is your ability to remember the difference between real-life charts and ETS charts.

Friends give you charts to display the information they want you to see, and to make that information easier to understand. ETS constructs charts to hide the information you need to know, and to make that information hard to understand.

On charts, look for information ETS is trying to hide.

The chart problems just recycle the basic arithmetic concepts we've already covered: fractions, percentages, and so on. You should use the techniques we've discussed for each type of question, but there are also two techniques that are especially important to use when doing chart questions.

DON'T START WITH THE QUESTIONS; START WITH THE CHARTS

Take a minute to look for and write on your scratch paper:

> **Information in titles:** If one chart is about Country A and the other is about Country B, write a big "A" on your scratch paper to represent Country A's chart and a big "B" to represent Country B's chart.

> **Asterisks, footnotes, parentheses, and small print:** Make sure you read these carefully and note the information from them on your scratch paper; they're almost always added to hide crucial information.

Funny units: Pay special attention when a title says "in thousands" or "in millions." You can usually ignore the units when you do the calculations, but you have to remember them to get the right answer.

APPROXIMATE, ESTIMATE, AND BALLPARK

You probably don't estimate enough! Like some of our other techniques, you have to train yourself to do it. You should estimate, not calculate exactly:

- Whenever you see the word "approximately" in a question
- Whenever the answer choices are far apart in value
- Whenever you start to answer a question and you justifiably say to yourself, "This is going to take a lot of calculation!" Since you can't use a calculator on this test, you'll never be asked "calculator" math questions

Review those "friendly" percentages and their fractions to use as reference

points. For example, 34% is a little more than $\frac{1}{3}$.

Try this:

What is approximately 9.6% of 21.4?

Here's how to crack it

Use 10% as a friendlier percentage and 20 as a friendlier number. One-tenth of 20 is 2 (it says "approximately"—who are you to argue?). That's all you need to do to answer most chart questions.

CHART PROBLEMS

Make sure you've read everything carefully, and take notes before you try the first question:

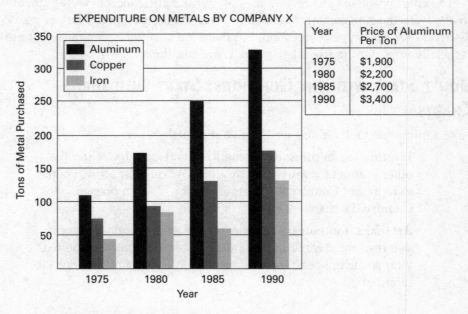

EXPENDITURE ON METALS BY COMPANY X

Year	Price of Aluminum Per Ton
1975	$1,900
1980	$2,200
1985	$2,700
1990	$3,400

Note: Graphs drawn to scale.

Approximately how many tons
of aluminum and copper combined were purchased in 1985?

- ⃝ 125
- ⃝ 255
- ⃝ 325
- ⃝ 375
- ⃝ 515

How much did Company X
spend on aluminum in 1980?

- ⃝ $675,000
- ⃝ $385,000
- ⃝ $333,000
- ⃝ $165,000
- ⃝ $139,000

Approximately what was the
percent increase in the price of
aluminum from 1975 to 1985?

- ⃝ 8%
- ⃝ 16%
- ⃝ 23%
- ⃝ 30%
- ⃝ 42%

Always write A, B, C, D, E on
your scratch paper to
represent the answer choices
(or A, B, C, D if it's Quant
Comp).

Okay, first question . . .

Here's how to crack it

First, we have to decide which chart to use. We need to find out how many tons
were purchased, so that would be the big chart. In 1985, the black bar (which
indicates aluminum) is at 250, and the gray bar (which indicates copper) is at
approximately 125. Add those up and you get the number of tons of aluminum
and copper combined that were purchased in 1985: 250 + 125 = 375. That's (D).
Notice that the question says "approximately," because the numbers in the
answer choices are pretty far apart.

Next question . . .

Here's how to crack it

We'll need both charts for this question, because we need to find the number of
tons of aluminum purchased in 1980 and multiply it by the price per ton of
aluminum in 1980 in order to figure out how much was spent on aluminum in
1980. The bar graph tells us that 175 tons of aluminum were purchased in 1980,
and the little chart tells us that aluminum was $2,200 per ton in 1980.
175 × $2,200 = $385,000. That's (B).

Last question . . .

Here's how to crack it

Remember that percent increase formula?

$$\text{Amount change} = \frac{x}{100} \times \text{original number}$$

We'll need the little chart for this one. In 1975, the price of aluminum was $1,900 per ton. In 1985, the price of aluminum was $2,700 per ton. Now use the formula. The amount of change is the difference between those two numbers:

$$2,700 - 1,900 = 800$$

So, $800 = \frac{x}{100} \times$ the starting point, or $1,900. Let's solve for the variable:

$$800 = \left(\frac{x}{100}\right)(1,900)$$

$$800 = \frac{1,900x}{100}$$

$$800 = 19x$$

$$\frac{800}{19} = \frac{(19x)}{19}$$

$$\frac{800}{19} = x$$

At this point, you could divide 800 by 19. But the question tells us to approximate, and that's always easier and more error-proof, so let's do that. What's 800 divided by 20? It's 40. Which answer choice is closest to 40? Answer choice (E), which is the correct answer.

AVERAGES

Averages shouldn't look foreign to you; they're used in baseball statistics and GPAs.

The average (arithmetic mean) of a set of numbers is the sum, or total value, of all the numbers divided by the number of numbers in the set. The average of the set {1, 2, 3, 4, 5} is the total of the numbers (1 + 2 + 3 + 4 + 5, or 15) divided by the number of numbers in the set (which is 5). Dividing 15 by 5 gives us 3, so 3 is the average of the set.

ETS always refers to an average as an "average (arithmetic mean)." This confusing parenthetical remark is meant to keep you from being confused by other kinds of averages, such as medians and modes. You'll be less confused if you simply ignore the parenthetical remark and know that average means total divided by number of elements. We'll tell you about medians and modes later.

THINK TOTAL

Don't try to solve Average problems all at once. Do them piece by piece. The critical formula to keep in mind is this:

$$\text{Average} = \frac{\text{the sum of the numbers being averaged}}{\text{the number of elements}}$$

You are always going to need the sum of the numbers being averaged: the total amount, the total height, the total weight, the total of the scores, the total distance. Averaging questions are always really about totals. In fact, an average is just another way of expressing a total; an average is the total divided by the number of elements. In averaging problems, you should always find the total first, before you do anything else.

Try this one:

For Average problems (arithmetic mean), think TOTAL.

Column A	Column B
the average	the average
(arithmetic mean)	(arithmetic mean)
of 7, 3, 4, and 2	of $2a + 5$, $4a$, and $7 - 6a$

○ the quantity in Column A is always greater
○ the quantity in Column B is always greater
○ the quantities are always equal
○ it cannot be determined from the information given

Here's how to crack it

Let's deal with Column A first. The average of 7, 3, 4, and 2 would be $7 + 3 + 4 + 2$, or 16, divided by 4, which gives us 4. Now let's deal with Column B. Let's add:

$$2a + 5 + 4a + 7 - 6a =$$
$$2a + 4a - 6a + 5 + 7 =$$
$$5 + 7 = 12$$

Don't forget that we have to divide the total, 12, by the number of things, which was 3. That's 4. So the answer is (C).

By the way, could you have plugged in for Column B? Sure, let's try it using 2:

$$2a + 5 + 4a + 7 - 6a =$$
$$2(2) + 5 + 4(2) + 7 - 6(2) =$$
$$4 + 5 + 8 + 7 - 12 =$$
$$9 + 15 - 12 =$$
$$24 - 12 = 12$$

Same thing, right?

UP AND DOWN

Averages are very predictable. You should make sure you know automatically what happens to them in certain situations. For example, suppose that you take three tests and earn an average score of 90. Now you take a fourth test. What do you know?

If the average goes up as a result of the fourth score, then you know that the fourth score was higher than 90. If the average stays the same as a result of the fourth score, then you know that the fourth score was exactly 90. If the average goes down as a result of the fourth score, then you know that the fourth score was less than 90.

MEDIAN, MODE, AND RANGE

The median is the middle value in a set of numbers; above and below it lie an equal number of values. For example, in the set {1, 2, 3, 4, 5, 6, 7} the median is 4, because it's the middle number (and there is an odd number of numbers in the set). If the set were {1, 2, 3, 4, 5, 6} the median would be the average of 3 and 4, or 3.5, because there is an even amount of numbers. Just think "median = middle."

The mode is the number or range of numbers in a set that occurs the most frequently. For example, in the set {2, 3, 4, 5, 3, 8, 6, 9, 3, 9, 3} the mode is 3, because 3 shows up the most. Just think "mode = most."

The range is the difference between the highest and the lowest numbers in your set. So, in the set {2, 6, 13, 3, 15, 4, 9}, the range is 15 (the highest number in the set) −2 (the lowest number in the set), or 13.

Here's an example:

$$F = \{4, 2, 7, 11, 8, 9\}$$

Column A	Column B
The range of Set F	The median of Set F

○ the quantity in Column A is always greater
○ the quantity in Column B is always greater
○ the quantities are always equal
○ it cannot be determined from the information given

Here's how to crack it

Let's put the numbers in order first, so it'll be easier to see what we have: {2, 4, 7, 8, 9, 11}. First to Column A: The range is the largest number, or 11, minus the smallest number, or 2. That's 9. Now to Column B: The median is the middle number of the set, but since there are two middle numbers, 7 and 8, we have to find the average. Or do we? Isn't the average of 7 and 8 clearly going to be smaller than the number in Column A, which is 9? Yes (remember, in Quant Comps, we always *compare*, not calculate). So, the answer is (A).

STANDARD DEVIATION

On a hard question you might be asked about standard deviation. The standard deviation of a set is a measure of the set's variation from its mean. You'll rarely, if ever, have to actually calculate it, so just remember this: The bigger the standard deviation, the more widely dispersed are the values. The smaller the standard deviation, the more closely grouped around the mean are the values in a set.

Here's an example:

Column A	Column B
The standard deviation of the sample numbers 4, 4, and 4	The standard deviation of the sample numbers 6, 0, and 6

- ◯ the quantity in Column A is always greater
- ◯ the quantity in Column B is always greater
- ◯ the quantities are always equal
- ◯ it cannot be determined from the information given

Since the numbers in Column B, 6, 0, and 6, are more widely dispersed than the numbers in Column A, 4, 4, and 4, the standard deviation in Column B is bigger than that in Column A, so the answer is (B).

Here's another example:

If the mean of a set of data is 15, and the standard deviation is 4, which of the following represents the interval that is two standard deviations from the mean?

- ◯ 7 to 15
- ◯ 7 to 23
- ◯ 11 to 19
- ◯ 15 to 23
- ◯ 19 to 23

Here's how to crack it
The mean is 15, and each standard deviation is 4. So, two standard deviations would be 8. The interval has to go in both directions away from the mean, or 15, so that's 15 − 8 and 15 + 8, or 7 − 23. That's (B).

RATE

Rate problems are similar to average problems. They might ask for average speed, or distance, or the length of a trip, or how long a trip (or a job) takes. Just use one of the following formulas:

$$\text{Rate} = \frac{\text{Distance}}{\text{Time}} \quad \text{or} \quad \text{Rate} = \frac{\text{Amount}}{\text{Time}}$$

Take a look:

It takes Carla 3 hours to drive to her brother's house at an average speed of 50 miles per hour. If she takes the same route home, but her average speed is 60 miles per hour, how long does it take her to get home?

○ 2 hours
○ 2 hours and 14 minutes
○ 2 hours and 30 minutes
○ 2 hours and 45 minutes
○ 3 hours

Here's how to crack it

Okay, for the trip to Carla's brother's house, we have a 3-hour drive (that's the Time) and an average speed of 50 (that's the Rate). Now we can find the Distance of the trip:

$$\text{Rate} = \frac{\text{Distance}}{\text{Time}}$$
$$50 = \frac{\text{Distance}}{3}$$
$$150 = \text{Distance}$$

Now that we know that the trip is 150 miles, we can figure out how long it takes Carla to get home at her new Rate (60):

$$60 = \frac{150}{\text{Time}}$$
$$2.5 = \text{Time}$$

So, it takes her two and a half hours to get home. That's choice (C).

Try another:

A machine can stamp 20 envelopes in 4 minutes. How many of these machines, working simultaneously, are needed to stamp 60 envelopes per minute?

○ 5
○ 10
○ 12
○ 20
○ 24

Here's how to crack it

First we have to figure out the rate of one machine per minute:

$$\text{Rate} = \frac{\text{Amount}}{\text{Time}}$$

$$\text{Rate} = \frac{20}{4}$$

$$\text{Rate} = 5$$

If one machine can stamp 5 envelopes per minute, how many machines do you need to stamp 60 per minute? 60 ÷ 5, or 12. That's (C).

RATIOS AND PROPORTIONS

Ratios, like fractions, percentages, and decimals, are just another way of representing division. Don't let them make you nervous.

EVERY FRACTION IS A RATIO, AND VICE VERSA

A fraction is a ratio between its numerator and its denominator. Every ratio can be expressed as a fraction. A ratio of 1:2 means that there can be a total of three

things (or a multiple of three), and the fraction $\frac{1}{2}$ means "1 out of 2."

On the GRE, you may see ratios expressed in several different ways:

- $x:y$
- the ratio of x to y
- x is to y

TREAT A RATIO LIKE A FRACTION

Anything you can do to a fraction you can also do to a ratio. You can cross-multiply, find common denominators, reduce, and so on.

COUNT THE PARTS

If you have three coins in your pocket and the ratio of pennies to nickels is 2:1, how many pennies and nickels are there? Two pennies and one nickel, right?

If you have 24 coins in your pocket and the ratio of pennies to nickels is 2:1, how many pennies and nickels are there? That's a little trickier. You have 16 pennies and 8 nickels. How did we find that answer? We counted "parts."

The ratio 2:1 contains 3 parts—there are 2 pennies for every 1 nickel, making 3 parts altogether. To find out how many of our 24 coins are pennies, we simply divide 24 by the number of parts (3) and then multiply the result by each part of the ratio. Dividing 24 by 3 yields 8—that is, each of the 3 parts in our ratio consists of 8 coins. Two of the parts are pennies; at 8 coins per part, that makes 16 pennies. One of the parts is nickels; that makes 8 nickels.

A ratio box can help you organize your ratio information.

Here's another way to understand ratios. It's called the ratio box. Again, the question is, if you have 24 coins in your pocket and the ratio of pennies to nickels is 2:1, how many pennies and nickels are there? This is what the ratio box would look like for this question, with all of the information we're given already filled in:

	pennies	nickels	Total
ratio	2	1	3
multiply by			
real			24

"Real" means what we really have, not in the conceptual world of ratios, but in real life. Again, the ratio total (the number you get when you add up the number of parts in the ratio) is 3. The real total number of coins is 24. How do we get from 3 to 24? We multiply by 8. That means our "multiply by" number is 8. This is what the ratio box would look like now:

	pennies	nickels	Total
ratio	2	1	3
multiply by	8	8	8
real			24

Now let's finish filling in the box by multiplying out everything else:

	pennies	nickels	Total
ratio	2	1	3
multiply by	8	8	8
real	16	8	24

Let's try a GRE example:

Flour, eggs, yeast, and salt are mixed by weight in the ratio of 11 : 9 : 3 : 2, respectively. How many pounds of yeast are there in 20 pounds of the mixture?

○ $1\frac{3}{5}$

○ $1\frac{4}{5}$

○ 2

○ $2\frac{2}{5}$

○ $8\frac{4}{5}$

Here's how to crack it

Let's make a ratio box and fill in what we know:

	flour	eggs	yeast	salt	Total
ratio	11	9	3	2	
multiply by					
real					20

First, add up all of the numbers in the ratio to get the ratio total:

	flour	eggs	yeast	salt	Total
ratio	11	9	3	2	25
multiply by					
real					20

Now, what do we multiply 25 by to get 20?

$$25x = 20$$
$$\frac{25x}{25} = \frac{20}{25}$$
$$x = \frac{20}{25}$$
$$x = \frac{4}{5}$$

So $\frac{4}{5}$ is our "multiply by" number. Let's fill it in:

	flour	eggs	yeast	salt	Total
ratio	11	9	3	2	25
multiply by	$\frac{4}{5}$	$\frac{4}{5}$	$\frac{4}{5}$	$\frac{4}{5}$	$\frac{4}{5}$
real					20

Okay, the question is asking for the amount of yeast, so we don't have to worry about the other ingredients. Just look at the yeast column. All we have to do is multiply 3 by $\frac{4}{5}$ and we have our answer $3 \times \frac{4}{5} = \frac{12}{5}$, or $2\frac{2}{5}$. That's answer choice (D).

PROPORTIONS

The GRE often contains problems in which you are given two proportional, or equal, ratios from which one piece of information is missing. These questions take a given relationship, or ratio, and project it onto a larger or smaller scale. Here's an example:

> If the cost of a one-hour telephone call is $7.20, what would be the cost of a ten-minute telephone call at the same rate?
> ○ $7.10
> ○ $3.60
> ○ $1.80
> ○ $1.20
> ○ $ .72

The key to proportions is setting them up correctly.

Here's how to crack it

The most important thing when doing a proportion problem is making sure you set it up correctly. Let's express the ratios here as dollars over minutes, since we're being asked to find the cost of a ten-minute call. That means that we have to convert the 1 hour to 60 minutes (otherwise it wouldn't be a proportion).

$$\frac{\$}{\min} = \frac{\$7.20}{60} = \frac{x}{10}$$

Now cross multiply:

$$60x = (7.2)(10)$$
$$60x = 72$$
$$\frac{60x}{60} = \frac{72}{60}$$
$$x = \frac{6}{5}$$

Now we have to convert $\frac{6}{5}$ to a decimal. But, first, we can ballpark and eliminate some choices. We know $\frac{6}{5}$ is a little more than 1, so that eliminates choices (A), (B), and (E). Now let's finish it off: $6 \div 5 = 1.2$, so the answer is (D).

MORE ON EQUATIONS AND FACTORING

Remember when we discussed factoring in the last chapter? Well, now we're ready to go into a little more detail.

FOIL

When you see two sets of parentheses, all you have to do is remember to multiply every term in the first set of parentheses by every term in the second set of parentheses. Use FOIL to remember the method. FOIL stands for First, Outer, Inner, Last—the four steps of multiplication. For example, if you see $(x + 4)(x + 3)$, you would multiply the first terms $(x \times x)$, the outer terms $(x \times 3)$, the inner terms $(x \times 4)$, and the last terms (4×3), as follows:

$$(x \times x) + (x \times 3) + (4 \times x) + (4 \times 3)$$
$$x^2 + 3x + 4x + 12$$
$$x^2 + 7x + 12$$

This also works in the opposite direction. For example, if you were given $x^2 + 7x + 12 = 0$, you could solve it by breaking it down as follows:

$$(x +)(x +) = 0$$

We know to use "plus" signs because the 7 and the 12 are both positive. Now we have to think of two numbers that when added together, give us 7, and when multiplied together, give us 12. Yep, they're 4 and 3:

$$(x + 4)(x + 3) = 0$$

Note that this will have two solutions for x. Either one of the equations can equal zero for the whole thing to equal 0. So, x can either be –4 or –3.

QUADRATIC EQUATIONS

There are three expressions of quadratic equations that can appear on the GRE. You should know them cold, in both their factored and unfactored forms. Here they are:

Expression 1:

Factored form: $x^2 - y^2$ (the difference between two squares)

Unfactored form: $(x + y)(x - y)$

Expression 2:

Factored form: $(x + y)^2$

Unfactored form: $x^2 + 2xy + y^2$

Expression 3:

Factored form: $(x - y)^2$

Unfactored form: $x^2 - 2xy + y^2$

Let's see how this would look on the GRE:

If x and y are positive integers,
and if $x^2 + 2xy + y^2 = 25$, then
$(x + y)^3 =$

○ 5
○ 15
○ 50
○ 75
○ 125

Here's how to crack it

This is why you have to memorize those quadratic equations. The equation in this question is Expression 2 from above: $x^2 + 2xy + y^2 = (x + y)^2$. The question tells us that $x^2 + 2xy + y^2$ is equal to 25, which means that $(x + y)^2$ is also equal to 25. Think of $x + y$ as one unit that, when squared, is equal to 25. Since this question specified that x and y are positive integers, what positive integer squared equals 25? Right, 5. So $x + y = 5$. The question is asking for $(x + y)^3$. In other words, what's 5 cubed, or $5 \times 5 \times 5$? It's 125. That's (E).

Here's another one:

Column A	Column B
$(4 + \sqrt{6})(4 - \sqrt{6})$	10

○ the quantity in Column A is
   always greater
○ the quantity in Column B is
   always greater
○ the quantities are always equal
○ it cannot be determined from the
   information given

Here's how to crack it

First, eliminate choice D—we only have numbers here, so the answer *can* be determined. Now, Column A looks like a job for FOIL! Multiply the first terms, and you get 16. Multiply the outer terms and you get $-4\sqrt{6}$. Multiply the inner terms and you get $4\sqrt{6}$. Multiply the last terms and you get –6. So, we have $16 - 4\sqrt{6} + 4\sqrt{6} - 6$. Those two inner terms cancel each other out, and we're left with $16 - 6$, or 10. What do you know? That's what we have in Column B, too! So, the answer is (C).

BUT WHENEVER YOU SEE VARIABLES . . .

Don't forget to plug in! You will save yourself a lot of trouble if you just plug in numbers for the variables in complicated algebraic expressions. Here's an example of a complicated algebraic expression:

$$(4x^2 + 4x + 2) + (3 - 7x) - (5 - 3x) =$$

Let's plug in 2 for the xs in the expression.

$$(4 \times 2^2 + 4 \times 2 + 2) + (3 - 7 \times 2) - (5 - 3 \times 2) =$$
$$16 + 8 + 2 + 3 - 14 - 5 + 6 = 16$$

Then you would plug in 2 for x in all the answer choices, and look for our target answer, 16.

SIMULTANEOUS EQUATIONS

ETS will sometimes give you two equations and ask you to use them to find the value of a given expression. Don't worry, you don't need any math-class algebra; in most cases, all you have to do to find ETS's answer is to add or subtract the two equations.

Here's an example:

If $5x + 4y = 6$ and $4x + 3y = 5$, then what does $x + y$ equal ?

Here's how to crack it

All you have to do is add together or subtract one from the other. Here's what we get when we add them:

$$\begin{array}{r} 5x + 4y = 6 \\ + \ 4x + 3y = 5 \\ \hline 9x + 7y = 11 \end{array}$$

A dead end. So let's try subtraction:

$$\begin{array}{r} 5x + 4y = 6 \\ - \ 4x + 3y = 5 \\ \hline x + \ y = 1 \end{array}$$

Bingo. The value of the expression $(x + y)$ is exactly what we're looking for. On the GRE, you may see the two equations written horizontally. Just rewrite the two equations, putting one on top of the other, then simply add or subtract them.

12

Figures

WHAT YOU NEED TO KNOW

The good news is that you don't need to know much about actual geometry to do well on the GRE. We've boiled geometry down to the handful of bits and pieces that ETS actually tests.

Before we begin, consider yourself warned: Since you'll be taking your test on a computer screen, you'll have to be sure to transcribe all the figures onto your scrap paper accurately. All it takes is one mistaken angle or line and you're sure to miss the problem. So, make ample use of your scratch paper and *always double check your figures*. Start practicing now, by using scratch paper with this book.

DEGREES, LINES, AND ANGLES

You need to know that:

1. A line (which can be thought of as a perfectly flat angle) is a 180-degree angle.

2. When two lines intersect, four angles are formed; the sum of the angles is 360 degrees.

3. When two lines are perpendicular to each other, their intersection forms four 90-degree angles. Here is the symbol ETS uses to indicate a perpendicular angle: ⊥

4. Ninety-degree angles are also called right angles. A right angle on the GRE is identified by a little box at the intersection of the angle's arms:

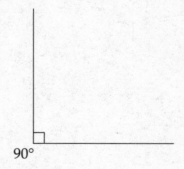

90°

5. A triangle contains 180 degrees.

6. Any four-sided figure contains 360 degrees.

7. A circle contains 360 degrees.

8. Any line that extends from the center of the circle to the edge of the circle is called a *radius* (plural is *radii*).

VERTICAL ANGLES

Vertical angles are the angles across from each other that are formed by the intersection of lines. Vertical angles are equal. In the drawing below, angle x is equal to angle y and angle a is equal to angle b.

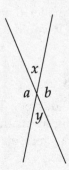

PARALLEL LINES

Don't worry about remembering what certain angles are called. Just remember: When two parallel lines are cut by a third line, only two angles are formed, big angles and small angles. All the big angles are equal. All the small angles are equal. The sum of *any* big and *any* small angle is always 180 degrees. Here's an example:

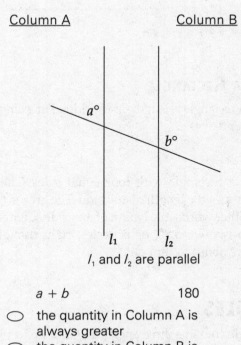

l_1 and l_2 are parallel

Column A	Column B
$a + b$	180

○ the quantity in Column A is
  always greater
○ the quantity in Column B is
  always greater
○ the quantities are always equal
○ it cannot be determined from
  the information given

ALWAYS write down A, B, C, D
for Quant Comps.

Here's how to crack it

Notice that you are told that the lines are parallel. You need to know that; you can't assume that they are just because they look like they are. As you just learned, only two angles are formed when two parallel lines are cut by a third line, a big angle (greater than 90 degrees) and a small one (smaller than 90 degrees). Look at angle *a*. Looks smaller than 90, right? Now look at angle *b*. Looks bigger than 90, right? So *a* + *b* would have to add up to 180. The answer is (C).

FOUR-SIDED FIGURES

Any figure with four sides has 360 degrees. That includes rectangles, squares, and parallelograms (a four-sided figure made out of two sets of parallel lines whose area can be found with the formula $A = bh$, where *h* is the height perpendicular to the base).

PERIMETER OF A RECTANGLE

The perimeter of a rectangle is just the sum of the lengths of the four sides.

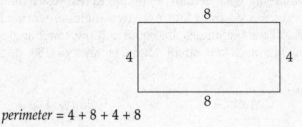

perimeter = 4 + 8 + 4 + 8

AREA OF A RECTANGLE

The area of a rectangle is length times width. For example, the area of the rectangle above is 32 (or 8 × 4).

SQUARES

A square is a rectangle with four equal sides. The perimeter of a square is, therefore, 4 times the length of any side. The area is the length of any side times itself, or in other words, the length of any side squared. The diagonal of a square splits it into two 45:45:90, or isosceles, right triangles. What was that? Don't worry, you're about to find out . . .

TRIANGLES

The three angles of a triangle ALWAYS add up to 180 degrees.

Every triangle contains three angles that add up to 180 degrees. You must know this. It applies to every triangle, no matter what it looks like. Here are some examples:

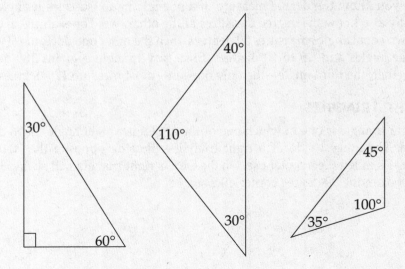

EQUILATERAL TRIANGLES

An equilateral triangle is one in which all three sides are equal in length. Because the sides are all equal, the angles are all equal, too. If they're all equal, how many degrees is each? We hope you said 60 degrees, because 180 divided by 3 is 60.

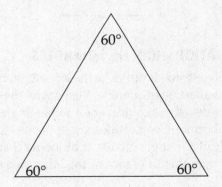

ISOSCELES TRIANGLES

An isosceles triangle is a triangle in which two of the three sides are equal in length. This means that two of the angles are also equal, and that the third angle is not (otherwise it would be equilateral, right?).

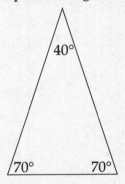

If you know the degree measure of any angle in an isosceles triangle, you usually also know the degree measures of the other two. For example, if one of the two equal angles measures 30 degrees, then the other one does, too. Two 30-degree angles add up to 60 degrees. Since any triangle contains 180 degrees altogether, the third angle—the only one left—must measure 120 degrees.

RIGHT TRIANGLES

A right triangle is one in which one of the angles is a right angle—a 90-degree angle. The longest side of a right triangle—the side opposite the 90-degree angle—is called the hypotenuse. On the GRE, a right triangle will always have a little box in the 90-degree corner, like so:

ANGLE/SIDE RELATIONSHIPS IN TRIANGLES

In any triangle, the longest side is opposite the largest interior angle; the shortest side is opposite the smallest interior angle. That's why the hypotenuse of a right triangle is its longest side—there couldn't be another angle in the triangle bigger than 90 degrees. Furthermore, equal sides are opposite equal angles.

Also, the third side of a triangle can never be longer than the sum of the other two sides, or shorter than the difference of the other two sides.

PERIMETER OF A TRIANGLE

The perimeter of a triangle is simply a measure of the distance around it. All you have to do to find the perimeter of a triangle is to add up the lengths of the sides.

AREA OF A TRIANGLE

The area of any triangle is the height (or "altitude") multiplied by the base, divided by 2 (that's $A = \frac{1}{2}bh$). After all, isn't a triangle really half of a rectangle or square? The altitude is defined as a perpendicular line to the base:

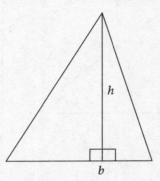

This formula works on any triangle:

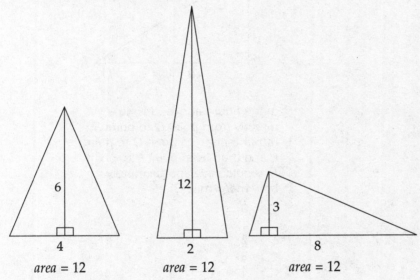

area = 12   *area = 12*   *area = 12*

PYTHAGOREAN THEOREM

The Pythagorean Theorem applies only to right triangles. The theorem states that in a right triangle, the square of the length of the hypotenuse (the longest side, remember?) equals the sum of the squares of the lengths of the two other sides. In other words, $c^2 = a^2 + b^2$, where c is the length of the hypotenuse:

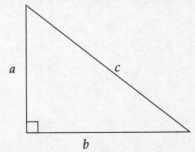

Problems on the GRE often involve right triangles whose sides measure 3, 4, and 5, or multiples of those numbers. Why is this? Because a 3-4-5 right triangle is the smallest one in which measures of the sides are all integers. Does $3^2 + 4^2 = 5^2$? It sure does. Here are three examples of right triangles based on the basic 3-4-5 right triangle:

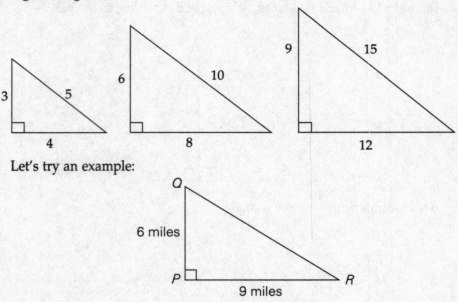

Let's try an example:

In the figure above, driving directly from point Q to point R, rather than from point Q to point P and then from point P to point R, would save approximately how many miles?

- ○ 0
- ○ 1
- ○ 2
- ○ 3
- ○ 4

Write everything down on scratch paper! Don't do anything in your head!

Here's how to crack it

Okay, we've got a right triangle here, with QR as the hypotenuse, or c. Let's use the Pythagorean Theorem to figure out the length of QR. That's $6^2 + 9^2 = c^2$. In other words, $36 + 81 = c^2$. So 117 is equal to c^2.

Now, 117 is not the square of an integer, but we can approximate the square root of 117. How? Well, try to zero in on it by thinking of easy nearby numbers.

For example, we know that 10^2 is 100, and we know that 11^2 is 121. So, $\sqrt{117}$ must be somewhere between 10 and 11. The question tells us to approximate, so we did.

Now, if we drove from Q to P (6 miles) and then from P to R (9 miles), we'd have traveled 15 miles. Going directly from Q to R is almost 11 miles. So, we'd be saving approximately 4 miles. That's (E).

The Pythagorean Theorem will sometimes be the key to solving problems involving squares or rectangles. For example, every rectangle or square can be divided into two right triangles. This means that if you know the length and width of any rectangle or square, you also know the length of the diagonal—it's the shared hypotenuse of the hidden right triangles. Here's an example:

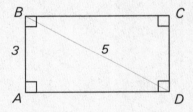

In the rectangle above, what is the area of triangle ABD?

- ⭕ 6
- ⭕ 7.5
- ⭕ 10
- ⭕ 12
- ⭕ 15

Here's how to crack it

We know this is a rectangle, which means triangle ABD is a right triangle. Not only that, but it's a 3-4-5 right triangle (with a side of 3 and a hypotenuse of 5, it must be). That means side AD is 4. So, the area of triangle ABD is $\frac{1}{2}$ the base (3) times the height (4). That's $\frac{1}{2}$ of 12, otherwise known as 6. The answer is (A).

Two Special Right Triangles

There are two special right triangles you may see on the GRE. The first is the **45:45:90**. This is also called an **isosceles right triangle**. In such a triangle, the two non-hypotenuse sides are equal. If the length of each short leg is x, then the length of the hypotenuse is $x\sqrt{2}$. Here's an example:

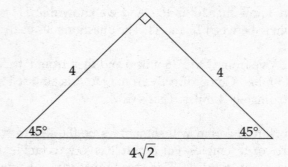

The second special right triangle is called the **30:60:90** right triangle. The ratio between the lengths of the sides in a 30:60:90 triangle is constant. If you know the length of any of the sides, you can find the lengths of the others. Here's the ratio of the sides:

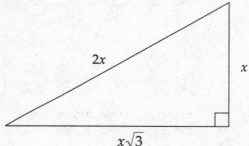

That is, if the shortest side is length x, then the hypotenuse is $2x$, and the remaining side is $x\sqrt{3}$.

Let's try an example involving a special right triangle:

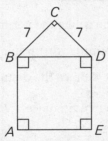

In the figure above, what is the
area of square *ABDE*?

○ $28\sqrt{2}$

○ 49

○ $49\sqrt{2}$

○ 98

○ $98\sqrt{2}$

Here's how to crack it

In order to figure out the area of square *ABDE*, we need to know the length of
one of its sides. We get the length of *BD* by using the isosceles right triangle
attached to it. *BD* is the hypotenuse, which means its length is $7\sqrt{2}$. To get the
area of the square we have to square the length of the side we know, or
$\left(7\sqrt{2}\right)\left(7\sqrt{2}\right) = (49)(2) = 98$. That's (D).

CIRCLES

THE WORLD OF PI

You may remember being taught in math class that the value of pi (π) is 3.14, or
even 3.14159. On the GRE, π = 3+ is a close enough approximation. You don't
need to be any more precise than that in order to find ETS's answer. There will
probably be questions on your GRE that you will be able to solve simply by
plugging in 3 for each π among the answer choices and comparing the results.
Just remember that π is a little bigger than 3.

Keep in mind the relationship that π expresses. Pi is the ratio between the
circumference of a circle and its diameter. When we say that π is a little bigger than
3, we're saying that every circle is about three times as far around as it is across.

> Pi has been calculated to
> hundreds of decimal places,
> but don't worry, you only
> need to know that it's
> three-ish.

RADII AND DIAMETERS

The *radius* of a circle is any line that extends from the center of a circle to the edge
of the circle. If the line extends from one edge of a circle to the other, and goes
through the circle's center, it's the circle's *diameter*. Therefore, the diameter is
twice as long as the radius.

CIRCUMFERENCE OF A CIRCLE

The circumference of a circle is like the perimeter of a triangle: It's the distance around the outside. The formula for finding the circumference of a circle is 2 times π times the radius, or π times the diameter:

$$\text{circumference} = 2\pi r \text{ or } \pi d$$

If the diameter of a circle is 4, then its circumference is 4π, or roughly 12+. If the diameter of a circle is 10, then its circumference is 10π, or a little more than 30.

An *arc* is a section of the outside, or circumference, of a circle. An angle formed by two radii is called a central angle (it comes out to the edge from the center of the circle). There are 360 degrees in a circle, so if there is an arc formed by, say, a 60-degree central angle, and 60 is $\frac{1}{6}$ of 360, then the arc formed by this 60-degree central angle will be $\frac{1}{6}$ of the circumference of the circle.

AREA OF A CIRCLE

The area of a circle is π times the square of the radius:

$$\text{area} = \pi r^2$$

Let's try an example involving circles:

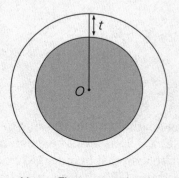

Note: Figure not drawn to scale.

In the wheel above, with center O, the area of the entire wheel is 169π. If the area of the shaded hubcap is 144π, then $t =$

- ○ 1
- ○ 2
- ○ 3
- ○ 5
- ○ 12.5

Here's how to crack it

We have to figure out what t is, and it's going to be the length of the radius of the entire wheel minus the length of the radius of the hubcap. If the area of the entire wheel is 169π, the radius is $\sqrt{169}$, or 13. If the area of the hubcap is 144π, the radius is $\sqrt{144}$, or 12. $13 - 12 = 1$, or (A).

Let's try another one:

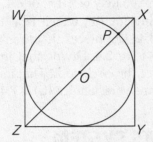

In the figure above, a circle with the center O is inscribed in square $WXYZ$. If the circle has radius 3, then $PZ =$

○ 6

○ $3\sqrt{2}$

○ $6 + \sqrt{2}$

○ $3 + \sqrt{3}$

○ $3\sqrt{2} + 3$

Ballparking answers will help you eliminate choices.

Here's how to crack it

"Inscribed" means the edges are touching. The radius of the circle is 3, which means PO is 3. If Z were at the other end of the diameter from P, this problem would be easy and the answer would be 6, right? But Z is beyond the edge of the circle, which means that PZ is a little more than 6. Let's stop there for a minute and glance at the answer choices. We can eliminate anything "out of the ballpark"—in other words, any answer choice that's less than 6, equal to 6 itself, or a lot more than 6. Remember when we told you to memorize a few of those square roots? Let's use them:

(A) Exactly 6? Nope.

(B) That's 1.4×3, which is 4.2. Too small.

(C) That's $6 + 1.4$, or 7.4. Not bad. Let's leave that one in.

(D) That's $3 + 1.7$, or 4.7. Too small.

(E) That's $(3 \times 1.4) + 3$, which is $4.2 + 3$, or 7.2. Not bad. Let's leave that one in, too.

So, we eliminated three choices with Ballparking. We're left with (C) and (E). You could take a guess here if you had to, but let's do a little more geometry to find the answer.

Because this circle is inscribed in the square, the diameter of the circle is the same as a side of the square. Draw in a diameter parallel to ZY to prove it to yourself. We already know that the diameter of the circle is 6, so that means that ZY, and indeed all the sides of the square, are also 6. Now, if ZY is 6, and XY is 6, what's XZ, the diagonal of the square? Well, XZ is also the hypotenuse of the isosceles right triangle XYZ. The hypotenuse of a right triangle with two sides of 6 is $6 \times \sqrt{2}$. That's approximately 6 × 1.4, or 8.4.

The question is asking for PZ, which is a little less than XZ. It's somewhere between 6 and 8.4. The pieces that aren't part of the diameter of the circle are equal to 8.4 – 6, or 2.4. Divide that in half to get 1.2, which is the distance from the edge of the circle to Z. That means that PZ is 6 + 1.2, or 7.2. Check your remaining answers: Choice (C) is 7.4, and choice (E) is 7.2. Bingo! The answer is (E).

THE COORDINATE SYSTEM

A coordinate system is shaped like a cross. The horizontal line is called the **X-axis**; the vertical line is called the **Y-axis**. The four areas formed by the intersection of these axes are called **quadrants**. The point where the axes intersect is called the **origin**. This is what it looks like:

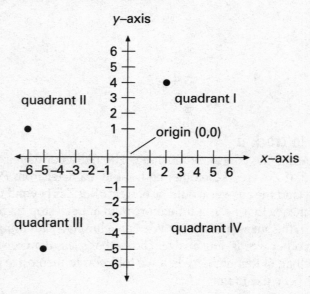

To express any point in the coordinate system, first give the horizontal value, then the vertical value, or (x, y). In the diagram above, the marked point above and to the right of the origin can be described by the coordinates (2, 4). That is, the point is two spaces to the right of the origin and four spaces above the origin. The point above and to the left of the origin can be described by the coordinates (–6, 1). That is, it is six spaces to the left and one space above the origin. What are the coordinates of the point to the left of and below the origin? Right, it's (–5, –5).

Here's a GRE example:

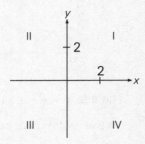

Points (x, 5) and (–6, y), not shown in the figure above, are in quadrants I and III, respectively. If $xy \neq 0$, in which quadrant is point (x, y)?

○ IV
○ III
○ II
○ I
○ It cannot be determined from the information given

ALWAYS write A, B, C, D, E on your scratch paper to represent the answer choices (or A, B, C, D if it's Quant Comp).

Here's how to crack it

If point (x, 5) is in quadrant I, that means x is positive. If point y is in quadrant III, that means y is negative. The quadrant that would contain a positive x and a negative y is quadrant IV. That's answer choice (A).

SLOPE

Trickier questions involving the coordinate system might give you the equation of a line on the grid, which will involve something called the slope. The equation of a line is:

$$y = mx + b$$

That's where the x and the y are points on the line, b stands for the **y-intercept**, or the point at which the line crosses the y-axis, and m is the **slope** of the line, or the change in y divided by the change in x. Sometimes on the GRE, the m is an a, as in $y = ax + b$. Let's see this in action on the following page:

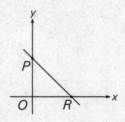

The line $y = -\dfrac{8}{7}x + 1$ is graphed on the rectangular coordinate axes.

Column A	Column B
OR	OP

○ the quantity in Column A is always greater
○ the quantity in Column B is always greater
○ the quantities are always equal
○ it cannot be determined from the information given

Here's how to crack it

The b in this case is 1. That means the line crosses the y-axis at 1. So the coordinates of point P are (0, 1). Now we have to figure out what the coordinates of point R are. We know the y coordinate is 0, so let's stick that into the equation (the slope and the y-intercept are constant, meaning they don't change):

$$y = mx + b$$

$$0 = -\frac{8}{7}x + 1$$

Now let's solve for x:

$$0 = -\frac{8}{7}x + 1$$

$$0 - 1 = -\frac{8}{7}x + 1 - 1$$

$$-1 = -\frac{8}{7}x$$

$$\left(-\frac{7}{8}\right)(-1) = \left(-\frac{7}{8}\right)\left(-\frac{8}{7}\right)x$$

$$\frac{7}{8} = x$$

So the coordinates of point R are $(\dfrac{7}{8}, 0)$. That means OR, in Column A, is equal to $\dfrac{7}{8}$, and OP, in Column B, is equal to 1. The answer is (B).

VOLUME

You can get the volume of a three-dimensional figure by multiplying the area of a two-dimensional figure by height (or depth). For example, to find the volume of a rectangular solid, you take the area of a rectangle and multiply by the depth. The formula is *lwh* (length times width times height). To find the volume of a circular cylinder, take the area of a circle and multiply by the height. The formula is πr^2 times the height (or $\pi r^2 h$).

DIAGONALS

There's a special formula to use if you are ever asked to find the length of a diagonal (the longest distance between any two corners) inside a three dimensional rectangular box. It is $a^2 + b^2 + c^2 = d^2$, where a, b, and c are the dimensions of the figure (kind of looks like the Pythagorean Theorem, huh?).

Take a look:

> What is the length of the longest distance between any two corners in a rectangular box with dimensions 3 inches by 4 inches by 5 inches?
>
> ○ 5
>
> ○ 12
>
> ○ $5\sqrt{2}$
>
> ○ $12\sqrt{2}$
>
> ○ 50

Here's how to crack it

Let's use our formula, $a^2 + b^2 + c^2 = d^2$. The dimensions of the box are 3, 4, and 5:

$$3^2 + 4^2 + 5^2 = d^2$$
$$9 + 16 + 25 = d^2$$
$$50 = d^2$$
$$\sqrt{50} = d$$
$$5\sqrt{2} = d$$

That's (C).

SURFACE AREA

The surface area of a rectangular box is equal to the sum of the areas of all of its sides. In other words, if you had a box whose dimensions were $2 \times 3 \times 4$, there would be two sides that are 2 by 3 (area of 6), two sides that are 3 by 4 (area of 12), and two sides that are 2 by 4 (area of 8). So, the surface area would be $6 + 6 + 12 + 12 + 8 + 8$, which is 52.

PLUG IN ON GEOMETRY PROBLEMS

Don't forget to PLUG IN on geometry questions. Just pick numbers according to the rules of geometry.

Remember, *whenever* you see variables in the answer choices, plug in. On geometry problems, you can plug in values for angles or lengths as long as the values you plug in don't contradict either the wording of the problem or the laws of geometry (you can't let the interior angles of a triangle add up to anything but 180, for instance).

Here's an example:

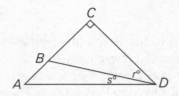

In the drawing above, if $AC = CD$, then $r =$

○ $45 - s$
○ $90 - s$
○ s
○ $45 + s$
○ $60 + s$

Here's how to crack it

See the variables in the answer choices? Let's plug in. First of all, we're told that AC and CD are equal, which means that ACD is an isosceles right triangle. So angles A and D both have to be 45 degrees. Now it's Plugging In time. The smaller angles, r and s, have to add up to 45 degrees, so let's make $r = 40$ degrees and $s = 5$ degrees. The question is asking for the value of r, which is 40, so that's our target answer choice. Now eliminate answer choices by plugging in 5 for s:

(A) $45 - 5 = 40$. Bingo! Check the other choices to be sure.

(B) $90 - 5 = 85$. Nope.

(C) 5. Nope.

(D) $45 + 5 = 50$. Eliminate.

(E) $60 + 5 = 65$. No way.

By the way, we knew that the correct answer couldn't be greater than 45 degrees, since that's the measure of the entire angle D, so you could have eliminated (D) and (E) right away.

Remember, plug in whenever you see variables!

DRAW IT YOURSELF

When ETS doesn't include a drawing with a geometry problem, it usually means that the drawing, if supplied, would make ETS's answer obvious. In that case, you should just draw it yourself. Here's an example:

Column A	Column B
The diameter of a	14
circle with area 49π	

- ⬭ the quantity in Column A is always greater
- ⬭ the quantity in Column B is always greater
- ⬭ the quantities are always equal
- ⬭ it cannot be determined from the information given

Here's how to crack it

Draw that circle on your scratch paper! If the area is 49π, what's the radius? Right, 7. And if the radius is 7, what's the diameter? Right, 14. The answer is (C). Isn't it helpful to see the picture?

REDRAW

On tricky Quant Comp questions, you may need to draw the figure once, eliminate two answer choices, and then redraw the figure to try to disprove your first answer, in order to see if the answer is (D). Here's an example:

For Quant Comp geometry, draw, eliminate, and REDRAW; it's like Plugging In twice.

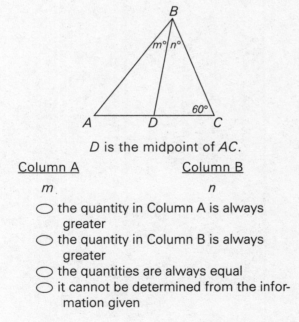

D is the midpoint of AC.

Column A	Column B
m	n

- ⬭ the quantity in Column A is always greater
- ⬭ the quantity in Column B is always greater
- ⬭ the quantities are always equal
- ⬭ it cannot be determined from the information given

Do we really know that this triangle looks like this? Nope. We know that the lengths of *AD* and *DC* are equal; from this figure, it looks like angles *m* and *n* are also equal. Since they could be, we can eliminate choices (A) and (B). But let's redraw the figure to try to disprove our first answer. Let's make the triangle a right triangle, since right triangles are very familiar.

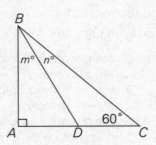

Remember that *D* is still the midpoint of side *AC*. But we can now see that the triangle with the 60-degree angle *C* also includes angle *BDC*, which is greater than 90 degrees. Let's plug in to be sure that angle *n* is smaller than angle *m*. Let's plug in 110 degrees for angle *BDC*, so angle *n* would have to be 10 degrees. If angle *BDC* is 110, then the angle next to it would have to be 70 degrees, and angle *m* would be 20 degrees. By redrawing the figure, the value of *m* is greater than the value of *n*, which eliminates (C). The correct choice must be (D).

PART IV

How to Crack the Analytical Writing Section

13

The Geography of the Analytical Writing Section

In October 2002 the Analytical section of the GRE will become the Analytical Writing section. (The Analytical Writing section is identical to the Writing Assessment Test that was offered separately prior to October 2002, but now it will be the third section of the GRE.)

The section is divided into two parts; for each part, you're presented with a topic on which you have to write an essay. The first part lasts 45 minutes and is entitled "Present Your Perspective on an Issue," while the second part lasts 30 minutes and is entitled "Analyze an Argument."

You will not be given the essay topics in advance, nor will you be given a choice of topics. However, there is a complete list of all the possible essay topics available for you to download for free on the GRE website. Simply go to www.gre.org and click on "Writing Assessment" under the heading "Prepare to Test" to find the essay topics. The topics you will be given on test day must be from this list, so there won't be any surprises if you prepare properly.

WHY ADD ESSAYS TO THE GRE?

ETS's official line is that many schools felt that applicants were not sufficiently prepared for academic writing, and that the current application requirements did not give admissions officials a way to measure writing ability. Therefore, ETS created the Analytical Writing section.

The real truth is that many schools complained that the current Verbal section simply did not test verbal skills in a way that was useful or applicable to graduate-level students. After all, why should an adult applying to earn a Master's in Psychology or a Ph.D. in Public Policy be taking a multiple-choice vocabulary test? At the same time, ETS had already developed the procedures for administering essay tests—the GMAT (the test used to determine admission to M.B.A. programs) has featured a writing assessment section for years. Combine these two factors, and the Analytical Writing section of the GRE was inevitable.

Interestingly, the point that ETS keeps making when they argue that the essays are good tools for admissions committees is that scores on the old GRE Writing Assessment essays correlate highly with grades earned in undergraduate writing classes. Sounds like a great argument, until you realize that since this is the case, schools could just as easily use students' undergraduate writing class grades and skip the Analytical Writing section entirely.

HOW DO THE SCHOOLS USE THE WRITING ASSESSMENT?

If you are a citizen of a non-English-speaking country, you can expect the schools to look quite closely at both the score you receive on the essays you write and the essays themselves. (Schools can obtain copies of the actual essays you type into the computer. Depending on the school and the program, they may or may not ever do this, and they may or may not ever read them.) If you are a native English speaker with a reasonably good Verbal score and solid English grades in college then the writing assessment is not likely to be a crucial part of your package.

On the other hand, if your verbal skills are not adequately reflected by your grades in college, or in the Verbal section of the GRE, then a strong performance on the writing assessment could be extremely helpful. In most cases, the Analytical Writing section of the GRE can only help you.

Ultimately, however, it really depends on how much your program values writing skills. If you are applying to a program in applied statistics, for example, the admissions committee might not care much about how you write. If this is the case, you should prepare for the Analytical Writing section adequately enough so that you'll receive a score that won't hurt the rest of your application, but not so extensively as to take preparation time away from what's really important to you—the Math section of the GRE.

If you're applying to a program that is likely to be more writing-intensive, you should prepare more thoroughly for the Analytical Writing section. It's far easier to improve your Analytical Writing skills than it is to improve your vocabulary, so your preparation time will be well spent.

How Will the Essays Be Scored?

When you get your GRE score back from ETS, you will receive separate scores for the Math and Verbal sections (on a scale of 200–800) and for the Analytical Writing section (on a scale of 0–6). Your Math and Verbal scores will be available instantly at the end of your testing section, but you will have to wait to receive your essay scores, because they are scored by humans. Each essay is read by two readers, each of whom will assign your writing a grade from 0 to 6, in half-point increments (6 being the highest score possible). If the two scores are within a point of each other, they will be averaged. If the spread is more than one point, the essays will be read by a third reader, and the scores will be adjusted to reflect the third scorer's evaluation.

ETS uses the "holistic" scoring method to grade essays; your writing will be judged not on small details but rather on its overall impact. The ETS essay readers are supposed to ignore small errors of grammar and spelling. Considering that these poor readers are going to have to plow through hundreds of thousands of essays each year, this is probably just as well. This doesn't give you license to be careless, however; essays riddled with spelling and grammatical mistakes will score lower than those with only a few mistakes.

Who Are These Readers Anyway?

We'll put this in the form of a multiple-choice question:
Your essays will initially be read by

(A) captains of industry

(B) leading professors

(C) college TAs working part time

If you guessed (C), you're doing just fine. Each essay will be read first by part-time employees of ETS, mostly culled from graduate school programs.

How Much Time Do They Devote to Each Essay?

The graders get two minutes, tops. They work in eight-hour marathon sessions (nine to five, with an hour off for lunch). They are each required to read a certain number of essays per hour—often dozens. Obviously, these poor graders do not have time for an in-depth reading of your essay. They probably aren't going to notice how carefully you thought out your ideas or how clever your analysis was. Under pressure to meet their quota, they are simply going to be giving it a fast skim. By the time your reader gets to your essay, she will probably have already seen over a hundred—and no matter how ingenious you were in coming up with original ideas, she's already seen them.

Is the Analytical Writing Section Fair?

Actually, it's probably the "fairest" of all three of the GRE sections. This is because all it purports to measure is how well you can write an essay in a limited amount of time with no outside reference materials. And that's what it tests.

On the other hand, the scoring of the section isn't necessarily set up for the average writer's benefit. Fortunately, it's really easy to learn what will give you a high score on the Analytical Writing section, and to practice writing essays that way.

So How Do You Score High on the Analytical Writing Essays?

On the face of it, you might think it would be pretty difficult to impress these jaded readers, but it turns out that there are some very specific ways to persuade them of your superior writing skills.

What ETS Doesn't Want You to Know

In a 1982 internal study, two ETS researchers analyzed a group of essays written by actual test-takers and the grades that those essays received. The most successful essays had one thing in common. Which of the following characteristics do you think it was?

- Good organization
- Proper diction
- Noteworthy ideas
- Good vocabulary
- Sentence variety
- Length
- Number of paragraphs

What Your Essay Needs in Order to Look Like a Successful Essay

The ETS researchers discovered that the essays that received the highest grades from ETS essay graders had one single factor in common: Length.

To ace the Analytical Writing section, you need to take one simple step: Write as much as you possibly can. Each essay should include at least four indented paragraphs.

So All I Have to Do Is Type "I Hate the GRE" Over and Over Again?

Well, no. The length issue isn't that easy. The ETS researchers did also control for the fact that high-scoring essays all made reasonably good points addressing the topic; after that condition was given, the winning factor was length. So you have to actually write something that covers the essay topic. We'll help you with that, though, so just read on.

Oh, Yes, You Can Plan Your Essays in Advance

In fact, there are some very specific ways to prepare for the essays that go beyond length and good typing skills. Of course, if all you had to worry about were the ETS graders, these techniques might not be necessary. However, your GRE essays are being sent to the schools to which you're applying. Just in case the admissions officers decide to read them, you want them to be good. So how can you prepare ahead of time?

Creating a template

When a builder builds a house, the first thing he does is construct a frame. The frame supports the entire house. After the frame is completed, he can nail the walls and windows to the frame. We're going to show you how to build the frame for the perfect GRE essay. Of course, you won't know the exact topic of the essay until you get there (just as the builder may not know what color his client is going to paint the living room), but you will have an all-purpose frame on which to construct a great essay no matter what the topic is. We call this frame the **template**.

Preconstruction

Just as a builder can construct the windows of a house in his workshop weeks before he arrives to install them, so can you pre-build certain elements of your essay. We call this **preconstruction**.

In the next two chapters we'll show you how to prepare ahead of time to write essays on two topics you won't see until they appear on your screen.

How Does the Word Processing Program Work?

ETS has created a very simple program to allow students to compose their essays on the screen. Compared to any of the commercial word processing programs, this one is extremely limited, but it does allow the basic functions: You can move the cursor with the arrow keys, and you can delete, copy, and paste. If you're a computer novice, don't worry. You don't have to use any of these functions. With just the backspace key and the mouse to change your point of insertion, you will be able to use the computer like a regular typewriter. However, if you can't type then you really do have a problem. You must type the essay on the computer; no hand-writing is allowed (unless you're in a country that still has paper administrations of the test). If you're not able to type for medical reasons, you should contact ETS to find out what accommodations they can make for you. If you simply have not learned to type, you will certainly need this skill for graduate school, so learn now.

Here's what your screen will look like during the Analytical Writing section of the test:

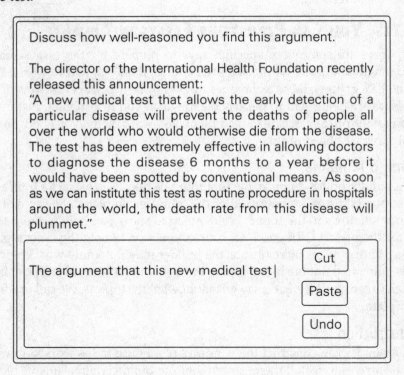

The question always appears at the top of your screen. Below it, in a box, will be your writing area (where you can see a partially completed sentence). When you click inside the box with your mouse, a winking cursor will appear, indicating that you can begin typing. As we said above, the program supports the use of many of the normal computer keys:

- The *backspace* key removes text to the left of the cursor.
- The *delete* key removes text to the right of the cursor.
- The *arrow* keys move the cursor up, down, left, or right.

- The *home* key moves the cursor to the beginning of a line.
- The *end* key moves the cursor to the end of a line.
- The *enter* key moves the cursor to the beginning of the next line.
- *Page up* moves the cursor up one page.
- *Page down* moves the cursor down one page.

You can also use the icons on the right of the screen to copy and paste words, sentences, or paragraphs. To do this, first you have to highlight the desired text by clicking on the starting point with your mouse and then holding down the mouse button while you drag it to the ending point. Then (while this may seem counterintuitive) click on the *cut* button. This deletes the text you've selected from the screen, but also stores it in the computer's memory. Now, just move the cursor to wherever you would like the selected text to reappear, and click on the *paste* button. The selected text will appear in that spot.

If you make a mistake, simply click on the *undo* button, which will undo whatever operation you have just done. You can undo a cut, a paste, or even the last set of words you've typed in. Unfortunately, unlike many word processing programs, ETS's program does not have a *redo* button, so be careful what you decide to undo.

Obviously, the small box on the screen is not big enough to contain your entire essay. However, by hitting the *page up* and *page down* buttons on your keyboard, or by using the arrows on your keyboard, you will be able to go forward and backward to reread what you have written and make corrections.

DOES SPELLING COUNT?

Officially, no. ETS essay readers are supposed to ignore minor errors of spelling and grammar. However, the readers wouldn't be human if they weren't influenced poorly by an essay with lots of spelling mistakes and improper grammar—it gives the impression that you just didn't care enough to proofread. Unfortunately, there is no spell-check function in the word processing program.

LOGISTICS OF THE ESSAYS

The two essay sections have important differences, besides the difference in the amount of time allotted. Let's see what ETS says about each one:

"The **Issue** task states an opinion on an issue of broad interest and asks test takers to address the issue from any perspective(s) they wish, so long as they provide relevant reasons and examples to explain and support their views.

"The **Argument** task presents a different challenge: it requires test takers to critique an argument by discussing how well reasoned they find it. Test takers are asked to consider the logical soundness of the argument rather than agree or disagree with the position it presents.

"Thus the two tasks are complementary in that one requires test takers to construct their own arguments by making claims and providing evidence supporting their position on the issue, whereas the other requires them to critique someone else's argument by assessing its claims and evaluating the evidence it provides."

Hmm. What that means in regular language is that the 45-minute Issue essay gives you a statement and you pick a side (pro or con) and argue for that side. The 30-minute Argument essay gives you an argument, and you critique the argument. All that stuff about the essays being complementary doesn't have anything to do with anything (and, frankly, is all in ETS's head), but it reinforces the idea that you need to approach the two essays in two very different ways.

WHAT WILL THE ESSAY TOPICS LOOK LIKE?

Again, there are two types of essay topics: Analysis of an Issue and Analysis of an Argument. Here's an example of each:

Analysis of an Issue

> *It is necessary for the entertainment industry to police itself by censoring television programs and popular music lyrics.*

Analysis of an Argument

> *The director of the International Health Foundation recently released this announcement:*

> *"A new medical test that allows the early detection of a particular disease will prevent the deaths of people all over the world who would otherwise die from the disease. The test has been extremely effective in allowing doctors to diagnose the disease 6 months to a year before it would have been spotted by conventional means. As soon as we can institute this test as routine procedure in hospitals around the world, the death rate from this disease will plummet."*

You will have to write one essay on each topic.

YOU'RE STARTING TO LOSE ME NOW

Okay, then, let's start getting into the meat of the essays. We'll start by showing you how to break down the Issue topic, and then we'll move on to writing the Issue essay. Then we'll do the same thing for the Argument topic. Ready?

14

The Basics of the Issue Topic

PRO VS. CON

Every Issue topic is essentially a pro vs. con statement. However, there's one small twist; the actual topic only states one side of the argument.

> Children need strict discipline in order to grow successfully to adulthood. Without it, they, and society as a whole, will have no sense of morals and will drift into depression and violence.

This Issue prompt (like the vast majority of Issue prompts on the GRE) gives you one side of an argument. Essentially, this prompt is saying (in Orwellian terms), "strict discipline good."

You can write a very good essay by agreeing with the prompt (if you can think of enough supporting examples and follow the steps we'll lay out for you in the next chapter, of course). But you can write a better essay if you at least acknowledge the opposing argument. The best way to acknowledge it is to make it absolutely explicit.

"Strict discipline bad."

Okay, so that's the opposing side of the topic, but you'll probably want to plump it up and make it match the language and tone used in the actual prompt as closely as possible. We also want to have a response of some sort to the second sentence of the prompt, which says that lack of discipline causes depression and violence. Think about what could result from too much discipline, and use that as part of your response.

"Too much discipline, however, can stifle children. Instead of providing them with a moral compass, it can actually suppress their personalities and lead them to be unthinking automatons, much more likely to resort to violence or succumb to depression than those who have been allowed to use their creativity."

Now we're talking! The statement above provides a counterweight to the actual essay topic and could serve as a great opening for your essay, simply by restating the actual topic and then typing in the opposing side.

Let's try another one:

> Whether a given book is literature or merely engaging fiction cannot be determined when the book is first published. The answer to this question can only be determined long after the book is published and the author is dead, when the book can be examined in relation to the political and cultural world in which it appeared.

What's this side of the issue saying? "You can't tell if a book is good when it's just published." So the opposing side would have to be, "You *can* tell if a book is good when it's just published." The topic says that you have to be able to look back and put a book in historical context to tell if it's really good, so we need to think of a response to that. How about that what makes a book good never really changes?

Now let's make it match the actual prompt:

"Others argue, however, that it is possible to judge the quality of a work of fiction when it is first published, because the qualities that constitute great literature never change."

Are you starting to get the hang of this? Let's break down exactly what we've been doing:

STEPS TO BREAKING DOWN THE ISSUE PROMPT

Step 1: Read the topic and summarize what it's saying (i.e., "Strict discipline good").

Step 2: Summarize the opposing side of the topic (i.e., "Strict discipline bad").

Step 3: Look at the evidence the topic gives for the side it argues, and come up with some points to challenge that side (i.e., "If lack of discipline causes depression and violence, then too much discipline stifles creativity and makes children unfeeling robots with a greater capability for depression and violence").

Step 4: Write down the opposing side and the evidence you've come up with, making it match the language used in the prompt as much as possible (i.e., "Too much discipline, however, can stifle children. Instead of providing them with a moral compass, it can actually suppress their personalities and lead them to be unthinking automatons, much more likely to resort to violence or succumb to depression than those who have been allowed to use their creativity").

DRILL

Time to practice breaking down the Issue topic. Work through these four example topics, and then check your answers against ours.

1. Parenthood is the defining event in human life. Anyone who does not become a parent misses out on the full understanding of what it is to be human.

Summary:

Opposing side:

Respond to points made in topic:

Now make it look like the topic:

2. With the blossoming of the Internet, traditional libraries are obsolete. Students should not be forced to learn traditional research skills, and public libraries should be demolished and the lands they stand on used for more efficient public purposes.

Summary:

Opposing side:

Respond to points made in topic:

Now make it look like the topic:

3. It is counterproductive for students to be forced to study non-contemporary works of art, literature, and philosophy. Since society has moved past these old forms of expression, it is more useful for students to focus on current and future forms of expression.

Summary:

Opposing side:

Respond to points made in topic:

Now make it look like the topic:

4. The phrase "By any means necessary" is the ultimate expression of American patriotism.

Summary:

Opposing side:

Respond to points made in topic:

Now make it look like the topic:

HERE'S HOW TO CRACK THEM

Here's how we'd approach these topics.

> *1. Parenthood is the defining event in human life. Anyone who does not become a parent misses out on the full understanding of what it is to be human.*

Summary: "Can't be human without being a parent."

Opposing side: "Can be human without being a parent."

Respond to points made in topic: Other ways to understand what it is to be human, other events can be defining, the same event may not be defining for everyone.

Now make it look like the topic:

"It can be argued, however, that other events in human life are equally, if not more, defining, or that no one event can be defining for everyone. There are other ways, besides being a parent, to understand what it is to be human."

> *2. With the blossoming of the Internet, traditional libraries are obsolete. Students should not be forced to learn traditional research skills, and public libraries should be demolished and the lands they stand on used for more efficient public purposes.*

Summary: "Get rid of libraries."

Opposing side: "Keep the libraries."

Respond to points made in topic: Internet can't take the place of books entirely, students should know as many ways to research as possible, what better use for public land can there be but to provide knowledge for everyone?

Now make it look like the topic:

"This view, however, fails to take into account the fact that the Internet cannot entirely take the place of books, so libraries will always be necessary. In addition, students benefit from knowing a variety of ways to do research, and there is no more efficient use of public lands than to provide knowledge for everyone."

3. It is counterproductive for students to be forced to study non-contemporary works of art, literature, and philosophy. Since society has moved past these old forms of expression, it is more useful for students to focus on current and future forms of expression.

Summary: "Studying old things is a waste of time."

Opposing side: "Studying old things is a good use of time."

Respond to points made in topic: Have we really moved past old forms? How can you really understand current things without understanding old things?
Now make it look like the topic:
"However, it can also be argued that studying non-contemporary works is anything but counterproductive, since there is no real evidence that we are truly free of these forms, and since an understanding of historical ideas is essential to an understanding of contemporary society."

4. The phrase "By any means necessary" is the ultimate expression of American patriotism.

Summary: "'By any means necessary' is patriotic."

Opposing side: "'By any means necessary' is unpatriotic."

Respond to points made in topic: Hmmm. . . No real back-up points here. This makes it both easier and harder to respond. Where would you go with this argument? Maybe that doing whatever had to be done was the way the country was founded and expanded, and has gone through any social and political change. So a good response could be that doing whatever had to be done suppressed the freedom of the individual, which is one of the foundations of America.
Now make it look like the topic:
"This statement, however, fails to take into account the fact that something done 'by any means necessary' often results in the suppression of individual rights, which are the basis of American freedom."

WHERE IS THIS ALL HEADING?

In the next section we're going to learn how to preconstruct an Issue essay, so that you can have your basic structure, and even some of your sentences, written before you even walk into the testing center. Knowing how to break down the topic quickly and efficiently will make your first paragraph a breeze and provide a solid base for the rest of your essay.

15

Writing the Issue Essay

Writing the Analysis of an Issue essay requires a series of steps.

Step 1: Read the topic and summarize it. Then summarize the opposing position, think of points to challenge those in the actual topic, and then write it out to match the wording of the topic.

Step 2: Decide the general position you are going to take—remember that you need to take a stand on the issue.

Step 3: Brainstorm. Come up with a bunch of supporting ideas or examples. It helps to write these down on your scratch paper. These supporting statements should help convince the reader that your main thesis is correct.

Step 4: Look over your supporting ideas and throw out the weakest ones. There should be three to five left over.

Step 5: Write the essay on screen, using all the preconstruction and template tools you're going to be learning in this chapter.

Step 6: Read over the essay and do some editing. The GRE readers will not take away points for spelling or grammatical mistakes, but you don't want too many (especially if officials from a grad school program are also reading the essay), and you want your organization to be as sound as possible.

WHAT THE READERS ARE LOOKING FOR

The essay topic for the Analysis of an Issue will ask you to choose a side on an issue and develop a coherent defense of your position. You aren't required to know any more about the subject than would any normal person. As far as ETS is concerned, it doesn't even matter which side of the argument you take—as long as your essay is well written. So what constitutes a well-written essay?

The essay readers will be looking for four characteristics as they skim at the speed of light through your Analysis of an Issue essay. According to a booklet prepared by ETS, "an outstanding essay...

- explores ideas and develops a position on the issue with insightful reasons and/or persuasive examples,

- is clearly well organized,

- demonstrates superior control of language, including diction and syntactic variety,

- demonstrates superior facility with the conventions of standard written English, but may have minor flaws."

To put it more simply, the readers are looking for good organization, good supporting examples for whatever position you've taken, and reasonably good use of the English language. Let's start with good organization, which is a snap—all you have to do is use what we call the template.

A Sample Template

You will want to come up with your own template, but here is an elementary example of one, just to get you started:

Paragraph 1:

The issue of _____

is a controversial one. On the one hand, _____

_____ .

On the other hand, _____

_____ .

However, in the final analysis, I believe that _____

_____ .

Paragraph 2:

One reason for my belief is that _____

_____

_____

_____ .

Paragraph 3:

Another reason for my belief is _____

_____

_____

_____ .

Paragraph 4:

Perhaps the best reason is _____

_____

_____

_____ .

Paragraph 5:

For all these reasons, I believe that _____

_____

_____

_____ .

Let's try fitting an Analysis of an Issue topic we've already seen into this organizational structure.

Essay topic 1:

> *It is necessary for the entertainment industry to police itself by censoring television programs and popular music lyrics.*

How would this topic fit into the first paragraph of our template? Take a look.

The issue of censorship of popular TV programs and music lyrics **is a controversial one. On the one hand,** increased crime and violence are causing a disintegration of the framework of our society. **On the other hand,** free speech is one of our most important freedoms, guaranteed by the constitution. **However, in the final analysis, I believe that** the dangers of subjecting impressionable young minds to questionable values makes self-censorship by the entertainment industry a viable alternative.

Notice that the author of this essay did exactly what we worked on in the previous chapter. She summarized the topic, then fleshed out the opposing side and wrote it down explicitly. Then she finished off the first paragraph by explicitly stating which side she would argue in the rest of the essay. Perfect.

If we were writing the rest of this essay, at this point we would start giving supporting examples and reasons for our position, but for now, let's concentrate on the first paragraph. Could we have used this template to take the other side of the argument? Sure. Here's how that would look:

The issue of censorship of popular TV programs and music lyrics **is a controversial one. On the one hand,** free speech is one of our most important freedoms, guaranteed by the constitution. **On the other hand,** increased crime and violence are causing a disintegration of the framework of our society. **However, in the final analysis, I believe that** the principle of free speech is too precious to allow censorship in any form.

Okay, It Works with That Topic, but Will It Work with Another?

Of course. Let's try the same template with another topic.

Essay topic 2:

> Everyone agrees that countries need governing, and yet the cost of government seems to increase every year. Government bureaucracy needs to be overhauled, since it is fundamentally unable to perform the function for which it was created.

Using our template:

The issue of the overhaul of our federal bureaucracy **is a controversial one. On the one hand,** federal jobs employ a huge number of Americans, making any attempt to prune the federal payroll both difficult and painful. **On the other hand,** the percentage of our tax-dollars spent simply on the upkeep of this huge bureaucratic juggernaut is rising at an alarming rate. **However, in the final analysis, I believe that** the political and financial price of bureaucratic reform would be too high.

As you can see, this template will fit practically any situation. To prove it, let's try it out on one of the great philosophical arguments of our time.

Now You Try It

Read the following topic carefully, then go through the steps to provide the other side of the argument. Decide which side of the argument you want to be on, and then fill in the blanks of the first paragraph of this template. You may have noticed in the previous examples that to make this particular template work most effectively, the first "on the one hand" should introduce the argument that you are ultimately going to support. The "on the other hand" should be the argument you are going to disprove. The sentence beginning "However, in the final analysis" will return to the point of view that you believe in.

Essay topic 3:

> The one quality essential for any political leader is the ability to change position based on the will of the people. A leader, especially in a democratic society, must be responsive to what the people want, above and beyond any personal beliefs.

The issue of _____

_____ is a controversial one. On the one hand,

_____

_____.

On the other hand, _____

_____.

However, in the final analysis, I believe that _____

_____.

THE ANALYSIS OF AN ISSUE ESSAY IN SIX STEPS

If you were completing the entire essay now, you would write paragraphs supporting your belief, but for right now let's concentrate on that first paragraph. Here's one way Topic 3 could have gone:

The issue of *a politician's primary responsibility* is a controversial one. On the one hand, *much of the reason we elect a politician is because we trust that person to use his or her own beliefs to govern wisely.* On the other hand, *a politician must serve the people who elected him or her.* However, in the final analysis, I believe that *a politician must be guided more by personal conviction than by what the constituency wants, even at the risk of not being reelected.*

ARE THERE OTHER TEMPLATES?

There are many ways to organize an Analysis of an Issue essay, and we'll be showing you a few variations, but the important thing is that you bring with you to the exam a template you have practiced using and with which you are comfortable. Whatever the topic of the essay and whatever your personal mood that day, you don't want to have to think for even a second about how your essay will be organized. By deciding on a template in advance, you will already have your organizational structure down before you get there.

That said, it's important that you develop your own template, based on your own preferences and your own personality. Of course, yours may have some similarities to one of ours, but it should not mimic ours exactly—for one thing, because it's pretty likely that when this edition of our book comes out, the folks who write the GRE will read it, and they might take a dim view of anyone who blatantly copies one of our templates word-for-word.

CUSTOMIZING YOUR TEMPLATE

Your organizational structure may vary in some ways, but it will always include the following elements: The first paragraph should illustrate to the reader that you have understood the topic and that you have chosen a position. To do this, first restate the topic and its opposing side, then say how you feel about it. The first paragraph does not have to be more than a couple of sentences.

In the second, third, and fourth paragraphs you will develop examples and ideas to support your thesis. The last paragraph should sum up your position on the topic, using slightly different wording from the first paragraph.

Here are some alternate ways of organizing your essay:

Variation 1:

1st paragraph: State both sides of the argument briefly before announcing what side you are on

2nd paragraph: Support your argument

3rd paragraph: Further support

4th paragraph: Further support

5th paragraph: Conclusion

Variation 2:

1st paragraph: State your position

2nd paragraph: Acknowledge the arguments in favor of the other side

3rd paragraph: Rebut each of those arguments

4th paragraph: Conclusion

Variation 3:

1st paragraph: State the position you will eventually contradict, i.e., "Many people believe that ..."

2nd paragraph: Contradict that first position, i.e., "However, I believe that ..."

3rd paragraph: Support your position

4th paragraph: Further support

5th paragraph: Conclusion

Write your own template for the Issue topic here

1st paragraph:

2nd paragraph:

3rd paragraph:

4th paragraph:

5th paragraph:

So Much for Organization, Now What About Support?

We've shown you how templates and structure words can be used to help the organization of your essay. However, organization is not the only important item on the essay reader's checklist. You will also be graded on how you support your main idea.

The Key to Good Support: Brainstorming

Learning to use the structural words we've just been discussing is in fact a way to bring pre-built elements into the GRE examination room with you. Along with a template, they will enable you to concentrate on your ideas without worrying about making up a structure from scratch. But what about the ideas themselves?

After reading the essay topic, you should take a couple of minutes to plan out your essay. First, decide which side of the issue you're going to take. Then, begin brainstorming. On a piece of scratch paper, write down all the reasons and persuasive examples you can think of in support of your essay. Don't stop to edit yourself; just let them flow out.

If you think better on the computer, you can write out your outline and supporting ideas directly on the screen. Just remember to erase them before the time for that essay is over.

Then go through what you've written, to decide on the order in which you want to make your points. You may decide, on reflection, to skip several of your brainstorms—or you may have one or two new ones as you organize.

Here's an example of what some brainstorming might produce in the way of support for Analysis of an Issue topic #1:

Main Idea

Censorship of television programs and popular music lyrics would be a mistake.

Support

1. Freedom of speech was one of the founding principles of this country. It has been too hard won for us to give it up.

2. Who would perform this censorship, and how would we ensure that there was no political agenda attached to it?

3. Once started, censorship of violent content is hard to stop or to curb. Where would we draw the line? Hamlet? Bambi?

4. So far, the evidence of different studies is contradictory. The causal link between violence on television and real violence has not yet been convincingly proven.

5. While upsetting to many, the lyrics of such entertainers as Snoop Doggy Dogg continue a long tradition of protest of social conditions that has stretched over the centuries and has included such artists as Bob Dylan and Woody Guthrie.

After you've finished brainstorming, look over your supporting ideas and throw out the weakest ones. In general, examples from your personal life are less compelling to readers than examples from history or current events. There should be three to five ideas left over. Plan the order in which you want to present these ideas. You should start with one of your strongest ideas.

GETTING SPECIFIC

The GRE essay readers are looking for supporting ideas or examples that are, in their words, "insightful " and "persuasive." What do they mean? Suppose you asked your friend about a movie he saw yesterday, and he said, "It was really cool."

Well, you'd know that he liked it, and that's good—but you wouldn't know much about the movie. Was it a comedy? An action adventure? Were the characters sexy? Did it make him cry?

The GRE readers don't want to know that the movie was cool. They want to know that you liked it because:

> "It movingly traced the development of two childhood friends
> as they grew up and grew apart."

or because:

> "It combined the physical comedy of the Three Stooges with
> the excitement of *Raiders of the Lost Ark*."

You want to make each example as precise and compelling as possible. After you have brainstormed a few supporting ideas, spend a couple of moments on each one, making it as specific as possible. For example, let's say we're working on an essay supporting the idea that the United States should stay out of other countries' affairs.

Too vague: When the United States sent troops to Vietnam, things didn't work out too well. (*How* didn't they work out? What were the results?)

More specific: Look at the result of the United States sending troops to Vietnam. After more than a decade of fighting in support of a dubious political regime, American forces suffered casualties numbered in the tens of thousands, and we may never know how many Vietnamese lost their lives as well.

ANALYSIS OF AN ISSUE: FINAL THOUGHTS

You've brought with you a template and some structure words; you've picked a position; you've brainstormed. Brainstorming should have taken about five minutes. Now it's time to write your essay. Start typing, indenting each of the four or five paragraphs. (By the way, the *tab* key on the GRE computer program does not work—to indent, just hit the spacebar a few times.) Use all the tools you've learned in this chapter. Remember to keep an eye on the time. You have only 45 minutes to complete the first essay.

It would be a smart idea to write your introduction and conclusion paragraphs first, and insert the example paragraphs between them. That way, if you run out of time, your essay will still sound finished and will leave the readers with a good impression.

If you have a minute at the end, read over your essay and do any editing that's necessary.

PRACTICE

Practice on the following sample Issue topic. If you have access to a computer, turn it on and start up a word-processing program (you may want to use a very rudimentary one like Notepad to simulate the ETS program you'll see on the real test). Then set a timer for 45 minutes. In that time, read the topic, brainstorm in the space provided in this book, and then type your essay into the computer.

A sample issue

> *Random stop-and-search procedures are necessary to preserve safety in modern urban neighborhoods.*

What's the opposing side?

Pick a position:

Write down as many supporting examples as you can think of:

Now circle the three strongest examples.

Spend the remaining time typing an essay, using the template you developed earlier in this chapter.

How to score your essay

Now it's time to put on your essay scoring hat and prepare to grade your own essay. (If you're lucky enough to have a friend who is also preparing for the GRE, you could switch essays and grade each other's like you used to do in sixth grade.) You'll need to be objective about the process. Remember, the only way to improve is to honestly assess your weaknesses and systematically eliminate them.

Set a timer for two minutes. Read the essay carefully but quickly, so that you do not exceed the two minutes on the timer.

Now ask yourself the following questions about the essay:

1. Overall, did it make sense?

2. Did you address the topic directly?

3. Did you address the topic thoroughly?

4. Did your introduction paragraph repeat the issue to establish the topic of the essay?

5. Did the first paragraph make your position on the topic obvious?

6. Did you have three strong paragraphs supporting your position?

7. Did your examples make sense?

8. Did you flesh out your examples?

9. Did your examples apply directly to the topic?

10. Did your essay have a strong concluding paragraph?

11. Was your essay well-organized?

12. Did you use language that made the organization of the essay obvious?

13. Did you use correct grammar, spelling, and language, for the most part?

14. Was your essay of an appropriate length (at least four paragraphs of three sentences each)?

If you could answer "yes" to all or almost all of those questions, congratulations! Your essay would receive a score in the 5-6 range. If you continue to practice, and write an essay of similar quality on the Analysis of an Issue part of the real test, you should score very well.

If you answered "yes" to fewer than 12 of the questions, you have room for improvement. Fortunately, you also know which areas you need to strengthen as you continue to practice.

If you answered "yes" to fewer than 5 of the questions, your essay would not score very well on a real GRE. An essay of this quality would not help you in the admissions process and could raise some red flags in the minds of the admissions people. You need to continue to practice, focusing on the areas of weakness that you discovered during this scoring process.

There are more Issue topics for you to practice in the back of this book. If you want to practice even more, go to www.gre.org and download the list of real Issue topics. **You cannot possibly practice writing essays on all of the real GRE topics, so don't even try.** However, you should spend time reading through the topics to become familiar with the variety of issues ETS could give you.

16

The Basics of
Arguments

You'll be able to use all the skills we've just been discussing on this type of essay as well, but in a slightly different way. Instead of asking for your opinion on a topic, the Argument topic asks you to critique someone else's argument. Before we jump into setting up templates and other preconstruction steps, let's take a look at how Analytical Writing arguments work.

THE PARTS OF AN ARGUMENT

An argument, for GRE purposes, is a short paragraph in which an author introduces a topic and uses reasoning or factual evidence to back up his or her opinion about that topic.

A really simplified example of an argument could be:

> *My car broke down yesterday, and I need a car to get to work. Therefore, I should buy a new car.*

The car argument above is composed of three parts:

- The conclusion—the author's opinion and recommendation for action
- The premises—the facts the author uses to back up his or her opinion
- The assumption—unstated conditions that must be true in order for the argument to make sense

In this argument, the author's conclusion is "I should buy a new car."

The premises the author uses to support this conclusion are that the car broke down yesterday, and that he or she needs a car to get to work.

The premises must support the conclusion the way table legs support a tabletop. The tabletop is the most obvious and useful part of a table—you see more of it, and you can put things on it. But without the legs to hold it up, it's just a slab of wood on the floor. The same is true for the conclusion of an argument. The conclusion is the part that gets all the attention, since it recommends some course of action. But without the premises to support this conclusion, the conclusion won't hold up.

THE WHY TEST

Remember that the conclusion is supported by the other statements in the argument. The "Why Test" is a way to check that the statement you identified as the conclusion is supported by the other statements. State what you think is the conclusion, then say, "Why?" The other statements should provide the reasons why.

Try using the "Why Test" on the car example.

Conclusion: "I should buy a new car."

Why? "My car broke down yesterday, and I need a car to get to work."

You can see how the other statements support the conclusion. Notice that if we had mistakenly chosen the wrong statement as the conclusion, the other sentences would not have supported it. Let's try it.

Conclusion: "My car broke down yesterday."

Why? "I should buy a new car, and I need a car to get to work."

Huh? It makes no sense. So you know that "My car broke down yesterday" isn't the conclusion.

FACT VS. OPINION

Another great way to tell the premises and conclusion apart is to glance at their form. The premises will be facts (even if you're not sure they're true, you still have to accept them as facts), and the conclusion will sound like an opinion.

CONCLUSION WORDS

Certain words indicate a conclusion:

- so
- therefore
- thus
- hence
- then
- consequently
- as a result
- concluded that
- showed that

When you see these words, you can be pretty sure that you've found the conclusion of the argument.

PREMISE WORDS

Certain words indicate premises:

- because
- since
- if
- given that
- in view of
- in light of
- assume

DRILL

Find the conclusions for the following arguments. (These are NOT like the more complicated arguments you'll see as essay prompts. We'll move on to those once you've mastered these.) Be sure to use the Why Test to check that you have the right conclusion.

1. A diet that is low in saturated fats reduces the risk of heart disease. Vegetables are low in saturated fats. Therefore, you should eat vegetables regularly to reduce your risk of heart disease.

Conclusion: _____

Why? _____

2. Making seat-belt use mandatory will reduce automobile fatalities. State X has one of the lowest automobile fatality rates in the country, and seat-belt use is required by law there.

Conclusion: _____

Why? _____

3. Traditional economic theory assumes that demand for a product will increase when the price of that product decreases, and that among products of equal quality, consumers will always choose to purchase the product at the lowest possible price. However, consumer demand for such products as apparel and sunglasses has been greater for higher-priced "designer" brands than it has been for lower-priced brands of comparable quality.

Conclusion: _____

Why? _____

Here's how to crack them

1. **Conclusion:** Therefore, you should eat vegetables regularly to reduce your risk of heart disease.

   Why? A diet that is low in saturated fats reduces the risk of heart disease. Vegetables are low in saturated fats. (Notice that the conclusion of this argument is a directive—it tells you what you should do.)

2. **Conclusion:** Making seat-belt use mandatory will reduce automobile fatalities.

   Why? State X has one of the lowest automobile fatality rates in the country, and seat-belt use is required by law there. (Notice that, in this example, the conclusion is given first, followed by the premises. Whether a statement is the conclusion of an argument depends on the logic of the argument, not on the location of the statement.)

3. **Conclusion:** The traditional assumption of economic theory—that demand for a product will increase when the price of that product decreases, and that among products of equal quality, consumers will always choose to purchase the product at the lowest possible price—may be wrong.

   Why? Because consumer demand for such products as apparel and sunglasses has been greater for higher-priced "designer" brands than it has been for lower-priced brands of comparable quality. (Notice that the conclusion in this example was not directly stated in the argument!)

ASSUMPTIONS

An assumption is an unstated premise that supports the author's conclusion. It's the connection between the stated premises and the conclusion. In the example of the table, the assumption is the nails or glue that hold the legs and the tabletop together. Without the glue or nails, the table will fall apart. Without the assumption, the argument will fall apart.

Sometimes the assumption is described as the **gap** between the facts that make up the premises and the conclusion. They don't always connect, so the assumption is the gap between them.

Let's take a look back at the car argument:

> My car broke down yesterday, and I need a car to get to work. Therefore, I should buy a new car.

The premises are that my car broke down yesterday and I need a car to get to work. The conclusion is that I should buy a new car.

When you first read this argument, you may have had some questions. These questions might have been along the lines of "Why can't the author just rent a car?" or "Why can't the author just fix the car?"

As you read an argument, identifying the premises and conclusion, questions may pop into your head. Those questions are pointing out the gap that leads to the assumption.

Here, the gap is between having a broken car and still needing a car to get to work on the one side, and having to buy a new car on the other side.

Therefore, the assumption must be:

There is no other way to have a car.

There are all sorts of smaller assumptions here—that the car can't be fixed, that a car can't be rented, that there's no other car the author can borrow—but those are all covered in the main assumption.

The assumption fills the gap between the premises and conclusion, and, in fact, functions as an unstated premise:

My car broke down yesterday, and I need a car to get to work. There is no other way to have a car. Therefore, I should buy a new car.

Three Common Types of Arguments and Their Assumptions

There are three very common types of arguments used on the GRE. If you become familiar with these three types, it will help you identify the assumptions in the argument more quickly when the clock is ticking on the real test.

The sampling assumption

Four out of five dentists surveyed recommend a certain brand of chewing gum.

Conclusion:

Why? (premises)

What is being assumed?

The conclusion is that this certain brand of gum is the best (and that you should buy that gum). Why? Because four out of five dentists surveyed recommend it. The assumption is that these dentists are representative of all dentists. (What if the dentists they surveyed were all working for the gum company?)

To spot a sampling argument, look for a conclusion that generalizes from a small sample of evidence. Sampling arguments always assume that the sample is representative, or not biased in any direction.

The analogy assumption

I've been able to ski the black diamond ski trails at ski areas in Colorado, so I will be able to ski the black diamond ski trails at New Hampshire ski areas.

Conclusion:

Why? (premises)

What is being assumed?

What's the conclusion? "I will be able to ski the black diamond ski trails at New Hampshire ski areas." Why? "Because I've been able to ski the black diamond ski trails at ski areas in Colorado." The assumption is that black diamond ski trails at New Hampshire ski areas will be similar to black diamond ski trails at Colorado ski areas.

To spot an analogy assumption, look for comparisons. Analogy assumptions always assume that the things being compared are, in fact, similar.

The causal assumption

Whenever I eat spicy foods for dinner, I have indigestion all night. Eating spicy foods causes my indigestion.

Conclusion:

Why? (premises)

Assumption:

What's the conclusion? That "eating spicy foods causes my indigestion." Why? Because "whenever I eat spicy foods for dinner, I have indigestion all night." Causal arguments on the GRE take a strict view of causality. If you argue that eating spicy foods causes your indigestion, one assumption is that if you don't eat spicy foods, you won't have indigestion. Also, strictly speaking, if you claim that eating spicy foods causes indigestion, you're also assuming that nothing else is causing the problem.

To spot causal arguments, look for indicator words like "causes," "responsible for," and "due to."

Causal arguments always assume that:

1. If you remove the cause, you will remove the effect.

2. There is no other cause.

DRILLS

For each of the following arguments, find the conclusion, premises, and assumptions. Try to think of as many assumptions as you can for each argument.

> 1. Studies show that most car accidents occur during the evening rush hour, when people are stressed and in a hurry to get home from work. Therefore, we could reduce the number of accidents by instituting stress-management programs so that employees wouldn't feel so much stress during the evening rush hour.

Conclusion:

Why? (premises)

Assumptions:

> 2. The board of directors of a major university recently decided to institute a salary freeze for faculty and staff to save money. They reason that this method worked to cut costs in 1978-79 without sacrificing the university's academic reputation, so it will work again without any negative effects.

Conclusion:

Why? (premises)

Assumptions:

> 3. A recent study found that children from an inner-city neighborhood in Rochester who spent at least 5 hours a day in daycare scored better on standardized tests than did children from that neighborhood who spent less time in daycare. They concluded that all children in the United States should spend at least 5 hours a day in daycare.

Conclusion:

Why? (premises)

Assumptions:

Here's how to crack them

1. The **conclusion** is that "we could reduce the number of accidents by instituting stress-management programs so that employees wouldn't feel so much stress during the evening rush hour." **Why?** Because "studies show that most car accidents occur during the evening rush hour, when people are stressed and in a hurry to get home from work." **Assumptions:** That stress actually causes the accidents, so that an absence of stress would reduce the number of accidents. That there are no other causes of the accidents besides stress. That stress-management programs would actually reduce stress in employees.

   This is a causal argument, so the assumptions are that a reduction in stress actually will reduce the number of accidents, and that there are no other causes for the stress. Pretty standard. Don't stop there, though. If the stress-management programs don't work, the argument falls apart, so the efficacy of the stress-management programs must also be an assumption.

2. Note that here the **conclusion** is simply what the board concluded, rather than the author's conclusion: "the board of directors of a major university recently decided to institute a salary freeze for faculty and staff to save money." Why? "They reason that this method worked to cut costs in 1978–79 without sacrificing the university's academic reputation, so it will work

again without any negative effects." What were the board's **assumptions**? That freezing salaries won't have negative effects on the university's reputation this year. That 1978-79 and now are similar. That there are no other factors that could hurt the university's reputation this year if they freeze salaries.

This is an analogy argument, so the core assumption is that 1978-79 and now are similar. All the other assumptions are just different angles of this same assumption.

3. The **conclusion** is "that all children in the United States should spend at least 5 hours a day in daycare." **Why?** Because "a recent study found that children from an inner-city neighborhood in Rochester who spent at least 5 hours a day in daycare scored better on standardized tests than did children from that neighborhood who spent less time in daycare." **Assumptions:** That what works in inner-city Rochester will work in the rest of the United States. That daycare is causing the increase in test scores.

This is primarily a sampling argument, so the main assumption is that the sample group of kids is representative of all kids in the U.S. There's also a causal angle to this argument, which is that the daycare caused the increase in test scores. The assumption is that there was no other cause for the test scores, and that the daycare actually did cause the increase.

HARDER DRILLS

Now let's practice on the kinds of arguments you'll see as topics on the real test. You'll notice that they're longer than the ones we've seen before. This means there are more assumptions to find and more ways to pick them apart. For each of the arguments, find the conclusion, premises, and assumptions. Try to think of as many assumptions as you can for each argument. Have fun.

> 1. The following appeared in a brochure for Pilgrim Hills, an assisted living facility for the elderly.

> "Deciding on a move to Pilgrim Hills is a serious matter, and all the relevant issues should be addressed. For instance, if you should become ill, can your family provide constant care for you in your home? At Pilgrim Hills, we are ready to provide you with 24-hour nursing care. How long will you be able to afford the costly upkeep of your home, including mortgage payments, taxes, and maintenance like lawn-mowing and painting services? At Pilgrim Hills, you don't worry about any of these things. One monthly bill includes your rent, care services, and even your meals. How easy is it to get out of the house to visit your friends, especially in bad winter weather? At Pilgrim Hills, your friends are right down the hall, so you can spend as much time with them as you'd like. It's clear that a move to Pilgrim Hills can solve your most pressing problems, as well as easing the burden your family feels caring for you."

Conclusion:

Why? (premises)

Assumptions:

Anything else?

2. The following appeared in a letter from the principal of Allentown High School to the teachers in the school.

"Backusville High School instituted a policy last year of requiring all its students to arrive at school half an hour early to finish all their homework before attending classes. Since the inception of this policy, 15% more students have enrolled at Backusville. The Board of Education reminds us that the more students we have enrolled at Allentown, the more federal funding we receive, so it is clear that to improve the quality of education for all Allentown students we need to institute an early-attendance policy similar to the one that Backusville has instituted."

Conclusion:

Why? (premises:)

Assumptions:

Anything else?

3. "The town of Titushaven, nicknamed 'The Football City,' has had an extremely high number of football fans per capita for the last several generations. 80% of the houses in Titushaven display yard decorations for their favorite professional football teams, and attendance at local high school football games (both home and away) is standing room only. In addition, Titushaven produces a football-related talk-radio show broadcast in the three surrounding counties. Revenues from advertising on this program have increased every year for the last 25 years. Based on these facts, the town council of Titushaven should open a football museum in Titushaven to increase the local economy."

Conclusion:

Why? (premises)

Assumptions:

Anything else?

Here's how to crack them

1. The **conclusion** is that moving to Pilgrim Hills will solve an
    elderly person's problems. The **premises** are that PH provides
    24-hour nursing care, full maintenance of housing units, and an
    enclosed community.

    The **assumptions** are that these three services will solve all
    your problems. Other assumptions are that you actually need
    these services, instead of other ones, that you can afford to live
    at Pilgrim Hills, that you want to live at Pilgrim Hills, and that
    by not moving to Pilgrim Hills you are being a burden on your
    family.

    All these assumptions are areas of weakness that you should
    expose in your essay. Bring up alternate scenarios that would
    refute the argument. For instance, if a person's house is already
    paid for, property taxes are low, and if her family does basic
    upkeep services for free, then moving to Pilgrim Hills would be
    much more of a financial burden than staying in her own house
    would be. Alternately, it doesn't really matter if you can see
    other people easily because they live down the hall if you don't
    like any of the other people at Pilgrim Hills. In fact, this could
    be a disadvantage to living at Pilgrim Hills.

    You get the idea.

2. The **conclusion** is that instituting early-attendance rules will
    increase the quality of education for all the students at Allen-
    town. The **premises** are that early-attendance policies increase
    enrollment, and increased enrollment causes an influx of
    federal money.

    The **assumptions** are that the increase in enrollment at
    Backusville was actually caused by this early attendance rule,
    that what happened at Backusville will happen at Allentown,
    that increased money for the school will improve the quality of
    education, and that any improvement in the quality of educa-
    tion caused by more federal money won't be negated by the
    increased number of students at Allentown.

    Whew. That's a lot of assumptions, all of them pretty large.
    This should be an easy essay to write. Just expose the weakness
    of each of these assumptions one by one.

3. The **conclusion** is that Titushaven should open a football museum. The **premises** are that Titushavenians are football nuts, as evidenced by their high rate of display of yard decorations, attendance at high school football games, and successful football radio show.

   The **assumptions** are that all these other factors have something to do with a football museum. Specifically, can the local football fans in Titushaven support a football museum by themselves? How will locals spending money to attend the museum really affect the economy of Titushaven? Won't they need to attract tourists from other places to the museum to see any local economic benefit? And how can the town council guarantee that anyone else will come, since there's no reason to believe that any of the population of surrounding areas has the same interest in football as Titushaven residents have?

Well, great, but why do I care?

You care about taking apart the argument, and finding the assumptions in particular, because the key to writing a great Argument essay on the Analytical Writing section is ripping apart the argument.

Think about it. The official instructions on the test ask you to "critique" the author's argument. However, if you claim that everything the author says makes sense, you won't be able to write an essay that's more than a few sentences long. This means that in order to write a great essay, you'll need to tear the author's argument apart.

Danger: The most common mistake people make in writing the Argument essay is expressing their own opinions. Don't do this! The Issue essay specifically asks you to give an opinion and then back it up. The Argument essay wants a critique of someone else's opinion, not your own.

17

Writing the Argument Essay

Writing the Analysis of an Argument essay requires a series of steps.

Step 1: Read the topic and separate out the conclusion from the premises.

Step 2: Since they're asking you to critique (i.e., weaken) the argument, concentrate on identifying its assumptions. Brainstorm as many different assumptions as you can think of. It helps to write these out on a piece of scratch paper or on the computer screen.

Step 3: Look at the premises. Do they actually help to prove the conclusion?

Step 4: Choose a template that allows you to attack the assumptions and premises in an organized way.

Step 5: At the end of the essay, remember to take a moment to illustrate how the argument could be made more compelling.

Step 6: Read over the essay and do some editing.

WHAT THE READERS ARE LOOKING FOR

An Analysis of an Argument topic presents you with an argument. Your job is to critique the argument's line of reasoning and the evidence supporting it and suggest ways in which the argument could be strengthened. Again, you aren't required to know any more about the subject than would any normal person — but you must be able to spot logical weaknesses. Make absolutely sure that you have read and understood the previous section about taking apart the argument, and that you can take apart all the arguments in the drills in that section.

The essay readers will be looking for four things as they skim through your Analysis of an Argument essay at the speed of light. According to a booklet prepared by ETS, "an outstanding argument essay...clearly identifies and insightfully analyzes important features of the argument; develops ideas cogently, organizes them logically, and connects them smoothly with clear transitions; effectively supports the main points of the critique; and demonstrates superior control of language, including diction, syntactic variety, and the conventions of standard written English. There may be minor flaws."

To put it more simply, the readers will be looking for all the same things they were looking for in the Analysis of an Issue essay, plus one extra ingredient: a cursory knowledge of the rules of logic.

DOING THE ACTUAL ANALYSIS OF THE ARGUMENT

In any Analytical Writing argument, the first thing to do is to separate the conclusion from the premises.

Let's see how this works with an actual essay topic. Here's the Analysis of an Argument topic you saw before:

Topic:

> The director of the International Health Foundation recently released this announcement:

> "A new medical test that allows the early detection of a particular disease will prevent the deaths of people all over the world who would otherwise die from the disease. The test has been extremely effective in allowing doctors to diagnose the disease 6 months to a year before it would have been spotted by conventional means. As soon as we can institute this test as routine procedure in hospitals around the world, the death rate from this disease will plummet."

The conclusion in this argument comes in the first line:

> A new medical test that allows the early detection of a particular disease will prevent the deaths of people all over the world who would otherwise die from that disease.

The premises are the evidence in support of this conclusion.

> The test has been extremely effective in allowing doctors to diagnose the disease 6 months to a year before it would have been spotted by conventional means.

The assumptions are the *unspoken* premises of the argument—without which the argument would fall apart. Remember that assumptions are often causal, analogical, or statistical. What are some assumptions of *this* argument? Let's brainstorm.

BRAINSTORMING FOR ASSUMPTIONS

You can often find assumptions by looking for a gap in the reasoning: **Medical tests allow early detection:** According to the conclusion, the medical test leads to the early detection of the disease. There doesn't seem to be a gap here.

Early detection allows patients to survive: In turn, the early detection of the disease allows patients to survive the disease. Well, hold on a minute. Is this necessarily true? Let's brainstorm:

- First of all, do we know that early detection will *necessarily* lead to survival? We don't even know if this disease is curable. Early detection of an incurable disease is not going to help anyone survive it.

- Second, will the test be widely available and cheap enough for general use? If the test is expensive or only available in certain parts of the world, people will continue to die from the disease.

- Third, will doctors and patients interpret the tests correctly? The test may be fine, but if doctors misinterpret the results or if patients ignore the need for treatment, then the test will not save lives.

Death rate will plummet: There's a huge gap here in that there's absolutely no explanation of how merely detecting the disease will immediately cause the death rate from it to plummet. This area is ripe for exploration.

THE USE OF THE EVIDENCE

Okay, we've uncovered some assumptions. Now, ETS also wants to know what we thought of the argument's "use of evidence." In other words, did the premises help to prove the conclusion? Well, in fact, no, they didn't. The premise here (the fact that the test can spot the disease 6 months to a year earlier than conventional tests) does not really help to prove the conclusion that the test will save lives. And it certainly doesn't explain how the test will cause an immediate drop in the death rate.

ORGANIZING THE ANALYSIS OF AN ARGUMENT ESSAY

We're now ready to put this into a ready-made template. In any Analysis of an Argument essay, the template structure will be pretty straightforward: You're simply going to reiterate the argument, attack the argument in three different ways (one to a paragraph), summarize what you've said, and mention how the argument could be strengthened. From an organizational standpoint, this is pretty easy. Try to minimize your use of the word "I." Your opinion is not the point in an Analysis of an Argument essay.

A SAMPLE TEMPLATE

Of course, you will want to develop your own template for the Analysis of an Argument essay, but to get you started, here's one possible structure: The argument that (restatement of the conclusion) is not entirely logically convincing, since it ignores certain crucial assumptions.

First, the argument assumes that _____

_____ .

Second, the argument never addresses _____

_____ .

Finally, the argument omits _____

_____ .

Thus, the argument is not completely sound. The evidence in support of the

conclusion _____ .

Ultimately, the argument might have been strengthened by _____

_____ .

The key to an Analysis of an Argument essay is how clearly you critique the argument.

How Would Our Brainstorming Fit into the Template?

Here's how the assumptions we came up with for this argument would have fit into the template:

The argument that the new medical test will prevent deaths that would have occurred in the past is not entirely logically convincing, since it ignores certain crucial assumptions.

First, the argument assumes that early detection of the disease will lead to an immediate drop in the mortality rate from this disease, yet it does nothing to explain how this will happen, etc.

Second, the argument never addresses the point that the existence of this new test, even if totally effective, is not the same as the widespread use of the test, etc.

Finally, even supposing the ability of early detection to save lives and the widespread use of the test, the argument still depends on the doctors' correct interpretation of the test and the patients' willingness to undergo treatment, etc.

Thus, the argument is not completely sound. The evidence in support of the conclusion that the test will cause death rates to plummet does little to prove that conclusion, since it does not address the assumptions already raised. **Ultimately, the argument might have been strengthened** if the author could have shown that the disease responds to early treatment, which can be enacted immediately upon receipt of the test results, that the test will be widely available around the world, and that doctors and patients will make proper use of the test.

Customizing Your Analysis of an Argument Template

Your organizational structure may vary in some ways, but it will always include the following elements: The first paragraph should sum up the argument's conclusion. The second, third, and fourth paragraphs will attack the argument and the supporting evidence. The last paragraph should summarize what you've said and state how the argument could be strengthened. Here are some alternate ways of organizing your essay.

Variation 1:

1st paragraph: Restate the argument.

2nd paragraph: Discuss the link (or lack of same) between the conclusion and the evidence presented in support of it.

3rd paragraph: Show three holes in the reasoning of the argument.

4th paragraph: Show how each of the three holes could be plugged up by explicitly stating the missing assumptions.

Variation 2:

1st paragraph: Restate the argument and say it has three flaws.

2nd paragraph: Point out a flaw and show how it could be plugged up by explicitly stating the missing assumption.

3rd paragraph: Point out a second flaw and show how it could be plugged up by explicitly stating the missing assumption.

4th paragraph: Point out a third flaw and show how it could be plugged up by explicitly stating the missing assumption.

5th paragraph: Summarize and conclude that because of these three flaws, the argument is weak.

WRITE YOUR OWN TEMPLATE FOR THE ARGUMENT TOPIC HERE

1st paragraph:

2nd paragraph:

3rd paragraph:

4th paragraph:

5th paragraph:

ANALYSIS OF AN ARGUMENT: FINAL THOUGHTS

You've separated the conclusion from the premises. You've brainstormed for the gaps that weaken the argument. You've noted how the premises support (or don't support) the conclusion. Now it's time to write your essay. Start typing, indenting each of the four or five paragraphs. Use all the tools you've learned in this chapter. Remember to keep an eye on the time. Again, if you have a minute at the end, read over your essay and do any editing that's necessary.

PRACTICE

Practice on the following sample argument topic. If you have access to a computer, turn it on and start up a word-processing program (you may want to use a very rudimentary one like Notepad to simulate the ETS program you'll see on the real test). Then set a timer for 30 minutes. In that time, read the topic, brainstorm in the space provided in this book, then type your essay into the computer.

A sample argument

> *The market for the luxury-goods industry is on the decline. Recent reports show that a higher unemployment rate, coupled with consumer fears, has decreased the amount of money the average household spends on both essential and nonessential items, but especially on nonessential items. Since luxury goods are, by nature, nonessential, this market will be the first to decrease in the present economic climate, and luxury retailers should refocus their attention to lower-priced markets.*

Conclusion:

Why? (premises)

Assumptions:

Ways you can pull the argument apart:

Way the argument could be made more compelling:

Now use the template you developed earlier in this chapter to type your essay on the computer.

How to score your essay

Now it's time to put on your essay scoring hat and prepare to grade your own essay. (If you're lucky enough to have a friend who is also preparing for the GRE, you could switch essays and grade each other's like you used to do in sixth grade.) You'll need to be objective about the process. Remember, the only way to improve is to honestly assess your weaknesses and systematically eliminate them.

Set a timer for two minutes. Read the essay carefully but quickly, so that you do not exceed the two minutes on the timer.

Now ask yourself the following questions about the essay:

1. Overall, did it make sense?

2. Did you address the argument directly?

3. Did you critique the argument thoroughly?

4. Did your introduction paragraph repeat the argument to establish the topic of the essay?

5. Did you avoid injecting your own opinion into the essay?

6. Did you have three strong paragraphs critiquing the arguments?

7. Did your critiques make sense?

8. Did you flesh out your points to make the weaknesses of the argument explicit?

9. Did the examples apply directly to the topic?

10. Did the essay have a strong conclusion paragraph?

11. Was the essay well-organized?

12. Did you use language that made the organization of the essay obvious?

13. Did you use correct grammar, spelling, and language, for the most part?

14. Was the essay of an appropriate length (4-5 paragraphs of at least three sentences each)?

If you could answer "yes" to all or almost all of those questions, congratulations! Your essay would receive a score in the 5-6 range. If you continue to practice, and write an essay of similar quality on the Analysis of an Argument essay of the real test, you should score very well.

If you answered "yes" to fewer than 12 of the questions, you have room for improvement. Fortunately, you also know which areas you need to strengthen as you continue to practice.

If you answered "yes" to fewer than 5 of the questions, your essay would not score very well on a real GRE. An essay of this quality would not help you in the admissions process and could raise some red flags in the minds of the admissions people. You need to continue to practice, focusing on the areas of weakness that you discovered during this scoring process.

There are more Argument topics for you to practice in the back of this book. If you want to practice even more, go to www.gre.org and download the list of real Argument topics. **You cannot possibly practice writing essays on all of these real ETS topics, so don't even try.** However, you should spend time reading through them to become familiar with the variety of topics about which ETS can ask you.

18
More Techniques

PRECONSTRUCTION

In both essays, the ETS readers will be looking for evidence of your facility with standard written English. This is where preconstruction comes in. It's amazing how a little elementary preparation can enhance an essay. We'll be looking at four tricks that almost instantly improve the appearance of a person's writing:

- Structure words
- Contrast words
- Short sentence/long sentence
- The impressive book reference

STRUCTURE WORDS

Let's think back to the Verbal section for a minute: Most students encounter the same problem when they get to the Reading Comprehension section—there isn't enough time to read the passages carefully and answer all the questions. To get around this problem, we showed you some ways to spot the overall organization of a dense reading passage in order to understand the main idea and to find specific points quickly.

When you think about it, the ETS essay readers are facing almost the identical problem: They have only a few minutes to read your essay and figure out if it's any good. There's no time to appreciate the finer points of your argument. All they want to know is whether it's well organized and reasonably lucid—and to find out, they will be looking for the same structural clues you have learned to look for in the Reading Comprehension passages. Let's mention them again:

1. When entire paragraphs contradict each other, there are some useful pairs of words that help to make this clear:

   - on the one hand/on the other hand
   - the traditional view/the new view

2. If you have three points to make in a paragraph, it helps to point this out ahead of time:

   There are three reasons I believe that the Grand Canyon should be strip-mined. First... Second... Third...

3. If you want to clue in the reader to the fact that you are about to support the main idea with examples or illustrations, the following words are useful:

   - for example
   - to illustrate
   - for instance
   - because

To add yet another example or argument in support of your main idea, you can use one of the following words to indicate your intention:

- furthermore
- in addition
- similarly
- just as
- also
- moreover

To indicate that the idea you're about to bring up is important, special, or surprising in some way, you can use one of these words:

- surely
- truly
- undoubtedly
- clearly
- certainly
- indeed
- as a matter of fact
- in fact
- most important

To signal that you're about to reach a conclusion, you might use one of these words:

- therefore
- in summary
- consequently
- hence
- in conclusion
- in short

HERE'S HOW IT WORKS

Here's a paragraph that consists of a main point and two supporting arguments:

I believe he is wrong. He doesn't know the facts. He isn't thinking clearly.

Watch how a few structure words can make this paragraph classier and clearer at the same time:

I believe he is wrong. **For one thing**, he doesn't know the facts. **For another**, he isn't thinking clearly.

I believe he is wrong. **Obviously**, he doesn't know the facts. **Moreover**, he isn't thinking clearly.

I believe he is wrong **because, first**, he doesn't know the facts, and **second**, he isn't thinking clearly.

Certainly, he doesn't know the facts, and he isn't thinking clearly **either**. **Consequently**, I believe he is wrong.

THE APPEARANCE OF DEPTH

You may have noticed that much of the structure we have been discussing thus far has involved contrasting viewpoints. Nothing will give your writing the appearance of depth faster than learning to use this technique. The idea is to set up your main idea by first introducing its opposite.

It is a favorite ploy of incoming presidents to blame the federal bureaucracy for the high cost of government, but I believe that bureaucratic waste is only a small part of the problem.

You may have noticed that this sentence contained a "trigger word." In this case, the trigger word "but " tells us that what was expressed in the first half of the sentence is going to be contradicted in the second half. We discussed trigger words in the Sentence Completion chapter of this book. Here they are again:

- but
- however
- on the contrary
- although
- yet
- while
- despite
- in spite of
- rather
- nevertheless
- instead

By using these words, you can instantly give your writing the appearance of depth.

Example:

Main thought: *I believe that television programs should be censored.*

Your sentence: While many people believe in the sanctity of free speech, I believe that television programs should be censored.

Or: Most people believe in the sanctity of free speech, but I believe that television programs should be censored.

Here are a few other words or phrases you can use to introduce the view you are eventually going to decide against:

- admittedly
- true
- certainly
- granted
- obviously
- of course
- undoubtedly
- to be sure
- one cannot deny that
- it could be argued that

CONTRASTING VIEWPOINTS WITHIN A PASSAGE

Trigger words can also be used to signal the opposing viewpoints of entire paragraphs. Suppose you saw an essay that began

> Many people believe that youth is wasted on the young. They point out that young people never seem to enjoy, or even think about, the great gifts they have been given but will not always have: physical dexterity, good hearing, good vision. However...

What do you think is going to happen in the second paragraph? That's right, the author is now going to disagree with the "many people" of the first paragraph. Setting up one paragraph in opposition to another lets the reader know what's going on right away. The organization of the essay is immediately evident.

RHYTHM

Many people think good writing is a mysterious talent that you either have or don't have, like good rhythm. In fact, good writing has a kind of rhythm to it, but there is nothing mysterious about it. Good writing is a matter of mixing up the different kinds of raw materials that you have available to you—words, phrases, dependent and independent clauses—to build sentences that don't all sound the same.

SHORT SENTENCES, LONG SENTENCES

The ETS graders won't have time to savor the language in your essay, but they know that effective writing mixes up short and long sentences for variety, and consequently they will be looking to see how you put sentences together. Here's an example of a passage in which all the sentences sound alike:

> Movies cost too much. Everyone agrees about that. Studios need to cut costs. No one is sure exactly how to do it. I have two simple solutions. They can cut costs by paying stars less. They can also cut costs by reducing overhead.

Why did all the sentences sound alike? Well, for one thing, they were all about the same length. For another thing, the sentences were all made up of independent clauses with the same exact setup: subject, verb, and sometimes object. There were no dependent clauses, almost no phrases, no structure words, and, frankly, no variety at all. Here's the same passage, but this time we varied the sentence length by combining some clauses and using conjunctions. We also threw in some structure words.

> Everyone agrees that movies cost too much. Clearly, studios need to cut costs, but no one is sure exactly how to do it. I have two simple solutions: Studios can cut costs by paying stars less and by reducing overhead.

THE IMPRESSIVE BOOK REFERENCE

In any kind of writing, it pays to remember who your audience will be. In this case, the essays are going to be graded by college teaching assistants. They wouldn't be human if they didn't have a soft spot in their heart for someone who can refer to a well-known book.

What book should you pick? Obviously it should be a book that you have actually read and liked. We do not advise picking a book if you've only seen the movie. Hollywood has a nasty habit of changing the endings.

You might think that it would be impossible to pick a book to use as an example for an essay before you even know the topic of the essay, but it's actually pretty easy. Just to give you an idea of how it's done, let's pick a famous work of literature that most people have read at some point in their lives: *Hamlet*.

Now let's take a few topics, and see how we could work in a reference to *Hamlet*.

Essay topic 1:

Should television and song lyrics be censored in order to curb increasing crime and violence?

Excerpt from our essay: Where would such censorship stop? In an attempt to prevent teen suicide, would an after-school version of Shakespeare 's *Hamlet* be changed so that the soliloquy read, "To be, or...whatever"?

Essay topic 2:

Is government bureaucracy to blame for the increased cost of government?

Excerpt from our essay: If you were to compare the United States government to Shakespeare's *Hamlet* the poor bureaucrats would represent the forgotten and insignificant Rosencrantz and Guildenstern, not the scheming pretenders to the throne.

Essay topic 3:

Should the maximum amount of a medical malpractice lawsuit be capped in the interest of lowering the cost of health care?

Excerpt from our essay: Malpractice awards are getting out of hand. If Shakespeare's era was, as some historians claim, the most litigious age in history, surely ours must come a close second. If he were writing today, you have the feeling Hamlet might have said, "Alas, poor Yorick, he should have gotten a better malpractice lawyer."

You get the idea. Since your essays may be read by the admissions officers at the schools to which you are applying, you might think it would be better to cite a book by a well-regarded economist, biologist, or psychologist rather than that of a playwright or novelist. As long as your example feels like an organic addition to your essay, it won't matter too much who you cite. But you may find that these more specific subject references are harder to work into your essay—and they will almost certainly go over the head of the essay *graders*.

SUMMARY

1. The Analytical Writing section will consist of two essays, each to be written using a rudimentary word processing program and the computer keyboard. For one essay, you will be allotted 45 minutes; for the other, 30 minutes. The essays will be given scores that range from 0 to 6, in half-point increments.

2. The essays may be read by the schools to which you apply, but the essays will be graded by underpaid, overworked college instructors who have only a few minutes to read each essay.

3. To score high on the writing assessment:
   - Write as many words as possible.
   - Use a pre-built template to organize your thoughts.
   - Use structure words, contrast words, and a combination of short and long sentences to give the appearance of depth to your writing.
   - Refer to a well-known work of literature or nonfiction.

4. For the Analysis of an Issue topic:

   Step 1: Read the topic.

   Step 2: Decide the general position you are going to take on the issue.

   Step 3: Brainstorm. Come up with a bunch of supporting ideas or examples. It helps to write these down on a piece of scratch paper, or on your screen as long as you remember to erase them. These supporting statements are supposed to help convince the reader that your main thesis is correct.

   Step 4: Look over your supporting ideas and throw out the weakest ones. There should be three to five left over.

   Step 5: Write the essay, using all the preconstruction and template tools you learned in this chapter.

   Step 6: Read over the essay and edit your work.

5. For the Analysis of an Argument topic:

   Step 1: Read the topic and separate out the conclusion from the premises.

   Step 2: Since you're being asked to critique (i.e., weaken) the argument, concentrate on identifying its assumptions. Brainstorm as many different assumptions as you can think of. It helps to write these on a piece of scratch paper, or on your screen as long as you remember to erase them.

Step 3:   Look at the premises. Do they actually help to prove the conclusion?

Step 4:   Choose a template that allows you to attack the assumptions and premises in an organized way.

Step 5:   At the end of the essay, remember to take a moment to illustrate how these same assumptions could be used to make the argument more compelling.

Step 6:   Read over the essay and edit your work.

PART V

Practice

19

Ready for Some GRE Aerobics?

So, you've shaken off some rust, and learned a ton of strategy, and now you're ready for some real practice. By now, you're probably wondering . . .

HOW DO I PRACTICE A CAT ON PAPER?

It's true that you can't take a computer-adaptive test on paper; after all, there's no way this book can act like a computer.

But, you can, and should, do the following practice questions that we have broken up into sets of easy, medium, and difficult questions. The sets were designed for you to find out if you're still rusty or confused about certain topics or techniques.

The directions for each question type aren't included in these practice questions, because, if you've been reading the book, you should already know the directions for each question type. But if you need to brush up on the directions before you begin practicing, go back through the book and find them in the preceding chapters.

PRACTICE SET DIRECTIONS

Everyone (and we mean *everyone*) should start with the easy set first. After all, you wouldn't start your exercise program by running 10 miles! You'd do some jogging and stretching first. Besides, and this can't be stressed enough, your performance on the first few questions on a computer-adaptive test is *crucial* to scoring high, so no matter what level you think you're at, you can't afford *any* careless errors on *any* questions, especially the easy ones, where careless errors most often occur.

So start with the easy sets, check your answers, and see how you do (explanations to each question follow in chapter 21). Use the questions you got wrong (if any!) as a guide to what topics you still need to review. Then go back through the book and review those topics.

When you've done that, move on to the medium sets, following the same process: Do the questions, check your answers, use the questions you got wrong (if any!) as a guide to what topics you still need to review, and go back through the book and review those topics. After that, do the same thing with the difficult question sets. Finally, try out our sample essay topics in chapter 22.

After you've completed the practice sets in this book, you should move onto the full-length practice tests on our website (see page viii for more information) and then to "real GREs" to practice our techniques on real questions from past GREs, and to estimate your score. This is absolutely the best way to prepare for the questions you'll see on your own GRE. Call ETS at 800-537-3160 or log on to www.gre.org to purchase *GRE POWERPREP® Software* or the book *Practicing to Take the GRE General Test*.

MAKE IT REAL

As you do these practice sets, don't time yourself, but move quickly, and use scratch paper as you would if you were taking the real test. DON'T WRITE IN THE BOOK! You might even want to stand this book up when taking the sections, to simulate the experience of looking at a computer screen. Remember that screen-to-scratch-paper conversion is *extremely* important; in fact, it's really a key technique for doing well on the GRE.

Try to find a place with no distractions like ringing phones or barking dogs. Simulate the testing environment as much as you can.

Here we go . . .

20

Practice Sets

1. MOUNT:
   - ⚪ descend
   - ⚪ disassemble
   - ⚪ upset
   - ⚪ hide
   - ⚪ go back

2. PLAYER : TEAM ::
   - ⚪ oil : liquid
   - ⚪ line : drawing
   - ⚪ scales : increase
   - ⚪ hiss : recording
   - ⚪ ingredient : mixture

3. There may be some validity in the facetious recent description of a pundit—a weatherman who talks every day about current events without being able to _____ them.
   - ⚪ outline
   - ⚪ begin
   - ⚪ dissect
   - ⚪ influence
   - ⚪ stop

4. ERADICATE:
   - ⚪ ignore
   - ⚪ undo
   - ⚪ smoke
   - ⚪ introduce
   - ⚪ boil

5. The sparring of the two lawyers appeared _____ ; however, it is well known that, outside the courtroom, the friendship between the two is _____.
   - ⚪ pointless. .cooperative
   - ⚪ hostile. .obvious
   - ⚪ lighthearted. .abrogated
   - ⚪ heightened. .concealed
   - ⚪ brilliant. .precluded

6. EXCRETION : KIDNEY ::
   - ⚪ respiration : lung
   - ⚪ lymphoma : cancer
   - ⚪ propulsion : engine
   - ⚪ information : media
   - ⚪ disinfection : soap

7. In radio, a morning broadcasting time often _____ a larger and more _____ audience and, thus, one that is more appealing to advertisers of expensive products.
   - ⚪ demands. .attractive
   - ⚪ denotes. .agreeable
   - ⚪ indicates. .prosperous
   - ⚪ overlooks. .practical
   - ⚪ encourages. .widespread

8. SNAKE : REPTILE ::
   - ⚪ fish : school
   - ⚪ beetle : insect
   - ⚪ elephant : land
   - ⚪ egg : chicken
   - ⚪ lamb : sheep

Questions 9-12

It is impossible to approach the question of overpopulation apolitically, because, not surprisingly, demographic patterns are dissimilar around the world, and questions of religion, culture, government, and degree of industrial development affect these patterns. In industrialized nations, birthrates are, for the most part, lower than death rates. But in Asia and Africa, many countries have annual growth rates of 2.5 to 3.5 percent. The ability of most of these rapidly increasing populations to find food, water, shelter, and warmth is diminished as the population increases; people are forced to try to grow food and raise livestock on marginal land, which only exacerbates problems of erosion and deforestation. Concerns about air and water pollution are ignored in the scramble for food and fuel, with the result that as the population grows, the land is less able to sustain those already living on it. Pressure on already depleted natural resources could result in fundamental changes to local or even global ecosystems, changes that may be permanent. In order to keep environmental damage from escalating to the point at which it is irreversible, industrialized nations should at least offer support to undeveloped countries in the form of education about sanitation and family planning, and ideally should begin work on the long-range goal of worldwide population stability.

9. The primary purpose of the passage is to
   - ⚪ point out that a potentially disastrous mistake was made when world leaders failed to take political responsibility for the problems of overpopulation
   - ⚪ argue that technology could be developed to counteract much of the environmental damage that has already taken place
   - ⚪ assert that overpopulation causes environmental damage, and suggest that industrialized nations take an active role in alleviating such damage
   - ⚪ criticize the leaders of industrialized nations for abdicating their responsibility to global environmental stability
   - ⚪ analyze the ways in which overpopulation affects the environment, and recommend international legislation that would force nations to take action

10. With which of the following statements would the author most likely agree?
   - ⚪ No country's citizens should be allowed unlimited reproductive freedom.
   - ⚪ Problems of overpopulation might be solved if society were properly managed, but the idea of a properly managed society is politically naive.
   - ⚪ Some of the problems associated with overpopulation may produce effects that are irreversible.
   - ⚪ Industrialized nations should share some of their agricultural abundance with developing nations, thereby relieving some of the pressure on the developing nations' natural resources.
   - ⚪ Overpopulation is the most dangerous threat to world stability, and industrialized nations should consider taking strong action to ensure that every country implements strict land-use guidelines and pollution laws.

11. The author mentions which of the following as a factor influencing a country's demographic patterns?
   - ⚪ the level of agricultural production
   - ⚪ the degree to which the climate has changed over time
   - ⚪ high rates of overconsumption
   - ⚪ the religious beliefs held by its citizens
   - ⚪ the quality of its natural resources

12. Which of the following is NOT an example of a kind of environmental degradation mentioned specifically by the author?

- ○ A livestock owner overgrazes his land, allowing the soil to be adversely affected by wind and rain.
- ○ An old factory does not comply with federal regulations on noise pollution, thereby diminishing the quality of life for those living near the factory.
- ○ On the outskirts of a small town, people scavenging for firewood cut down one of the few remaining stands of trees in the area.
- ○ When a city expands beyond its sewer lines, outlying residents dispose of waste in a nearby stream.
- ○ Consumption of gases leads to a widening of the hole in the ozone layer.

13. LUCIDITY:

- ○ glistening
- ○ obscurity
- ○ gravity
- ○ attractiveness
- ○ quiescence

14. FERTILIZER : GROWTH ::

- ○ glaze : pottery
- ○ yeast : leavening
- ○ cotton : texture
- ○ illumination : interest
- ○ octane : speed

15. FRUSTRATE:

- ○ facilitate
- ○ moderate
- ○ climb
- ○ judge
- ○ assemble

16. BOLSTER:

- ○ infect
- ○ compound
- ○ untie
- ○ generate
- ○ undermine

17. DISARM : WEAPONS ::

- ○ limit : abilities
- ○ soothe : difficulties
- ○ restrain : movement
- ○ disguise : identity
- ○ usurp : power

18. STONE : SCULPTOR ::

- ○ brick : house
- ○ words : poet
- ○ bust : portrait
- ○ scalpel : surgeon
- ○ mine : ore

19. Jenson worked _____ on her thesis, cloistering herself in her study for days on end without food or sleep.

- ○ carelessly
- ○ creatively
- ○ tirelessly
- ○ intermittently
- ○ voluntarily

20. EVICT:

- ○ tear down
- ○ answer quickly
- ○ bring together
- ○ set free
- ○ admit into

Column A | Column B

1. $(3 + 0) \times 4$ $0 \times (3 + 4)$

- ○ the quantity in Column A is always greater
- ○ the quantity in Column B is always greater
- ○ the quantities are always equal
- ○ it cannot be determined from the information given

Column A | Column B

$a = 15$

$a + b = 29$

2. a^2 b^2

- ○ the quantity in Column A is always greater
- ○ the quantity in Column B is always greater
- ○ the quantities are always equal
- ○ it cannot be determined from the information given

3. Of team A's victories this year, sixty percent were at home. If team A has won a total of twenty games this year, how many of those games were won away from home?

- ○ 5
- ○ 7
- ○ 8
- ○ 12
- ○ 15

Column A | Column B

$a = b$

4. $4a + b$ $a + 4b$

- ○ the quantity in Column A is always greater
- ○ the quantity in Column B is always greater
- ○ the quantities are always equal
- ○ it cannot be determined from the information given

5. $652(523) + 427(652)$ is equal to which of the following?

- ○ $523 (652 + 427)$
- ○ $652 (523 + 427)$
- ○ $(652 + 427)(523 + 652)$
- ○ $(652 + 523)(427 + 652)$
- ○ $(652 + 652)(523 + 427)$

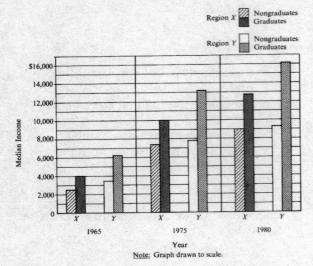

MEDIAN INCOME OF
COLLEGE GRADUATES *VS.* NONGRADUATES
IN REGIONS *X* AND *Y*

Region *X* — Nongraduates / Graduates
Region *Y* — Nongraduates / Graduates

Median Income

Year
Note: Graph drawn to scale.

6. The median income of graduates in Region *Y* increased by approximately how much between 1965 and 1980?

   ◯ $6,000
   ◯ $7,000
   ◯ $8,000
   ◯ $10,000
   ◯ $16,000

Column A   Column B

The diameter of circle *M* is greater than the radius of circle *N*.

7. The circumference   The circumference
   of circle *M*   of circle *N*

   ◯ the quantity in Column A is always greater
   ◯ the quantity in Column B is always greater
   ◯ the quantities are always equal
   ◯ it cannot be determined from the information given

8. If $a = 4$ and $4a - 3b = 1$, what is the combined value of a and b?

   ◯ 5

   ◯ $5\dfrac{2}{3}$

   ◯ 9

   ◯ $14\dfrac{2}{3}$

   ◯ $21\dfrac{2}{3}$

Column A   Column B

9. $\dfrac{3}{4} + \dfrac{3}{4}$ $\left(\dfrac{3}{4}\right)^2$

   ◯ the quantity in Column A is always greater
   ◯ the quantity in Column B is always greater
   ◯ the quantities are always equal
   ◯ it cannot be determined from the information given

10. If $k = 6 \times 17$, then which of the following is a multiple of k?
- ⟋ 68
- ⟋ 78
- ⟋ 85
- ⟋ 136
- ⟋ 204

Column A	Column B

$ab = a$ and $a = 0$

11. a b
- ⟋ the quantity in Column A is always greater
- ⟋ the quantity in Column B is always greater
- ⟋ the quantities are always equal
- ⟋ it cannot be determined from the information given

12. What is the value of $(4 + a)(4 - b)$ when $a = 4$ and $b = -4$?
- ⟋ −64
- ⟋ −16
- ⟋ 0
- ⟋ 16
- ⟋ 64

Column A	Column B

n cases of soda N contain a total of 36 bottles of soda.

13. The total number of bottles in x cases of soda X $\dfrac{36x}{n}$
- ⟋ the quantity in Column A is always greater
- ⟋ the quantity in Column B is always greater
- ⟋ the quantities are always equal
- ⟋ it cannot be determined from the information given

Column A	Column B

14 more than a is −9

14. $a + 9$ −14
- ⟋ the quantity in Column A is always greater
- ⟋ the quantity in Column B is always greater
- ⟋ the quantities are always equal
- ⟋ it cannot be determined from the information given

15. The illumination E, in footcandles, provided by a light source of intensity I, in candles, at a distance D, in feet, is given by $E = \dfrac{I}{D^2}$.

For an illumination of 50 footcandles at a distance of 4 feet from a source, the intensity of the source must be
- ⟋ 50 candles
- ⟋ 200 candles
- ⟋ 800 candles
- ⟋ 1,600 candles
- ⟋ 2,500 candles

Column A	Column B

The product of x and y is positive.

16. x y

- ○ the quantity in Column A is always greater
- ○ the quantity in Column B is always greater
- ○ the quantities are always equal
- ○ it cannot be determined from the information given

17. If $x + y = z$, then $x^2 + 2xy + y^2 =$

- ○ $4z$
- ○ $yz - x$
- ○ z^2
- ○ $z^2 + 4(x + z)$
- ○ $z^2 + yz + x^2$

Column A	Column B

18. 25×6.28 $\dfrac{628}{4}$

- ○ the quantity in Column A is always greater
- ○ the quantity in Column B is always greater
- ○ the quantities are always equal
- ○ it cannot be determined from the information given

19. $\dfrac{0.6 + 0.6 + 0.6 + 0.6 + 0.6}{5} =$

- ○ $\dfrac{2}{5}$
- ○ $\dfrac{3}{5}$
- ○ $\dfrac{30}{12}$
- ○ 4
- ○ 6

Column A	Column B

$M\%$ of 51 is 17.

20. 30 M

- ○ the quantity in Column A is always greater
- ○ the quantity in Column B is always greater
- ○ the quantities are always equal
- ○ it cannot be determined from the information given

1. DODGE:

   ○ release
   ○ create
   ○ assert aggressively
   ○ admire greatly
   ○ face directly

2. TEETH : SAW ::

   ○ cog : wheel
   ○ pick : ice
   ○ bit : drill
   ○ pulley : rope
   ○ wood : screw

3. INDUSTRY:

   ○ politics
   ○ density
   ○ lethargy
   ○ tolerance
   ○ vastness

4. Although the candidate obviously wanted to _____ the euphoria that has infused her campaign of late, she refrained from implying that the momentum had turned against her and might result in her defeat.

   ○ authenticate
   ○ moderate
   ○ maintain
   ○ clarify
   ○ revive

Questions 5-7

In analyzing the poetry of Mona Devon, we are confronted with three different yardsticks by which to measure her work. We could consider the poems as the
5 product of a twentieth-century artist in the tradition of James Joyce, T.S. Eliot, and Wallace Stevens. But to do this would be to ignore a facet of her which informs every word she writes, and which stems
10 from her identity as a woman. Could Joyce or Eliot have written the line, "the mumbo-jumbo of the stubble-cheeks"? But to characterize her solely as a woman poet is to deny her cultural heritage, for Mona
15 Devon is also the first modern poet of stature who is also Native American.

Stanley Wilson, the noted author of literary criticism, has argued compellingly that the huge popularity Devon enjoys
20 among the Native American schoolchildren is creating a whole new generation of poetry enthusiasts in an age when the reading of poetry, to say nothing of reading in general, is on the wane. While
25 this is undoubtedly true, Mr. Wilson's praise gives the impression that Devon's readership is limited to those of her own culture—an impression which suggests that Mr. Wilson is himself measuring her
30 by only one yardstick.

5. The main idea of this passage is that

   ○ Stanley Wilson is a product of the same tradition as Joyce, Eliot, and Stevens.
   ○ Analyzing poetry is often too subjective to be worthwhile.
   ○ Mona Devon's poetry should only be interpreted in terms of her heritage.
   ○ Mona Devon should not be put in the same category as Joyce, Eliot, or Stevens.
   ○ There is more than one way to interpret Mona Devon's poetry.

6. The author mentions the "the mumbo-jumbo of the stubble-cheeks" (lines 11-12) in order to
   - differentiate Devon from her male contemporaries
   - prove that Devon is more talented than her contemporaries
   - show that Wilson's critique of Devon's work is limited
   - imply that all literary criticism is just "mumbo-jumbo"
   - indicate the level of influence Devon's Native American heritage has on her work

7. It can be inferred from the passage that Stanley Wilson's praise of Devon is
   - completely endorsed by the author
   - focused too much on her status as a Native American poet
   - meant to disguise his opinion of Devon as a poet lacking in talent
   - helping to create a whole new generation of poetry enthusiasts
   - based on all facets of her poetry

8. CONTRITION : PENITENT ::
   - caution : driver
   - speculation : philosopher
   - obstinacy : athlete
   - sanguinity : partner
   - wisdom : sage

9. LUMINOUS:
   - distant
   - broken
   - dull
   - impractical
   - inconsiderate

10. Until about 1980, almost all economists assumed that economic growth is fueled by demand pressure at the level of the consumer; after the combination of high inflation and unemployment experienced in the 1990s, however, economists detected no _____ this previously _____ view of economic growth.
    - deviations from. .revolutionary
    - ground for. . ubiquitous
    - preference for. .unquestioned
    - forerunners of. .modern
    - disagreements with. .popular

11. TEMERITY : TREPIDATION ::
    - oration : publicity
    - strength : permanence
    - superfluity : necessity
    - axiom : confidence
    - indemnity : security

12. The treatment of waste water has been _____ through _____ the contaminants, but perhaps it may be more practical to neutralize the pollution in the water by adding certain chemical compounds that cause the harmful waste particles to become inert.
    - authorized. .screening
    - attempted. .tracing
    - initiated. .avoiding
    - simplified. .identifying
    - undertaken. .removing

13. COUNTERMAND : ORDER ::
    - corroborate : document
    - restate : claim
    - reopen : investigation
    - prejudice : testimony
    - revoke : license

14. PREDISPOSED:
    - ◯ directed
    - ◯ stubborn
    - ◯ disinclined
    - ◯ nostalgic
    - ◯ tranquil

15. Recent investigation into business and morality reveals the way in which apparently _____ business decisions, typically lost sight of in the ordinary operations of commerce, in reality _____ moral choices of major importance.
    - ◯ unimportant. .represent
    - ◯ unreliable. .provoke
    - ◯ unparalleled. .symbolize
    - ◯ unprecedented. .allow
    - ◯ untrammeled. .impel

16. SHEARING : WOOL ::
    - ◯ shredding : paper
    - ◯ breathing : wine
    - ◯ trimming : hedge
    - ◯ reaping : grain
    - ◯ weaving : silk

17. EXHUME:
    - ◯ breathe
    - ◯ inter
    - ◯ approve
    - ◯ assess
    - ◯ facilitate

18. While many people enjoy observing rituals and customs not _____ their culture, they _____ participating in them.
    - ◯ sanctioned by . . encourage
    - ◯ endemic to. . eschew
    - ◯ upheld in . . condone
    - ◯ central to . . relish
    - ◯ accustomed to. . avoid

19. INVARIABLE: CHANGE ::
    - ◯ incurable : disease
    - ◯ unfathomable : depth
    - ◯ extraneous : proposition
    - ◯ ineffable : expression
    - ◯ variegated : appearance

20. HEDGE:
    - ◯ attack repeatedly
    - ◯ risk commitment
    - ◯ seek advantage
    - ◯ lose pressure
    - ◯ become interested

Column A   Column B

$$3 + k = 5 - k$$

1. k 2

○ the quantity in Column A is always greater
○ the quantity in Column B is always greater
○ the quantities are always equal
○ it cannot be determined from the information given

Column A   Column B

2. $\dfrac{7}{8} - \dfrac{1}{6}$ $\dfrac{3}{4} - \dfrac{1}{8}$

○ the quantity in Column A is always greater
○ the quantity in Column B is always greater
○ the quantities are always equal
○ it cannot be determined from the information given

3. $\dfrac{0.2\left(0.0002\right)}{0.002}$

○ 0.02
○ 0.002
○ 0.0002
○ 0.00002
○ 0.000002

Column A   Column B

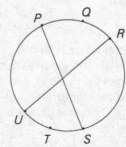

P, Q, R, S, T, and *U* are points on the circle as shown.

4.   The length of   The length of
     arc *PQR*   arc *STU*

○ the quantity in Column A is always greater
○ the quantity in Column B is always greater
○ the quantities are always equal
○ it cannot be determined from the information given

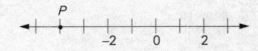

Note: Drawn to scale.

5.   If *Q* is a point to the right of 0 on the number line above and the distance between *P* and *Q* is 11, then the coordinate of *Q* is

○ −15
○ 7
○ 8
○ 11
○ 15

Column A | Column B

6. The number of minutes in y weeks

The number of of hours in $60y$ weeks

○ the quantity in Column A is always greater
○ the quantity in Column B is always greater
○ the quantities are always equal
○ it cannot be determined from the information given

Column A | Column B

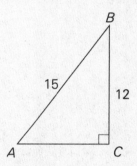

7. The area of △ ABC

90

○ the quantity in Column A is always greater
○ the quantity in Column B is always greater
○ the quantities are always equal
○ it cannot be determined from the information given

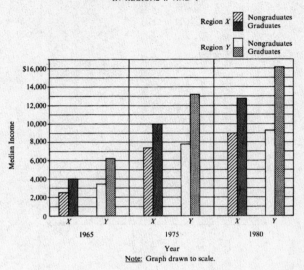

MEDIAN INCOME OF
COLLEGE GRADUATES VS. NONGRADUATES
IN REGIONS X AND Y

Note: Graph drawn to scale.

8. In 1975, the median income of nongraduates in Region X was approximately what fraction of the median income for graduates in Region X?

○ $\frac{3}{5}$

○ $\frac{5}{8}$

○ $\frac{3}{4}$

○ $\frac{10}{13}$

○ $\frac{4}{5}$

9. $12m^2 - 8m - 64 =$

- ○ $4(3m + 8)(m - 2)$
- ○ $4(3m - 8)(m + 2)$
- ○ $4(3m - 2)(m + 8)$
- ○ $4m^2 - 64$
- ○ $4m - 64$

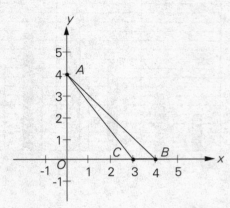

10. What is the area of triangle ABC in the figure above?

- ○ 2
- ○ 4
- ○ $4\sqrt{2}$
- ○ 7
- ○ 8

Column A   Column B

It takes Michael 3 hours at an average rate of 60 miles per hour to drive from his home to the state park. In contrast, it takes 2.5 hours at an average speed of 65 miles per hour for Michael to drive from his home to his lake house.

11. Michael's driving distance from his home to the state park   Michael's driving distance from his home to his lake house

- ○ the quantity in Column A is always greater
- ○ the quantity in Column B is always greater
- ○ the quantities are always equal
- ○ it cannot be determined from the information given

Column A   Column B

$$100 = \frac{10}{x}$$

12. x 10

- ○ the quantity in Column A is always greater
- ○ the quantity in Column B is always greater
- ○ the quantities are always equal
- ○ it cannot be determined from the information given

13. What is the greatest possible value of integer n if $6^n < 10,000$

- ○ 5
- ○ 6
- ○ 7
- ○ 8
- ○ 9

Column A   Column B

$$x^2 + 8x = -7$$

14. x 0

- ○ the quantity in Column A is always greater
- ○ the quantity in Column B is always greater
- ○ the quantities are always equal
- ○ it cannot be determined from the information given

15. In the equation $ax + b = 26$, x is a constant. If $a = 3$ when $b = 5$, what is the value of b when $a = 5$?

- ○ –11
- ○ –9
- ○ 3
- ○ 7
- ○ 21

Column A   Column B

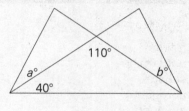

16.   *a*   *b*

- ◯ the quantity in Column A is always greater
- ◯ the quantity in Column B is always greater
- ◯ the quantities are always equal
- ◯ it cannot be determined from the information given

17. How many square tiles, each with a perimeter of 64 inches, must be used to completely cover a bathroom floor with a width of 64 inches and a length of 128 inches?

- ◯ 2
- ◯ 4
- ◯ 8
- ◯ 32
- ◯ 128

Column A   Column B

a is a positive number and *ab* < 0.

18.   *a*(*b* + 1)   *a*(*b* − 1)

- ◯ the quantity in Column A is always greater
- ◯ the quantity in Column B is always greater
- ◯ the quantities are always equal
- ◯ it cannot be determined from the information given

19. An office supply store charged $13.10 for the purchase of 85 paper clips. If some of the clips were 16¢ each and the remainder were 14¢ each, how many of the paper clips were 14¢ clips?

- ◯ 16
- ◯ 25
- ◯ 30
- ◯ 35
- ◯ 65

Column A   Column B

$y > 0$ and $(-1)^y = 1$

20.   *y*   2

- ◯ the quantity in Column A is always greater
- ◯ the quantity in Column B is always greater
- ◯ the quantities are always equal
- ◯ it cannot be determined from the information given

1. FLAG:
   - ⬭ break down
   - ⬭ regain energy
   - ⬭ resume course
   - ⬭ push forward
   - ⬭ show pride

2. SYNOPSIS : CONDENSED ::
   - ⬭ digression : repeated
   - ⬭ mystery : enticing
   - ⬭ excursion : pleasant
   - ⬭ antiquity : forgotten
   - ⬭ plagiarism : pirated

3. To examine the _____ of importing concepts from one discipline to enhance another, merely look at the degree to which words from the first may, without distortion, be _____ the second.
   - ⬭ danger. .meaningless for
   - ⬭ popularity. .created within
   - ⬭ etiquette. .revitalized by
   - ⬭ pace. .supplanted by
   - ⬭ validity. .employed by

4. CONSUMMATE:
   - ⬭ refuse
   - ⬭ undermine
   - ⬭ satiate
   - ⬭ abrogate
   - ⬭ suspect

5. ADMONISH : COUNSEL ::
   - ⬭ mollify : intensity
   - ⬭ necessitate : generosity
   - ⬭ enervate : vitality
   - ⬭ manufacture : opinion
   - ⬭ remunerate : payment

Polymer chemistry has entered a new dimension. Most polymers are nothing more than identical molecular units, or monomers, that are linked to form one-

5 dimensional chains. Now chemists have stitched together two-dimensional polymer sheets that have a variety of unusual properties. "There is a possibility of transforming all known monomers into

10 two-dimensional objects," says Samuel I. Stupp, leader of the team that synthesized the polymer sheets.

Indeed, Stupp has already demonstrated that the polymer sheets have remarkable

15 flexibility, strength, and durability. The polymers might serve as lubricants, semiconductors, optical materials, or selective membranes.

Stupp's sheet polymers are among the

20 largest molecules ever made by chemists, winning them the unattractive moniker "gigamolecules." The mass of a polymer is typically measured in daltons; a single carbon atom has a mass of 12 daltons.

25 Amylopectin, one of the largest known polymers and the principal component of starches, has a mass of 90 million daltons. Stupp estimates that his molecules weigh considerably more than 10 million daltons.

30 To make the polymer sheets, Stupp first prepares a precursor molecule by performing 21 different chemical reactions. The result is a rod-like molecule with two reactive sites: one in the center of the

35 molecule and the other at one end. It is perhaps easiest to understand how these precursors are assembled if one imagines that they are sharpened pencils. The eraser corresponds to the reactive end,

40 and the brand name stamped on the pencil represents the central reactive site. In this case, the "brand name" encourages the pencils to align side by side in the same direction. The pencils, therefore, form a

45 layer with the erasers on one side and the points on the other. A second layer forms directly on top of the first in such a way that the erasers in one layer touch those in

the other. One of Stupp's key insights was

50 to figure out how to sew these layers together. When heat is applied to the stacked layers, bonds are formed between the erasers and also between the brand names, thereby making connections within

55 the two layers and between them.

Although materials scientists have had little opportunity to characterize the gigamolecules, they are already thinking about some unusual applications. If the

60 sheets are exposed to heat or placed in an acidic environment, they tend to roll up like a tobacco leaf around a cigar. Various substances could be wrapped up inside the polymer—a trick that might be useful

65 for delivering pharmaceuticals into the body. Another possible use of the polymers is to build membranes that allow only certain molecules through.

6. The primary purpose of the passage is to

○ argue that advances in polymer chemistry will revolutionize the pharmaceutical industry

○ discuss new advances in the field of one-dimensional polymer chemistry and how those advances might be used for new technological challenges

○ discuss the invention and synthesis of two-dimensional polymer sheets and point out some of their possible uses

○ consider the new technological uses of the recently synthesized gigamolecules

○ review Samuel Stupp's contributions to polymer chemistry and his radical method of synthesizing gigamolecules

7. It can be inferred from the passage that which of the following could have posed a problem for scientists prior to Stupp when they attempted to synthesize two-dimensional polymers?

- The polymers were stronger and more flexible than had been expected, and proved difficult to manipulate.
- It was unclear what method to use to bond the stacked layers of the precursor molecules.
- The excessive weight of the polymers, in daltons, made them cumbersome and awkward in the bonding process.
- The large number of chemical reactions necessary were extremely time-consuming.
- The locations of the two reactive sites in the rod-like precursor molecule made it difficult to align them when the molecules were stacked.

8. The passage suggests that which of the following could be possible applications of gigamolecules?

I. A membrane of gigamolecules is used to filter out molecular impurities in water.

II. A sheet of gigamolecules is wrapped around a medicinal substance and given to a patient.

III. A gigamolecule is placed in a solution and then screened through a semipermeable membrane.

- I only
- I and II only
- I and III only
- II and III only
- I, II, and III

9. The passage is most probably directed at which type of audience?

- a governmental commission deciding whether to fund future studies of polymer chemistry
- a university committee considering tenure for Samuel I. Stupp
- a panel of chemists charged with determining the direction that future monomer research should take
- scientifically-literate laypersons interested in understanding the formation of the new gigamolecules
- experts in the field of polymer chemistry who are attempting to synthesize gigamolecules in their own labs

10. HYPERBOLE:

- dietary supplement
- strange sensation
- direct route
- employee
- understatement

11. Just as midwifery was for hundreds of years _____ practice, something that women retained control over for themselves, so too the increasingly independent role of the midwife in the process of childbirth is a _____ domination by institutional medicine.

- a personal. .reaction of
- a controversial. .tolerance of
- an autonomous. .liberation from
- a communal. .celebration of
- a dangerous. .protection from

12. EPIDEMIOLOGY : DISEASE ::

- radiology : fracture
- paleontology : behavior
- epistemology : knowledge
- ichthyology : religion
- numerology : formulas

13. Modernity appears to be particularly _____ mistaken notions, perhaps because in breaking free from the fetters of convention, the result is that we are very likely to be _____ unexamined hypotheses and unprepared actions.

- immune to. .accepting of
- contrary to. .reliant on
- fraught with. .susceptible to
- disposed of. .suspicious of
- insensitive to. .liberated from

14. PUISSANCE:

- impotence
- poverty
- flexibility
- grace
- vigor

15. OFFICIOUS : OBLIGING ::

- dubious : peculiar
- malevolent : corrupt
- effusive : demonstrative
- placid : merciful
- radical : cautious

16. The _____ issues that arise inherently from the very nature of social scientific investigation must be judged separately from the solely _____ issues, which are hotly debated one moment and forgotten the next.

- reiterated. .pragmatic
- innate. .realistic
- habitual. .discerning
- theoretical. .arbitrary
- perpetual. .temporal

17. EFFERVESCENT:

- vapid
- intercepted
- dispersed
- disaffected
- disconcerted

18. APOSTATE : FAITH ::

- apostle : leader
- altruist : literature
- defector : allegiance
- potentate : religion
- patriot : principle

19. Although bound to impose the law, a judge is free to use her discretion to _____ the anachronistic _____ of some criminal penalties.

- enforce . . judiciousness
- impose . . legality
- exacerbate . . severity
- mitigate . . barbarity
- restore . . impartiality

20. PERFIDY:

- flippancy
- optimism
- aptitude
- loyalty
- humility

Column A	Column B

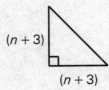

Triangle A   Triangle B

1. The area of Triangle A   The area of Triangle B

  ○ the quantity in Column A is always greater
  ○ the quantity in Column B is always greater
  ○ the quantities are always equal
  ○ it cannot be determined from the information given

Column A	Column B

2. $\dfrac{1}{2}(56)^{15}$ $28(56)^{14}$

  ○ the quantity in Column A is always greater
  ○ the quantity in Column B is always greater
  ○ the quantities are always equal
  ○ it cannot be determined from the information given

3. In the set of numbers {12, 5, 14, 12, 9, 15, 10}, f equals the mean, g equals the median, h equals the mode, and j equals the range. Which of the following is true?
  ○ $f > g > h > j$
  ○ $g = h > f > j$
  ○ $f = h > g > j$
  ○ $g > h > f = j$
  ○ $j > f > g = h$

Column A	Column B

4. $(3\sqrt{7} + 4\sqrt{7})^2$ 343

  ○ the quantity in Column A is always greater
  ○ the quantity in Column B is always greater
  ○ the quantities are always equal
  ○ it cannot be determined from the information given

5. Which of the following CANNOT be an integer if the integer k is a multiple of 12 but not a multiple of 9?

  ○ $\dfrac{k}{3}$

  ○ $\dfrac{k}{4}$

  ○ $\dfrac{k}{10}$

  ○ $\dfrac{k}{12}$

  ○ $\dfrac{k}{36}$

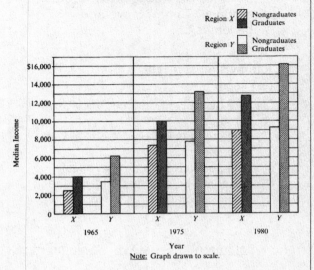

MEDIAN INCOME OF
COLLEGE GRADUATES *VS.* NONGRADUATES
IN REGIONS *X* AND *Y*

Note: Graph drawn to scale.

6. For how many of the four categories given did the median income increase by at least 30 percent from 1975 to 1980?

○ None
○ One
○ Two
○ Three
○ Four

7. Which of the following is equivalent to $(3a - 5)(a + 6)$?

I. $(3a + 5)(a - 6)$

II. $-5(a + 6) + 3a(a + 6)$

III. $3a^2 - 30$

○ II only
○ III only
○ I and II only
○ II and III only
○ I, II, and III

Column A   Column B

A rectangular bathroom measures $9\frac{1}{2}$ feet by 12 feet. The floor is covered by rectangular tile measuring $1\frac{1}{2}$ inches by 2 inches.

8. The number of $6 \times 48 \times 19$
tiles on the
bathroom floor

○ the quantity in Column A is always greater
○ the quantity in Column B is always greater
○ the quantities are always equal
○ it cannot be determined from the information given

9. A professor is choosing students to attend a special seminar. She has 10 students to choose from, and only four may be chosen. How many different ways are there to make up the four students chosen for the seminar?

○ 24
○ 120
○ 180
○ 210
○ 360

Column A   Column B

k is an integer such that
$9(3)^3 + 4 = k$.

10. The average   16
of the prime
factors of *k*

○ the quantity in Column A is always greater
○ the quantity in Column B is always greater
○ the quantities are always equal
○ it cannot be determined from the information given

Column A	Column B

11. $(6 + \sqrt{10})(6 - \sqrt{10})$ 27

- ⬭ the quantity in Column A is always greater
- ⬭ the quantity in Column B is always greater
- ⬭ the quantities are always equal
- ⬭ it cannot be determined from the information given

Column A	Column B

$$a = b + 2$$

12. $a^2 - 2ab + b^2$ $2a - 2b$

- ⬭ the quantity in Column A is always greater
- ⬭ the quantity in Column B is always greater
- ⬭ the quantities are always equal
- ⬭ it cannot be determined from the information given

13. If the dimensions of a rectangular crate, in feet, are 5 by 6 by 7, which of the following CANNOT be the total surface area, in square feet, of two sides of the crate?

- ⬭ 60
- ⬭ 70
- ⬭ 77
- ⬭ 84
- ⬭ 90

Column A	Column B

Tommy's average after 8 tests is 84. If his most recent test score is dropped, Tommy's average becomes 85.

14. Tommy's most recent test score   83

- ⬭ the quantity in Column A is always greater
- ⬭ the quantity in Column B is always greater
- ⬭ the quantities are always equal
- ⬭ it cannot be determined from the information given

Column A	Column B

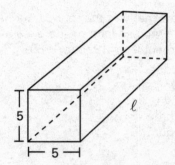

A rectangular box has a surface area of 190 square feet.

15. The length ℓ of the box   7 feet

- ⬭ the quantity in Column A is always greater
- ⬭ the quantity in Column B is always greater
- ⬭ the quantities are always equal
- ⬭ it cannot be determined from the information given

16. In the set of positive, distinct integers {a, b, c, d, e} the median is 16. What is the minimum value of a + b + c + d + e?

○ 26
○ 48
○ 54
○ 72
○ 80

Column A	Column B
17. On a cube, the number of faces that share an edge with any one face	Number of sides of a square

○ the quantity in Column A is always greater
○ the quantity in Column B is always greater
○ the quantities are always equal
○ it cannot be determined from the information given

18. If m + n = 24, and m − n + p = 15, then 4m + 2p =

○ 13
○ 26
○ 39
○ 64
○ 78

Column A	Column B
19. The length of the diagonal of a rectangle with perimeter 16.	The length of the diagonal of a rectangle with perimeter 20.

○ the quantity in Column A is always greater
○ the quantity in Column B is always greater
○ the quantities are always equal
○ it cannot be determined from the information given

Column A	Column B
20. $\sqrt{13} + \sqrt{51}$	$\sqrt{13 + 51}$

○ the quantity in Column A is always greater
○ the quantity in Column B is always greater
○ the quantities are always equal
○ it cannot be determined from the information given

21

Answers and Explanations

1. **A** Remember to make your own opposites for the stem words instead of looking at the choices ETS gives you right away. Also, if it helps, "translate" the stem word they give you into another word you are more comfortable with before making an opposite. So an opposite for MOUNT might be "get off," or "dismount." Choice A will be closest, but make sure you look at all the choices.

2. **E** Make a sentence expressing the relationship between the stem words. PLAYER is part of a TEAM is okay. Now try on the answer choices. A: OIL is part of a LIQUID? Yuck. B: LINE is part of a DRAWING? Not bad. Keep it for now. C: SCALES are part of an INCREASE? Huh? D: HISS is part of a RECORDING? Remember clear and necessary, and lose D! E: INGREDIENT is part of a MIXTURE? Not bad. We could make another sentence with the stem words to help decide between B and E. Something like a TEAM is a group of PLAYERs. Just remember to reverse the words in the answers now. B—DRAWING is a group of LINEs does not sound as good as MIXTURE is a group of INGREDIENTs. LINE and DRAWING is also not a particularly strong relationship. That's E!

3. **D** Remember to cover the answer choices. We can get a good idea of what the answer should be without even looking at them. Look for trigger words that indicate the direction of the sentence, and clues that tell us what's going on. The dash is a trigger here; it tells us that the first part of the sentence says the same thing as the later part. So a pundit, even if you don't know what it means, is like a weatherman, who can tell us about the weather (or current events, in the case of a pundit) without being able to _____ it. How about something like "control"? Check answers. Choice A isn't a match and neither is C. B and E aren't quite like control, and either one suggests that the other is just as good (or bad). D, "influence," is much like our "control."

4. **D** Remember to make synonyms for the stem, translating into language you're a bit more comfortable with. THEN make the opposite, and look at the answers for the choice that best matches. ERADICATE means get rid of. The opposite of get rid of is something like "cause" or "start." Check answers—A: IGNORE is not good. Neither is B: UNDO. Not much like opposites, these two. C: SMOKE? Maybe if we're smoking something. Otherwise . . . lose it. D: INTRODUCE is a lot like "cause" or "start." We like it. Good thing, too, because E is nuts. Boil indeed. Pick D.

5. **B** This sentence has a nice changing direction trigger, "however," in the middle of it. So we know the two parts of the sentence are saying two opposing things. The first part of the sentence discusses the sparring, or fighting, of the two lawyers and how it appeared. It probably looked like fighting. A word like "nasty" or "fighting" or "real" might be good for that first blank. Look at the first words in the answers. Choice A stinks. B's first word, "hostile," is a good word to keep. C—if they were fighting, is "light-hearted" good? No. D—"heightened" isn't awful; it could be that the fighting seemed intense. E, "brilliant," is not. On to the other blank. Oh, now we know that despite their seeming to fight, these guys are really friends? That changes things. That's what "however" is doing here. So what do we do with the second blank? Outside the court, their friendship is good, well known, strong. We have a choice now between B's "obvious," and D's "concealed." If it's well known, it's not concealed! B is the only answer for which both words work. Read it through to make sure.

6. **A** EXCRETION is regulated by the KIDNEY. Try A: RESPIRATION is regulated by the LUNG? Okay. B: LYMPHOMA is regulated by the CANCER? No. C: PROPULSION is regulated by the ENGINE? Not. D: INFORMATION is regulated by the MEDIA? Only if you're fond of conspiracy theories. E: DISINFECTION is regulated by SOAP? Nope. That leaves A. Another sentence you might have used is KIDNEY performs EXCRETION, or KIDNEY is the organ of EXCRETION.

7. **C** The answer is C. Do this one blank at a time, whichever one you think is easier to come up with a word for first. How about the first blank? Something like "gets" or "draws"? Now look at only the first words; we want to get rid of the ones

that are nothing like our word. "Overlooks" in D is pretty bad. Cross off answer choice D completely, making sure you don't consider it when we look at the rest of the answers' second words. But the other choices aren't that bad; leave them alone, and we'll go to the other blank. The second blank describes the audience, and the second part of the sentence tells us that this audience is "appealing to advertisers of expensive products." This is here to tell us that the audience can afford the advertised products. "Wealthy" is a good word. Look for something like it and remember—we're looking only at the second words in the answers! A—"attractive" is nice, as is B—"agreeable," but these don't address the "expensive products" mentioned. C—"prosperous" is like wealthy. We like it. E is likewise far from "wealthy." Both words in C are good. Make sure to read the sentence through with your answer choice; make sure it sounds reasonable.

8. **B** SNAKE is a type of REPTILE, right? Let's go. A: FISH is a type of SCHOOL? How about B? BEETLE is a type of INSECT? Sure. Keep it. C: ELEPHANT is a type of LAND? No way. D: EGG is a type of CHICKEN? Not really. Of course, they are related, but remember we are looking to see if they have the same relationship as the stem words. They don't. And E: LAMB is a type of SHEEP is okay. We have two choices that work; we can either make a more specific sentence with the stem, or work backward with the answers, making different sentences for them. B's sentence pretty much needs to be something like BEETLE is a type or kind of INSECT, which certainly works with the stem words. But D's sentence is something like a LAMB is a baby SHEEP, which doesn't work with the stem. Therefore, B is the best answer.

9. **C** What is this passage saying? It's saying that overpopulation causes environmental damage, so we better do something about it. Let's go to the answers. A: This seems extreme, and a mistake is not referred to in the passage. Eliminate. B: We don't really know much about technology from the passage. Eliminate. C: Sounds good. D: "Criticize" is too strong. No one is being criticized here. Eliminate. E: International legislation is not mentioned in the passage. Eliminate. So, C is the closest answer to what we said is the main idea.

10. **C** The answer must flow with the passage, since it's something the author would agree with. Remember to avoid anything too extreme. Choice A sounds really extreme. No one should be allowed unlimited reproductive freedom ever? Eliminate! B: There's no discussion of management in the passage. Eliminate. C: Sounds good. Line 27 does use the word "permanent" to describe the changes in the ecosystems. D: The passage does say that industrialized nations should help with education, but there was no suggestion of sharing resources. Eliminate. E: "... the most dangerous threat" is pretty extreme, and so is "strong action." So the best answer is C.

11. **D** We must go back into the passage to find this answer, using the lead words "demographic patterns." Remember—if it's not in the passage, it's not the answer. A: Can you find agricultural production in the passage? Bet you can't. Eliminate. B: Can you find climate change in the passage? Bet you can't. Eliminate. C: Can you find overconsumption in the passage? Bet you can't. Eliminate. D: Religion is mentioned on line 5. This one can stay. E: Can you find resource quality in the passage? Bet you can't. Eliminate. The answer is D—it's the only one mentioned in the passage.

12. **B** Careful—the question says NOT. That means four of these choices CAN be found in the passage. Find those four, and the one left is the answer. Choice A is in the passage—on lines 15–18. Eliminate. B: Quality of life is not really a concern in the passage, and noise pollution isn't mentioned either. Keep this choice. C is in the passage—on line 18. Eliminate. D is in the passage—on lines 18–22. Eliminate. E is in the passage—on lines 23–27. Eliminate.

13. **B** LUCIDITY means clarity. The opposite of this could be "unclearness." Not an elegant word, but it will do the trick. Don't even worry if the word you make is real, as long as it will help you get an answer. OBSCURITY, B, partially or completely hidden from sight, is best.

14. **B** A good sentence for the stem would be FERTILIZER encourages or causes GROWTH. Now try the answer choices: A: GLAZE encourages or causes POTTERY. No good for this sentence. Dump A. B: YEAST causes or encourages LEAVENING? It sure does. Keep it. C: COTTON causes or encourages TEXTURE? Nonsense. D: ILLUMINATION causes or encourages INTEREST—totally unrelated. E: OCTANE causes or encourages SPEED? Octane in gasoline has no relationship to speed. Eliminate E. So, the only answer that made any sense with the sentence we made with the stem was B. We're happy.

15. **A** FRUSTRATE means to annoy, make difficult. "Make easier" would be a good opposite. A: FACILITATE means just that—to make easier. But we need to look at all the answers. Don't take the chance of screwing this up. We might also like B: MODERATE. But that means make less severe. If you couldn't decide between these two choices, you'd make opposites for the answer choices, and see which is closer to the stem. The opposite for choice A would be to make harder. The opposite of B would be to make more severe. A is better.

16. **E** BOLSTER means support. The opposite of that would be "take away support." That gives us "undermine."

17. **E** A good sentence defining this relationship might be DISARM is to take away WEAPONS. How's A: LIMIT is to take away ABILITIES? Well, it's not taking them away. B: SOOTHE is to take away DIFFICULTIES? No, it just makes us feel better. C: RESTRAIN is to take away MOVEMENT? It's not awful, so keep it. D: DISGUISE is to take away IDENTITY? No, just to hide it. E: USURP is to take away POWER? Looks good. Now we need to choose between C and E. We could make another sentence for the stem, or we can work backward with C and E. A good relationship sentence for C is: RESTRAIN is to prevent MOVEMENT. Is DISARM to prevent WEAPONS? Not really. E: USURP is to forcibly take away POWER. Is DISARM to forcibly take away WEAPONS? Yes, it is, and it's a better choice than C.

18. **B** First we make a sentence: STONE is shaped by a SCULPTOR. Let's go to the answers. A: Is BRICK shaped by a HOUSE? No. Bricks are used to build a house. Eliminate. B: Are WORDS shaped by a POET? Yes, figuratively speaking. A possibility. Let's leave it, and check the other choices. C: Is a BUST shaped by a PORTRAIT? No. A bust could be a portrait and made of stone by a sculptor, but the relationship between BUST and PORTRAIT is not the same as the relationship between STONE and SCULPTOR. Eliminate. D: Is a SCALPEL shaped by a SURGEON? No. A surgeon might wield a scalpel like the same way a sculptor wields a chisel, but there's no *chisel* in the stem. Eliminate. E: Is a MINE shaped by ORE? Don't get too clever here. You might stretch matters and say that a mine takes its shape from the removal of ore, but that's not what we're looking for. Eliminate. The answer must be B, the only choice we haven't eliminated. And it is.

19. **C** Don't know what "cloistering" means? Don't worry. The clue in the sentence is that Jenson was "in her study for days on end without food or sleep." That describes someone working very hard. Let's put "hard" in the blank, and go to the answers. A: Does "carelessly" mean hard? No. Eliminate. B: Does "creatively" mean hard? No. Eliminate. C: Does "tirelessly" mean hard? Maybe; she did work "for days on end without food or sleep." Let's keep this. D: Does "intermittently" mean hard? Be careful! Are you sure you know the dictionary definition of the word? If not, you'd have to keep this choice and keep going. E: Does "voluntarily" mean hard? Definitely not. Eliminate. We're down to two choices, but we know that "tirelessly" fits, because we know that Jenson worked "for days on end without food or sleep." So the answer must be C. By the way, "intermittently" means stopping and starting at intervals. Learn that vocab!

20. **E** EVICT means to eject or remove someone, like a tenant from an apartment. Eject is not the opposite of TEAR DOWN, ANSWER QUICKLY, BRING TOGETHER, or SET FREE. But it is the opposite of ADMIT INTO.

EASY MATH PRACTICE SET EXPLANATIONS

1. **A** The first thing to do is to write down A, B, C, D. In this case, we can ditch D because all there are here are numbers, no variables. Now we need to evaluate each side. Remember PEMDAS, the order of operations. In Column A, we do the parentheses first, which will be 3. Then 3 times 4 is 12. So Column A is 12. In Column B, we also do the parentheses first—that will be 7. But then we multiply that times 0. And anything times 0 = 0. That's what Column B is. So A will always be larger.

2. **A** Write down A, B, C, D to use Process of Elimination. They tell us that $a = 15$ and $a + b = 29$. Plug the given value of a, 15, into the equation with a and b, and solve for b. $15 + b = 29$, so $b = 14$. Now Column A is 15 squared. Don't multiply this yet! Column B is 14 squared. Without actually multiplying out for each column, you should see that A will be larger. We were given a value for a—it was fixed, so we didn't really need to plug in to know that A is always larger. 15 squared must be greater than 14 squared.

3. **C** We are told that the team won 20 games, and that 60 percent of these were won at home. But we are being asked how many games the team won AWAY from home. That's the other 40 percent. To find exactly how many games were won AWAY from home, we need to take 40 percent of the 20 games. Use translation for this:

   "40 percent of 20 is" . . . can be translated as $\frac{40}{100} \times 20$, which will equal 8. The correct answer is C.

4. **C** Here we will need to plug in, so write down A, B, C, D. We're told that a and b are equal. So let's pick something like $a = b = 4$. Column A in this case is $4(4) + 4$, which equals 20. Column B is $4 + 4(4)$ which will also equal 20. So far they're equal. So cross out A and B. Are they always equal? Let's plug in again. Maybe $a = b = -1$? So Column A will give $4(-1) + (-1)$ which will equal -5. And Column B is $-1 + 4(-1)$, which will also be -5. Looks equal indeed. So it's C.

5. **B** Hope you didn't feel inclined to multiply this out! The ugliness of the numbers should deter you. Annoying multiplication is not what this test is about; *avoiding* it is. Can we rearrange this? After all, that's what the answers are: rearranged numbers, not actual products. We can factor a 652 out of each term like this: 652 (523 + 427), which is the same thing as (652) (523) + (652) (427). And that's B.

6. **D** To find the *amount* that the median income of graduates in Region Y increased from 1965 to 1980, find each individual amount. In 1965, median income was about $6,200. In 1980, it was about $16,200. So it increased by about $10,000. We don't really know the exact numbers, but the question says approximately. So don't make yourself crazy.

7. **D** Write down A, B, C, D to use Process of Elimination. We're told the diameter of circle M is greater than the radius of circle N. Plug in some values for the diameter and radius of these circles, making sure that they fit the info we're given. Let's say the diameter of M is 10, and the radius of N is 3. Column A asks for the circumference of circle M. Circumference = 2 times π times radius, or π times diameter. Using the 10 we picked for the diameter of M, the circumference of circle M is 10π. Using 3 for the radius of circle N will get us 6π as its circumference. For the time being it looks like A is larger, because 10π is larger than 6π, so eliminate B and C, since neither of these can always be true. We're left with A and D as choices. So plug in again, trying to make a different answer happen. If we keep the diameter of M as 10, but make the radius of $N = 9$, Column A is still 10π, but Column B becomes 18π. Now B is larger, so A cannot be the correct answer, since we found a case where Column A is not larger than Column B. Dump A. The only choice left is D.

8. **C** Put the value of a that they give us into the equation. It will become $4(4) - 3b = 1$. That's $16 - 3b = 1$. Subtract 16 from each side, and we now have $-3b = -15$. Divide each side by -3, and we find that $b = 5$. Make sure to read the question before picking an answer! The question asks for "the combined value of a and b." That's $4 + 5 = 9$—C. Notice how the value of b is sitting there also, waiting for us to be in a hurry and pick it. Don't.

9. **A** Write down A, B, C, D. Here again we know to eliminate D, because all we have are numbers. Column A is $\frac{3}{4} + \frac{3}{4}$, which are don't even need to use the Bowtie for, because the bottom numbers are the same. $\frac{3}{4} + \frac{3}{4} = \frac{6}{4}$, which we can also call $1\frac{1}{2}$. Column B, even though it also has $\frac{3}{4}$ in it, is asking us to *square* it. For multiplying $\frac{3}{4}$ by $\frac{3}{4}$, remember we multiply the top numbers across to get a top number. It'll be 9 in this case. And we multiply across the bottom for the bottom number, in this case 16. So the product is $\frac{9}{16}$. We don't need to use the Bowtie to compare these either. Column A is clearly larger than 1, and Column B is less. So, A is the answer.

10. **E** Here, we really can't easily escape doing the multiplication, but multiplying 17 by 6 shouldn't kill us. It's 102. And we are looking for a multiple of 102, or in other words, what we get when we multiply 102 by any integer. It could be -102, or 102, not that either of those are here. Of the ones that are here, only 204 is a multiple of 102. It's 102 times 2. So, E is the winner.

11. **D** Don't forget to write A, B, C, D on your scratch paper, and plug in! They tell us that $ab = a$, and that $a = 0$. Put in that value of a in the first equation. That makes it 0 times $b = 0$. Plug in a value of b that makes this true. Yes, it can be just about anything! Say we make $b = 5$. Then Column A is 0 and Column B is 5. Column B is larger, so we can eliminate choices A and C. But you know we're not done; we must plug in again. So, try another value for b, maybe something a bit wacky, like 0. Column A is still 0, but now so is Column B. So the columns can be equal. We've already crossed out A and C, and now we can cross out B, because we just found a case when the answer could be C. We're left with D, because we really had two different answers depending on what we plugged in for b.

12. **E** Watch the signs carefully. In order to evaluate this expression, we need to put in the values of a and b we are given. The $(4 + a)$ becomes $(4 + 4)$ which equals 8. And the $(4 - b)$ becomes $(4 - (-4))$ which is also 8. Subtracting a negative number is the same thing as adding, remember? To finish this problem, don't forget that we need to multiply the 8s together, getting 64. That's E.

13. **D** Write down A, B, C, D! The question says that n cases of soda N have a total of 36 bottles of soda. We can decide that $n = 6$, for example, so each case has 6 bottles. Now we go to the two columns. Column A asks us the total number of bottles in x cases of soda X. That's right, a different number of cases of a different soda. Cute, huh? It could be *anything*—the conditions above only apply to soda N. So even though we made $n = 6$, we can pick anything for x. And we can change our n, too, for that matter. So the answer is D.

14. **C** We are told that 14 more than a is –9. Let's translate this into an equation. Moving left to right, we see that this equation is $14 + a = -9$. Now solve it by subtracting 14 from each side; a equals –23. So put it into the columns. Column A is $-23 + 9$, which is –14. Ooh! Look at Column B! It's –14, too. We can't use any other values for a—it was a set value and we've plugged it in. Both columns are always –14, so the answer is C.

15. **C** Be careful here about which variable is which. Set up the equation as it's given, and substitute the numbers in the problem:

$$E = \frac{I}{D^2} \text{ becomes } 50 = \frac{I}{4^2}, \text{ or } 50 = \frac{I}{16}.$$

To solve, we multiply both sides by 16. I will equal 50 times 16, or 800. Bingo. That's C. Don't be thrown by the sciencey-sounding wording. We just need to put in the given values.

16. **D** Knowing that the product of x and y is positive only tells us that they are either both positive or both negative. But it doesn't tell us what they actually *are*. Plug in any numbers you like: 3 and 4, then 4 and 3. No way to tell, so the answer is D (hey, that rhymes!).

17. **C** Let's use our favorite technique. Plug in 2 for x, 3 for y, and 5 for z in the equation given and in all the answer choices. Then plug those numbers into the question. You get $2^2 + (2)(2)(3) + 3^2$, which equals $4 + 12 + 9$, or 25. That's our target answer. Let's look for it in the answer choices. A: 4 times 5 = 20. Eliminate. B: 15 – 2 = 13. Eliminate. C: $5^2 = 25$. Bingo. D: 25 + more. Eliminate. E: 25 + more. Eliminate. The answer is C.

18. **C** The first thing you should do is eliminate D as a choice—both columns contain numbers, so the answer *can* be determined. And remember, you are *comparing*, not calculating. So let's get rid of the fraction in Column B by multiplying *both columns* by 4. We end up with 100×6.28 in Column A, and 628 in Column B. Now, what's 100×6.28? It's 628. The columns are equal, so the answer is C.

19. **B** Hopefully you didn't calculate the numerator, because all you had to do was simplify it. Change it to 5(0.6). Now we can cancel the 5 in the numerator with the 5 in the denominator. We're left with 0.6, which is the same as $\frac{3}{5}$. That's B.

20. **B** Let's translate: $\frac{M}{100}(51) = 17$. Now we cross-multiply and get $51M = 1700$. Divide and get 33 and $\frac{1}{3}$ percent. That's bigger than 30, so the answer is B.

MEDIUM VERBAL PRACTICE SET EXPLANATIONS

1. **E** Maybe we can't define DODGE right away. Word association will help us here. Where have you seen this word used? Ever play dodgeball? What's the idea? Not getting hit. The opposite of that would be getting hit. Look for something like that. Or, if we can dodge a ball, we ought also to be able to do its opposite with a ball. A: RELEASE ball? Okay. B: CREATE ball? Out of what? Not so good. C: ASSERT AGGRESSIVELY ball, or ASSERT ball AGGRESSIVELY? This is plain weird. D: ADMIRE GREATLY a ball? Sure it's lovely and round, but does it make much sense? No. E: FACE DIRECTLY a ball, or FACE a ball DIRECTLY? Sounds good. And that's it. You could also use DODGE the draft. But you can't dodge the question even if you can't come up with a perfect definition of the word.

2. **C** Careful with the sentence here. We don't want to get too specific too quickly. Let's try TEETH are part of a SAW. A: COG is part of a WHEEL? Could be. Don't chuck it yet. B: PICK is a part of ICE? No. C: BIT is part of a DRILL. Yes. D: PULLEY is part of a ROPE? Well, it works with one sometimes, but it's not part of one. E: WOOD is a part of a SCREW? No way. So there's A and C to look at more closely. Can we make a more specific sentence with the stem? What do teeth have to do with a saw besides being a part of one? They cut. TEETH are the cutting part of a SAW. Back to choice A: COG is the cutting part of a WHEEL? There is no cutting part of a wheel. C? BIT is the cutting part of a DRILL? Yes, that's the part that does the damage. C is our answer.

3. **C** INDUSTRY has at least two meanings, one of which does not have a clear opposite. It won't be used here in the sense of "I'm in the plastics industry." Here it will mean hard work, diligence. The opposite of that will be something like lazy, without hard work. The closest to that is C— LETHARGY.

4. **B** Here we have "although" acting as a trigger, telling us that the start of the sentence is not the same as the end. The blank is in the first part, and we know the first part should be different from the second part of the sentence. The second part of the sentence says the candidate didn't want to let on that she might lose. What would she want to do to the "euphoria that has infused her campaign?" Calm it down, but not completely destroy it. She wanted to be realistic without being defeatist. Look for something like "calm." Choice A is no good. B, "moderate" is a lot like calm. Keep it. C—"maintain" is keeping the same, which she didn't want to do. Lose it. D and E are not like "calm." That's B.

5-7   Remember, the first thing we need to do when dealing with a Reading Comp passage is find the main idea. In this case, it's that Mona Devon's work should be measured by more than one "yardstick"—in other words, her work should be interpreted in terms of her heritage, gender, and the literary tradition from which it comes.

5.   **E**   We're looking for the main idea here, so let's remember our little summary and go to the answers. A: Careful. Wilson is mentioned, but he and his work are not the focus of the passage. Eliminate. B: Well, you might secretly believe this, but it is never mentioned in the passage. Eliminate. C: Her heritage is ONE thing we should use to interpret her work, but not the ONLY thing. Too narrow and extreme. Eliminate. D: The author doesn't disagree that Devon belongs in the same category as these poets. Also, they are only mentioned in the first paragraph, so are not likely to be mentioned in the correct answer to a main idea questions. Eliminate. E: Yes. A nice paraphrase of our summary, and the only choice left!

6.   **A**   Go to the line in question, and read a little above and a little below. The passage says that if you only consider Devon as a contemporary of Joyce and friends, you miss that she's a woman. "Stubble-cheeks" refers to men, and the implication is that male poets wouldn't use that type of description. A: Yes, this is exactly what mentioning the "stubble-cheeks" does. It distinguishes Devon as a female poet. B: Careful, no one is judging the level of talent in the passage. And that line would not necessary prove talent. Eliminate. C: Careful. The author does think this, but that's not why the "stubble-cheeks" are mentioned. Besides, Wilson doesn't come up until the second paragraph, and this line reference is in the first paragraph. Eliminate. D: This is pretty extreme. It's all mumbo-jumbo? Besides, the line is about the "stubble-cheeks," not the critics. Eliminate. E: The line quoted does not show the influence of her ethnic heritage. It shows the influence of her gender. Eliminate. The only answer that mentions gender is A.

7.   **B**   The answer to this question comes from the second paragraph, where Wilson's praise of Devon is mentioned. A: According to the last lines of the passage (". . . Mr. Wilson is himself measuring her by only one yardstick"), the author isn't sure Wilson's praise is as open-minded as it should be. And the word "completely" makes this choice pretty extreme. Eliminate. B: This is a nice paraphrase of that last line in the second paragraph. Keep it. C: Careful—the passage never says that Wilson doesn't think Devon has talent. Eliminate. D: It's not Wilson's praise that's creating new poetry readers on the reservation. It's Devon's work. Eliminate. E: The author seems to be saying that Wilson's praise may be based mostly on ONE facet of her poetry, not ALL. Also, the word "all" is pretty extreme. Eliminate. B is best.

8. **E** A good sentence is a PENITENT is characterized by CONTRITION. Since we reversed the order of the stem words, remember to do the same when we look at the answer choices. So, choice A gives us a DRIVER is characterized by CAUTION. You'd hope so, but you can't define the words in terms of each other. Strike A. A PHILOSOPHER is characterized by SPECULATION? Contemplation, perhaps, but not speculation. Out goes B. An ATHLETE is characterized by OBSTINACY? All athletes are stubborn? No. Eliminate C. D: A PARTNER is characterized by SANGUINITY? If you don't know what sanguinity means, leave this choice in. If you do know the word, you should want to eliminate the choice. And E: a SAGE is characterized by WISDOM. Yup. E is the best choice whether or not you knew what sanguinity meant. At least we know E has a good relationship. If you also didn't know what sage meant, then just pick between D and E. But learn that vocab!

9. **C** LUMINOUS has something to do with light, specifically "filled with light" or "giving off light." So we are looking for something that means "not giving off light" or "not being filled with light." Don't fall for A—DISTANT—which at a glance might be interesting. Make sure you look at all of the answers. That way we won't miss DULL, choice C, which is used here in the sense that something dull has no shine, or light, coming off it.

10. **B** There is a semicolon separating the two parts of the sentence, suggesting the second part continues in the same direction as the first, but there's also a "however" in the second part, which tells us something changes direction there. So the first part is telling us about "until about 1980" and the second part about the 1990s. If the economists believed that "growth is fueled . . . consumer" before 1980, the "however" suggests their view was different in the 1990s. The second part of the sentence should say this. It has two blanks—let's try the second first, since it talks about the economists' view. We know "almost all economists presumed" it. Let's look for something for the second blank that means assumed by nearly all. A: "revolutionary" may sound good in the blank, but it doesn't mean something assumed by most. Dump A and don't look back. For B: how's "ubiquitous"—everywhere at once? Okay. Leave it. C: "unquestioned" is also much like assumed by all. D: "modern" isn't supported by the rest of the sentence. E: "popular" isn't terrible. So we still have B, C, and E. Time for the first blank. Before 1980 the economists held the view that economic growth blah, blah, blah. After the 1990s, *however*, that changed— and economists detected no ____ this view. Support for? Belief in? Look at the first words in our remaining choices. B: "ground for" is lovely. C: "preference for" is not as good. And E: "disagreements with"—is way off. So B is the choice that works best in each blank. Be sure to read the sentence through after you've picked an answer, making certain it makes sense.

11. **C** Here we've got a couple of harder words as the stem. A good sentence to make would be TEMERITY is lacking TREPIDATION. Then go through the answer choices. Choice A doesn't work and has no relationship to boot. Same with B. C: SUPERFLUITY is lacking NECESSITY? Okay. D: AXIOM is lacking CONFIDENCE? No, but if you didn't know what "axiom" meant, you should leave it. E: INDEMNITY is lacking SECURITY is no good; if anything, "indemnity" would be more like "security." So C is best. If you didn't know one of the stem words, you could work backward from the answer choices, making sentences with each and trying out the sentences on the stem. Or if you didn't know either of the stem words, eliminate non-relationships like A, B, and D (if you knew "axiom"), and guess. It's not bad to get a question down to two or three answer choices when you don't even know what the stem words mean!

12. **E** It's a two–blanker; do one at a time, whichever you like better first. In this case, it's probably the second that is easier to deal with. We have a "but" partway through the sentence, telling us that what comes before the "but" is different from what comes after it. What comes after it tells us that another way to neutralize pollution is to add something to the water that will combine with the pollutants and make them harmless. The treatment alluded to in the first part of the sentence must be different. Second blank? Treating waste water is probably done by taking out, removing, or getting rid of the pollutants. Look for something like that for the second blank. Choice A's "screening" isn't bad. Keep it and go on. B's "tracing" is nothing like getting rid of. Lose it. C: "avoiding"? Oh look, here comes the pollution! Let's avoid it! Don't think so. And D? "Identifying" contaminants is not a way of treating waste water. But E's "removing" is fine. Now to the other blank. This is a bit weird. Seems like the blank doesn't even need to be here, but it is and we need to fill it. The treatment has been accomplished, or done by taking out the icky stuff? Look for something like either of those words. We only have two choices remaining. Choice A is "authorized" and we are authorized to dump it because it isn't much like the words we want. E's "undertaken" means done or accomplished. We are happy with E.

13. **E** The sentence would be COUNTERMAND is to take back an ORDER. Try it out. A: CORROBORATE is to take back a DOCUMENT? No. Maybe to agree with it, or verify it? B: RESTATE is to take back a CLAIM? No. Let me restate that: No. C: REOPEN is to take back an INVESTIGATION? Nonsense. D: PREJUDICE is to take back TESTIMONY? No, it stinks, and isn't related to boot. We boot it. E: REVOKE is to take back a LICENSE? You bet. Go with E.

14. **C** PREDISPOSED means likely to do something, as in "When I guess on a multiple-choice test, I'm predisposed to picking C." So the opposite of this will be a word that will convey the idea of "unlikely to do something." Careful here. B and C may interest us. Make precise opposites for them if you're not sure which to pick. For B—STUBBORN—the opposite might be easy to lead, which is not that close to PREDISPOSED. For C—DISINCLINED—however, an opposite might be liking or likely to do something. C it is!

15. **A** When you see a two-blank sentence completion, do whichever blank first you feel you know more about. The first blank, which describes the business decisions, looks good. What else do we know about the business decisions? The sentence says they are "apparently" something, and that they are "typically lost sight of." These clues help us put something like "lost sight of" in the first blank. Now go to the first words in the answer choices, looking for something comparable to "lost sight of." In A, "unimportant" is okay. In B, "unreliable" is not like "lost sight of," so lose it. C and D, "unparalleled" and "unprecedented," don't describe something easy to lose sight of—more the opposite, so eliminate them. And in E, "untrammeled" may be a word we don't know, so keep it. (If you do know it, you'll want to eliminate it.) On to the second blank. This blank describes the moral choices; what else do we know about them? The sentence changes direction, which we can see in the "apparently" this, but "in reality" that construction. So the decisions that are apparently no big deal, in reality are moral choices. In A, "represent" is good. But in E, "impel," which means "to force" just doesn't fit. So dump it. Choice A is left, and if you know "untrammeled" you'd pretty much be done after doing one blank. But make sure you check the other anyway.

16. **D** Make a sentence for the stem, such as SHEARING is how you get WOOL. SHREDDING is how you get PAPER? No, so kill A. In B, is BREATHING how you get WINE? Um, no. TRIMMING is how you get HEDGE? No—bye, C. REAPING is how you get GRAIN? It works if you know the words, and if you don't know what reaping is, you leave it anyway. WEAVING is how you get SILK? Nope. So D is either the only one that worked, or the only one left. Because another good sentence would be SHEARING is the harvesting of WOOL, and yes, REAPING is the harvesting of GRAIN.

17. **B** Let's assume we don't know the meaning of EXHUME. Work through the choices, turning each into its opposite. A: Not breathe? Is there really a word for this? There's probably not a direct opposite, so let's eliminate it. B: If you don't know this word, don't eliminate it! C: Disapprove. Okay, it's worth keeping. D: There's no clear opposite, so eliminate it. E: Make difficult. Okay, it's worth keeping. So, we've got three choices left. Your chances of finding the answer now depend on whether narrowing down the choices made anything click in your mind. Inter means bury; exhume means dig up.

18. **B** Use that trigger word "while"—it means that the two halves of the sentence, and therefore the two blanks, must be opposites. Since the clue is "enjoy observing rituals," the second blank has to be something like "don't enjoy" or "avoid." So we can eliminate A, C, and D. We're left with B and E. Now, to the first blank. The sentence is saying that people might like to observe these rituals, but they don't actually participate in them. If these rituals were part of their culture, they would already be participating in them, so they must not be. So, the first blank can be "part of." That's what "endemic" means, and that's not what "accustomed" means, so the answer is B.

19. **D** Make a sentence: "Something INVARIABLE is without CHANGE." Notice that "change" is a noun, not a verb. How do we know? We checked the answer choices! Okay, it's POE time. A: Is something that's INCURABLE without DISEASE? No. Eliminate this choice. B: Is something that's UNFATHOMABLE without DEPTH? Nope. Eliminate this choice too. C: Is something that's EXTRANEOUS without PROPOSITION? Do you know the dictionary definition of "extraneous?" If not, keep this choice and move on. D: Is something that's INEFFABLE without EXPRESSION? If you don't know the definition of "ineffable," you'd better keep this choice. E: Is something that's VARIEGATED without APPEARANCE? Even if you don't know the exact definition of "variegated," it probably doesn't mean "without appearance." Now we're guessing between C and D. So, do you think it's more likely that some word means "without proposition" or that some word means "without expression?" Well, it turns out that extraneous and proposition are not related, and ineffable does, indeed, mean incapable of being expressed.

20. **B** Do you think they mean a row of closely planted shrubs? Not likely. After all, what's the opposite of a row of closely planted shrubs? Not only that, but this word is not a noun, but a verb—you know that because all of the words in the answer choices are verbs. Maybe you've heard the phrase "to hedge your bets." Let's use POE. Choice A: There is no direct opposite for ATTACK REPEATEDLY. Eliminate. Choice B: Does "not risk commitment (with) your bets" make sense? Sure. Keep this choice. C: Does "not seek advantage (with) your bets" make sense? Maybe. D: Does "gain pressure (with) your bets" make sense? Not really. Eliminate. E: Does "become uninterested (in) your bets" make sense? Probably not. So, we're down to two choices, and we have to decide if we think it's more likely that "to hedge your bets" means to not take risks, or to not seek advantage? Well, the answer is B— to hedge a bet is to counterbalance it with other transactions so as to limit risk.

MEDIUM MATH PRACTICE SET EXPLANATIONS

1. **B** We are given an equation with one variable, k. Solve it by adding k to each side, so the k on the right of the equal sign goes away. Now we have $3 + 2k = 5$. Subtract 3 from each side, and we end up with $2k = 2$. Divide both sides by 2, and we get $k = 1$. Now put that into the columns. Column A is 1, and Column B is 2. There's only that one value, so there's nothing else to do. Column B will always be larger, so B's the answer.

2. **A** Remember to write down A, B, C, D, and realize that there are only numbers here, no variables, so D is not a viable option. Lose it. Use the Bowtie to subtract the fractions. In Column A, multiply 6 and 8 for a denominator of 48. The top will be $42 (7 \times 6) - 8 (8 \times 1) = 34$. We get $\frac{34}{48}$. We can reduce this to $\frac{17}{24}$. In Column B, the denominator is 32, and the top will be $24 (8 \times 3) - 4 (4 \times 1) = 20$. That's $\frac{20}{32}$, which is reduced to $\frac{5}{8}$. Now Bowtie to compare the values for Columns A and B, $\frac{17}{24}$ and $\frac{5}{8}$. Eight times 17 is 136 for Column A, and 24 times 5 is 120 for Column B. The Column A number is larger, and so is Column A.

3. **A** Lots of numbers with decimals, all in a fraction. Yikes. We can't have decimals in a fraction, and the answer choices are all decimals, so we need to convert this to a decimal. In order to do this, we need first to multiply out the top: 0.2 (0.0002). The most important thing is to keep track of the number of decimal places. The product will be 4, with a total of five decimal places. So that's 0.00004 on top. Now we have:

$$\frac{0.00004}{0.002}$$

We still need to get rid of decimals. In order to turn this into a decimal with no fractions, we need to make the bottom a whole number. Do this by moving the decimal three places to the right on the bottom, and three places to the right on the top. It's all right to move the decimals as long as we do it the same number of places on the top and bottom. So now we have:

$$\frac{0.04}{2}$$

and can just do "long" division to get the decimal:

$$2 \overline{)0.04} \quad \frac{0.02}{}$$

So it's 0.02, A.

4. **D** The two arcs certainly look equal, don't they? But we are really not given information that tells us this is the case. While the instructions tell us that points are in the order shown, they don't tell us some things that would be useful in this problem. If we were told that PS and RU intersect at the center, then we'd know that the arcs were the same length. That point where they do intersect might be the center, or it might not, so the best answer here is D. In this case, we really don't have enough info.

5. **B** The picture says it's drawn to scale, which might be useful. Each mark on the number line is 1 unit, which means P is -4. If we are told that Q is to the right of the 0, and the distance between P and Q is 11, all you need to do is count it off, extending the line. Mark Q, and then just see what its coordinate is by counting again from 0. It will be 7. That's B. Just read carefully, but you always do that anyway, right? Or you could have said that Q is the result of adding 11 to P, or $-4 + 11$, which is also 7.

6. **C** This looks really frightening; we might have to do some serious multiplying here. Avoid it. Don't try and set up any proportions, either. It'll just make you nuts. Go with common sense and write it all down. In Column A, we want to know the number of minutes in y weeks. "Lots," is the answer, but let's get specific and plug in, say, $y = 2$. So, how many minutes in 2 weeks? That's 14 days. Each day is 24 hours, so that's really how many minutes in 14 times 24 hours. And if there are 60 minutes in each hour, then there are 14 times 24 times 60 minutes in those 2 weeks. Don't multiply this out. Leave it for now. So far, in Column A, we have (14) (24) (60).

Do the same thing in Column B. Use the same value for y. So how many hours in 120 weeks? Well, each of those weeks is 7 days, so they really want to know how many hours there are in 7 times 120 days. And there's 24 hours in a day, so it's 7 times 120 times 24 hours in those 120 weeks. So Column B is (120)(7)(24). Don't multiply that out either. We can compare these without multiplying. How? Remember that we can do anything we want to each side in a Quant Comp question, as long as we do it to both sides. So now the columns are really this:

Column A	Column B
(14) (24) (60)	(120) (7) (24)

There's a 24 on each side; cancel them out. What we're really doing here is dividing each side by 24, but who cares—as long as we do it on both sides, it's cool. Now:

Column A	Column B
(14) (60)	(120) (7)

And if we divide both sides by 60 now, Column A is just 14, and Column B is 7 times 2, which is also 14. They're equal. Dump A and B. We can do it again with a different y, and should, but guess what happens. Equal every time, so, it's C. Anytime you're getting what look like potentially big ugly numbers that will need to be multiplied out, see if you can deal with them by factoring or dividing both sides of a Quant Comp by the same number.

7. **B** We need to find the area of the triangle, but we only know the height. Never fear—it's a right triangle. Guess what will get us that third side: The Pythagorean theorem—that $a^2 + b^2 = c^2$ thing. The a side and the b side are the legs, and c is the hypotenuse. We have two of the three, and can solve for the third. So, $12^2 + b^2 = 15^2$, or $144 + b^2 = 225$. Subtract 144 from each side. Now it's $b^2 = 81$. So $b = 9$, and we now have both the base and height of the triangle. For area, we do $\frac{1}{2}$ times the base times the height. So $\frac{1}{2} \times 9 \times 12 = 54$. That's the area. And Column B is 90, which is larger. The answer is B.

8. **C** To find the fraction, just put the first amount over the second. The median income of nongraduates in Region X in 1975 was approximately \$7,500. The median income for graduates in Region X in the same year was \$10,000. So it's $\frac{7,500}{10,000}$, which will reduce to $\frac{3}{4}$. That's C.

9. **B** It's meant to be a case of factoring, but we don't even really need to do it that way. We could plug in for m, picking a value like $m = 2$. In that case $12m^2 - 8m - 64$ would equal $12(4) - 8(2) - 64$. That makes it $48 - 16 - 64$ which equals -32. Then plug $m = 2$ into each of the answer choices and see which gives you a value of -32:

A) $4(6 + 8)(2 - 2) = 0$. No.

B) $4(6 - 8)(2 + 2) = -8(4) = -32$. Okay!

C) $4(6 - 2)(10) = 160$. Nope.

D) $4(4) - 64 = -48$. Uh uh.

E) $8 - 64 = -56$. No.

Isn't Plugging In splendid? When you see algebra-ish questions with variables in the answer choices, plug in!

10. **A** There are two ways to find the area of triangle ABC. We can find it directly using the area of a triangle formula: Area = $\frac{1}{2} bh$. In this case, the base of the triangle, segment CB, is 1. The height of the triangle, segment AO, is 4 (remember, the "height" of a triangle must be perpendicular to the base—it's really the "altitude"). Yes, that's right, the height can be outside the triangle, as long as it is drawn from the base to the vertex (corner) of the angle opposite the base. So, now it's just $\frac{1}{2}$ times 1 times 4, which equals 2. Voila! An equally valid way to get the area would be to find the area of large triangle AOB: $\frac{1}{2}$ times 4 times $4 = 8$, and then subtract the area of smaller triangle AOC. Triangle AOC's area would be $\frac{1}{2}$ times 3 times $4 = 6$. Subtracting the area of the larger triangle from the smaller would leave us with 2. That's still A.

11. **A** To find the value of Column A, multiply Michael's rate of 60 mph by his time of three hours. That's 180 miles. From his home to his lake house (Column B), he travels for 2.5 hours at a speed of 65 miles. That will be a distance of 2.5 times 65, which equals 162.5 miles. So, Column A is larger. Notice that we didn't plug in; we were given the numbers, so we can't fool around with them, and so, we're done.

12. **B** Write A, B, C, D on that scratch paper! In order to compare x and 10, we need to solve for the value of x. Here we can cross-multiply to get $100x = 10$ (put the 100 over 1, if it helps, before you cross-multiply). Divide both sides by 100, and you get $x = \frac{1}{10}$. Column A is $\frac{1}{10}$ and Column B is 10, so Column B is bigger. We're done here; there's only one value for x, and we have to use it.

13. **A** Don't forget to look at the answers; they're part of the question. We've got a question that smells like algebra with numbers in the answer choices. What to do? Plug in the answer choices. Though we usually start with the middle value, we want 6 to the n power to be less than 10,000. So we're going to start with A, which will yield the smallest number $n = 5$. The last number that gives us a number under 10,000 is the answer. Yes, we have to do a bit of multiplication, but we can also do some approximating. Six times 6 is 36, and 6 times that is 216. That's 6 to the third power. But let's just call it 200 now. Six to the fourth power is 200 times 6 = 1,200. Six to the fifth power is 1,200 times 6, or 7,200. That's still under 10,000. But is 5 the greatest possible value of integer n? Try $n = 6$. That would be 7,200 times 6. More than 40,000. So A is the greatest integer value for n that makes this less than 10,000. Don't you love plugging in the answer choices?

14. **B** Did you recognize this? It's a quadratic equation, meaning that one of the terms is a variable that's been squared. This also means that there are <u>two</u> values of x. First, we need to arrange the equation so it equals 0, so we need to add 7 to each side. Now we have $x^2 + 8x + 7 = 0$. To find the values of x here, we now need to factor this, or unFOIL. it. So set up two sets of parentheses:

$$(\quad)\ (\quad)$$

Since the last sign in the expression is positive, both signs will be the same in each set of parentheses. And, since the other sign in the expression is positive, that means that each of the signs in the parentheses will be a plus sign. So now it's

$$(\ +\ )\ (\ +\ )$$

Each of the first terms needs to be x, because that's where the x squared comes from when we FOIL.

$$(\,x +\ )\ (\,x +\ )$$

So now we play with the factors of the last term, the 7, and using trial and error, see what will give us the original expression when we FOIL. Not a big problem here, because there's only one pair of factors for 7. So it will be

$$(\,x + 7\,)\ (\,x + 1\,) = 0$$

In order for this to equal 0, either the first set of parentheses or the second set of parentheses needs to equal 0. $x = -7$ is the value that will make the first equal 0, and $x = -1$ is the value that works for the second. So the solution is $x = -1$ or -7. Plug each of these values in and compare the columns. Column A can be -1, and if Column B is 0, then Column B is larger in this case—and if Column A is -7, Column B is still 0, and is still larger. So no matter what, Column B is still larger, which means B is the answer.

15. **B** X is a constant, and all that means is that it stands for a number—the *same number* no matter what the values of the other variables are. We can figure out the value of x with the first set of a and b that we're given. Put in $a = 3$ and $b = 5$, and we have $3x + 5 = 26$. Now we do a little solving. Subtract 5 from each side, and it's $3x = 21$. Divide both sides by 3, and we get $x = 7$. Always. No matter what a and b are later, x is *constantly* 7. Now, $a = 5$, and we want to know the value of b. We can put $a = 5$, and $x = 7$ into the original equation, and solve for b. That would be $5\,(7) + b = 26$, or $35 + b = 26$. Subtract 35 from both sides, and we get $b = -9$. And that's B.

16. **D** Watch out. This is nastier than it looks. Sometimes we can eyeball pictures, and get a fair idea of approximate lengths and angles. But unless our notions are backed up by other information given to us with the problem, that notion is spurious (hey—look it up). In this case, some things look equal, but the picture never TELLS us they're equal. Some of these angles must be certain measures, but not all of them. The angle on the lower right corner of the middle triangle must be 30. We know two other angles of that triangle, and they total 150 degrees, and all triangles have a total of 180 degrees, so there's 30 left for that angle. Okay. We also know that the angles adjacent to the 110 degree angle at the top of the middle triangle are each 70 degrees. Why? Because straight lines have a total of 180 degrees, and each of those angles plus the 110-degree angle form straight lines. And not that we need it, but the vertical angle on top of the 110-degree angle is also 110, because vertical angles are equal. That's everything we know exactly. We know that the two angles in the left triangle (the ones besides the 70 we just found) must add up to 110 degrees. That 110 can be broken up any way we like. We can say that angle a is 50 degrees, and the other is 60. The right-hand triangle works the same way. We know that the other two angles must equal 110, and we can break it down however we like. If we make angle b 50 degrees, Column A and Column B will be equal. But there is no reason angle b couldn't be 60 degrees, and the other angle in that triangle be 50. That would make the answer B. Since we just got two different answers depending on what we used for angle measures, the answer is D. Even though angles a and b look equal, they don't have to be.

17. **D** Draw yourself a picture, and be careful. If the tiles have a *perimeter* of 64, then they have sides of 16. Perimeter is the sum of the four sides, right? So we have tiles 16 inches on each side that we are using to cover a floor that's 64 by 128 inches. How many will we need along each side? On the 64-inch side, the width, four tiles will do it. On the 128-inch side we will fit eight tiles. So the width will be 4 tiles and the length 8 tiles. That makes 4 rows of eight tiles (or we can think of it as 8 rows of 4 tiles). Either way, that's a total of 32 tiles, D.

18. **A** A nice, classic plug-in Quant Comp. Write down A, B, C, D to use Process of Elimination. We're told that *a* is a positive number, while *ab* is less than 0. Pick some numbers that go along with this. Our *a* can be 3, and *b*, which looks like it needs to be negative in order for *ab* to be less than zero, can be –4. So now we evaluate the columns. Column A is 3 (–4 + 1) which equals –9. Column B is 3 (–4 – 1) which equals –15. For now Column A is larger. Remember that –9 is bigger than –15, since it's closer to 0. Anyway, we can eliminate B and C. Now, plug in again. Try something a little weirder this time. Maybe make *a* = 1, and *b* = –1. Now Column A is 1 (–1 + 1) which equals 0. And Column B is 1 (–1 – 1) which equals –2. Column A is still bigger, so the answer is A.

19. **B** If we are being asked how many of the paper clips were the 14¢ clips, why not plug in the answers, and see if they work out? Start in the middle with C. Say there were 30 14¢ clips. If there were 85 clips altogether, then 55 of them were the 16¢ clips. Will this give us the $13.10 total mentioned in the question? We'd have 30 clips times 14¢, which is $4.20, and 55 clips times 16¢, which is $8.80. That would total $13.00 exactly, which is not enough money. What do we do now? The office spent more money, and the number of clips has to stay at 85, so they must have bought more of the expensive ones. We want fewer 14¢ clips and more 16¢ ones. Eliminate C, D, and E and go to choice A or B. B seems a good choice to try next because C was only off by 10¢. Let's do it. If we have 25 14¢ clips, then we'll have 60 16¢ clips. That's $3.50 plus $9.60, which, that's right, equals $13.10. We are pleased to introduce B, the correct answer.

20. **D** Don't forget to write down A, B, C, D. We're being asked to compare *y* with 2. Pick a "normal" number for *y*. Hmm . . . how's 2? (–1) squared = 1, so that's okay. So Column A and Column B can be equal, so strike A and B, since neither column is always bigger. But we have to plug in for *y* again. Can we mess this up? We can't plug in 0 or a negative number because the problem says *y* has to be greater than 0. One doesn't work with the other requirement, that $(-1)^y = 1$, but another even number, like 4, does work. Column A is bigger now, so lose C. All that's left is D, a fitting end since we were able to get two different answers when we used different values for *y*.

1. **B** FLAG is not being used as a noun here; we can see this by looking at the answer choices, which are verbs. Okay, so we know flag is a verb here. We may have heard it used as in "to mark" something, or "flag down" a taxicab. But these meanings don't have clear opposites. Here FLAG means to become worn down, to lose energy. B is the best opposite of that.

2. **E** SYNOPSIS is something that's CONDENSED. Choice A? Digressions are wanderings, not repetitions. Eliminate it. B and C are not good relationships. D: ANTIQUITY isn't something FORGOTTEN, just old. Dump D. Hope it's E! PLAGIARISM is something that's PIRATED? Bingo.

3. **E** Which blank first? Maybe the second, but you can do whichever you feel more comfortable with. For the second blank, the phrase "from one discipline to enhance another" is a helpful clue. That's what will happen in the second part of the sentence. "Words from the first may" be *used to enhance* the second? Look for something like "used to enhance." It doesn't matter that it's not just one word, or more words than there are in the answer choices. We just want the meaning to be similar. So A is out, based on this second blank. B isn't much good either. C: "revitalized by" isn't at all bad; this is something like used to enhance. D: "supplanted by" isn't terrible either; it would be something like replace. And E: "employed by" would be a lot like used. So we still have C, D, and E going into the other blank. How about something like "possibility" for the first blank? C: "etiquette"? Nonsense. D: "pace" is out. That leaves E: "validity," which isn't at all bad. Sometimes we need to settle for the best of a so-so bunch.

4. **D** CONSUMMATE is used as more than one part of speech. Here it's used as a verb. You may not know exactly what it means, but there's a phrase that you've probably heard that uses it: to consummate a marriage. What does that mean? Really, to make it official, partners must engage in traditional wedding night/honeymoon activity. The opposite of this is not to not have sex, but rather to declare not official, to cancel, declare null and void. And whatever the answer is, it should be something that can be done to a marriage. A: REFUSE? Well, you could do this to a marriage, but it doesn't really sound great, and there are four more answers to look at. B: UNDERMINE? One could certainly do this to a marriage, and it has a negative connotation, whereas if anything, the stem is positive. So, not bad. C: SATIATE. Well. We'll just skip the jokes, but somebody might make the association. Anyway, it can't really be done to a marriage, and it's not negative. D: ABROGATE is the answer choice that we're least likely to know, which makes it immediately suspect. We can't get rid of it if we don't know the word. E: SUSPECT is very weird with marriage, and what's the clear opposite of suspect, to "not suspect"? So we have A, B, and D. Learn that vocab. We can take a shot at this point, but it is D—ABROGATE—that is the correct opposite. It means to void, cancel, declare null and void.

5. **E** If you know the stem words, a good sentence is: ADMONISH is to provide COUNSEL. A: MOLLIFY is to provide INTENSITY? No, it's to lessen it. B: totally non-related. C: ENERVATE is to provide VITALITY? No, it's to deprive of it. So lose it. D: is not related. E: REMUNERATE is to provide PAYMENT? Yes, indeed. And if you don't know most of these words, good counsel would be to study the vocabulary list!

6-9   This is a big one, huh? What's it about? Basically, how Stupp advanced polymer chemistry by inventing polymer sheets (AKA gigamolecules). Don't worry if you don't know anything about science—you're not supposed to! Just remember—Reading Comp is not really about comprehension. It's a treasure hunt.

6. **C**   It's a main idea question, so let's keep in mind our little summary, and go to the answers. A: This is specific to the fifth paragraph, so it's not the whole purpose of the passage. Eliminate. B: Well—gigamolecules are two-dimensional. Eliminate. C: That's a nice paraphrase of our main idea. By inventing polymer sheets (gigamolecules), Stupp has advanced polymer chemistry big time. D: Too specific. The answer should mention something about how gigamolecules are made. E: The answer should mention the fact that he advanced polymer chemistry. Eliminate.

7. **B**   Go back to the passage—the answer is in the passage. The fourth paragraph is where the actual synthesis is discussed. A: This may be true, but we don't know that it gave scientists any trouble. Eliminate. B: Good. Line 49 told us that heating the layers was ". . . one of Stupp's insights." This implies that others before him might not have known how to bond the layers. Keep it. C: That may be true, but we don't know that it gave scientists any trouble in terms of bonding. Eliminate. D: We don't know this, because it is not IN the passage. Same with E. B works best, and it's in the passage.

8. **B**   Check each Roman numeral separately. Once we determine one is right or wrong, we can go directly to the answers and eliminate some answers. Roman numeral I: It's in the passage (on line 18—"selective membranes"), so that eliminates any choice that doesn't contain Roman numeral I. So, eliminate D. Roman numeral II: It's found on lines 63-64 ("substances could be wrapped up inside a polymer..."), so let's get rid of any choice that doesn't contain Roman numeral II—that's choices A and C. Roman numeral III: It's never mentioned in the passage, so we can eliminate any choice that contains Roman numeral III—that's C (already gone), D (already gone), and E. The only choice left is B.

9. **D**   To answer this general question, just think to yourself, "Polymer chemistry...who would care?" And stay within the scope of the passage (just like we do on Arguments). A: Is funding an issue in the passage? Nope. Eliminate. B: Too specific. The passage is really more about polymer chemistry. C: But what about polymers? Eliminate. D: Seems logical. The only people who would really get the most out of reading this passage are those who are scientifically literate. E: Is this a how-to passage? Not really. It would have to be even more detailed than it already is. Eliminate. The best answer is D.

10. **E** Here's a word you might remember from high school English classes. HYPERBOLE means exaggeration. The opposite of that would be "not exaggerating," or "understating." And whaddya know—there's choice E—UNDERSTATEMENT. Even if we didn't remember the meaning of HYPERBOLE, we can eliminate at least a couple of answers. A and D have no clear opposites. What the heck is the opposite of an employee? Don't forget that elimination is just as good a way to get close to the correct answer as is actually knowing the word. Another thing we might have made use of here is the prefix "hyper," which suggests a lot of something, or too much of it. The opposite should then be something that is a little of something— like UNDERSTATEMENT.

11. **C** There's an excellent clue for the first blank, which describes what kind of practice midwifery is. We're told it's "something that women retained control over for themselves." This is in the sentence to tell us to put something very much like it in the first blank. Do any of the first words mean anything like "something . . . retained control over themselves"? Choice A has "a personal"—not bad. B: "a controversial" is not very good. C: "an autonomous" is excellent. "A communal"—choice D, isn't awful. But E: "a dangerous" is. So we have A, C, and D. Next blank. The "independent role of the midwife. . . is a ____ domination by institutional medicine." An exception to? Choice A says "reaction of," but this would be a "reaction of domination," which doesn't make much sense. We would prefer something like reaction against, which this isn't, so lose it. On to C. "Liberation from" is a lot like exception to. We like it. Be sure to look at D, though. "Celebration of"? Don't think so. So C it is, with its lovely definition of autonomous as retaining control over something for themselves.

12. **C** Once again Process of Elimination will save the day. EPIDEMIOLOGY is the study of DISEASE. How's A? That's right, it stinks. B? If you think PALEONTOLOGY is the study of BEHAVIOR, go see *Jurassic Park*. C: EPISTEMOLOGY is the study of KNOWLEDGE. Either we know that it is, or we don't know the word. Either way, it's a keeper. D: ICHTHYOLOGY is the study of RELIGION? Well, we might not know what ICHTHYOLOGY is, but we'd likely know that it wasn't the study of religion; that would probably be a word we were more familiar with. If you're not sure, keep it. E: NUMEROLOGY is the study of FORMULAS? Yikes. It's like horoscopes; we can find it on the back page of *Cosmopolitan* magazine. C is the best answer. Incidentally, ICHTHYOLOGY is the study of fish. Ich!

13. **C** Here the two parts of the sentence are continuous, because of the "because" acting as a trigger. It's probably easier to deal with the first blank first. The "mistaken notions" in the first part of the sentence are similar to the "unexamined hypotheses" and "unprepared actions" of the second part. And modernity and "breaking free . . . of convention" also seem to be linked. So, if that's what's going on when we are playing around with modernity, it is probably full of, connected to, or leading to those mistaken notions. Look for something like that in the first words. Choices A, B, and E are all very much not like "connected to." Lose them. C's "fraught with" is just a fancy schmancy way of saying full of, and "disposed of,"—choice D—just really isn't clearly like or different from it. Let's let the other blank do the work for us. When breaking those fetters, we are probably using or doing something positive with those unexamined hypotheses. We should be suspicious of D, since it's negative. C is the best answer, and "susceptible" is much closer to using or doing or open to using.

14. **A** Here's another stem word that we're unlikely to know. And it doesn't look particularly positive or negative. In a case such as this, make opposites for the answer choices. This is unlikely to shake loose a recollection of the meaning of the word PUISSANCE, but it will help us spot answer choices that don't have clear opposites. Choice A—IMPOTENCE—has got an opposite—potency. B's opposite would be wealth, C's inflexibility, D's clumsiness, and E's lack of vigor, or no strength. They all have decent opposites, so we'll just pick one. It's nice to know that puissance means power, as opposed to say, A—impotence. Eat those vocab words for breakfast, but on the test, if stumped, take your best shot, and move on.

15. **C** The stem sentence is OFFICIOUS is overly OBLIGING. Choice A is not a good relationship, and in B, somebody MALEVOLENT isn't necessarily CORRUPT, much less overly corrupt. So they're out. C: EFFUSIVE is overly DEMONSTRATIVE? It certainly is! How about D? PLACID is overly MERCIFUL is weak, and not related. E: RADICAL is overly CAUTIOUS? No way. So C looks best. If you couldn't make a sentence for the stem, you still should have been able to eliminate at least A and D as bad relationships, and then work backward with the other choices you knew the words in.

16. **E** Okay, we've got two kinds of issues that we know are different from each other. We know they are different because the sentence emphasizes that they must be judged separately. Which issues do we know more about? The ones in the second blank are "hotly debated one moment and forgotten the next." That's lovely. We want a word that sums that up. Exercise your vocabulary if possible. Something like transitory, fleeting, ephemeral, temporary. Looking at the second words in the answer choices, we see that A, B, and C are way off the mark. D and E look like "temporary." And now for the first blank. We know the second bunch of issues are the temporary ones, so the first must be the real or permanent ones. D's "theoretical" is too fuzzy, but E's "perpetual" is a lot like permanent. We'll go with E.

17. **A** EFFERVESCENT means bubbly, bouncy, energetic. We want the opposite of that: not bubbly, not bouncy, not energetic. How about something like "blah"? Sure, it's not a pretty vocab word, but it doesn't have to be; let's see what happens. A: VAPID is like not having energy, not bouncy, kind of "blah." We'll keep it. B: INTERCEPTED is not like "blah" at all. Lose it. C: DISPERSED isn't like "blah," and is in fact closer to being a synonym for our stem than an antonym. Eliminate it. D: DISAFFECTED is probably the hardest word among the answer choices. If you don't know it, you can't eliminate it. Choice E, DISCONCERTED, means confused. Is this anything like "blah"? Not really, so dump it. So now we have two left, A and D. If you know what DISAFFECTED means (unfriendly, antagonistic), then you already know the answer is A. But if you didn't, at least you got it down to two choices on a hard antonym. Learn that vocab!

18. **C** Okay, let's assume we don't know what APOSTATE means, and go to the answers. Choice A: Is there a good relationship between APOSTLE and LEADER? Maybe. Do you know the dictionary definition of "apostle?" If not, you'd have to leave it. An apostle is one who pioneers an important reform movement, cause, or belief. Related to leader? Well, you could say that an apostle is a leader, but is an APOSTATE a FAITH? No, that sounds wrong. Let's eliminate this. B: How about ALTRUIST and LITERATURE? No. An altruist is a generous or selfless person. This has nothing to do with literature. Eliminate. C: A DEFECTOR is someone who gives up an ALLEGIANCE, such as to a country. Could an APOSTATE give up FAITH? A possibility. Keep it. D: POTENTATE and RELIGION? Are you sure you know the definition of potentate? If not, you can't eliminate this choice. But a potentate is one who has the power and position to rule over others, so the word is not related to religion. E: Is there a clear and necessary relationship between PATRIOT and PRINCIPLE? Be careful. A patriot might have principles, but there is nothing clear or necessary about the relationship between these two words. Eliminate. The more vocab you know, the less you'll be guessing. An APOSTATE is one who gives up his FAITH, so the answer is C.

19. **D** The word for the first blank will be something relatively positive, since the judge is "free to use her discretion" to do it. Let's take that to the answers and check the first words in the answer choice pairs. This eliminates C, since "exacerbate" means to make worse. The word for the second blank will be something negative, since the word "anachronistic," which means "out of date," is the clue. That eliminates A, B, and E—all of these words are either positive or neutral. We're left with D.

20. **D** Did you "sort of know" that "perfidy" is a negative word? Since "perfidy" is negative, eliminate negative choices, like choice A, and then guess. PERFIDY means deliberate breach of faith, or treachery. The opposite of treachery is loyalty—that's D.

HARD MATH PRACTICE SET EXPLANATIONS

1. **A** Write down A, B, C, D. This is a great place to plug in and avoid messy algebra. Instead of multiplying icky stuff like $(n + 3)$ and $(n + 3)$, let's just pick some values for n. Say $n = 5$. Okay, that makes the legs of Triangle A each 8, and the legs of Triangle B 7 and 9. The area of Triangle A is $\frac{1}{2}$ times 8 times 8, and the area of Triangle B is $\frac{1}{2}$ times 7 times 9. We're just comparing the values for the two columns (remember this is called Quantitative *Comparison*, not calculation). So we can disregard the $\frac{1}{2}$ on both sides. Column A is 64 and Column B is 63—this time. Column B isn't always bigger, so eliminate B, and they're not always equal, so eliminate C. We have two choices left, so we plug in again. Try something weird this time, like 0, 1, or –1. Let's use –1 for n. Now the legs of Triangle A are each 2, and the legs of triangle B are 1 and 3. Column A is $\frac{1}{2}$ times 2 times 2, and Column B is $\frac{1}{2}$ times 1 times 3. Ignoring the $\frac{1}{2}$ on both sides gives us 4 for Column A and 3 for Column B. Column A is still bigger, so A is the answer.

2. **C** Write down A, B, C, D on your scratch paper, and start factoring! We want to factor out the biggest "piece" we can from both columns—that's 56^{14}. Then eliminate it, since it's in both columns. What we are really comparing now is 1/2 (56) (that's Column A) and 28 (that's Column B). Since one half of 56 is, indeed, 28, we have 28 in both columns, so our answer is C.

3. **B** Let's start with the easier calculations first: The mode (h) is 12, because that's the only number in the set that shows up more than once. Put the numbers in order and you'll see that 12 is also the median (g). So, we can go right to the answers and eliminate any answer choice that does NOT say "$g = h$." That eliminates choices A, C, and D. The range is the largest number in the set (15) minus the smallest number in the set (5), so $j = 10$. Now we can eliminate any of the remaining choices that have j greater than $g = h$ (because obviously 10 is not greater than 12!). That eliminates E, and we're left with B, without even having to calculate the mean!

4. **C** Write down A, B, C, D and don't forget PEMDAS! In Column A, we take care of the parentheses first, and add $3\sqrt{7}$ and $4\sqrt{7}$ to get $7\sqrt{7}$. Next, we have to square $7\sqrt{7}$: that's 7 squared, which is 49, times $\sqrt{7}$ squared, which is 7. 49 times 7 equals 343. Hey, that's what we have in Column B! The answer is C.

5. **E** We are being asked which of the fractions in the answer choices WILL NOT be an integer if k is a multiple of 12 but not a multiple of 9. This CANNOT question is a good place to remember some of what we learned on "Sesame Street": One of these things is not like the others. See which four are alike, and the answer will be the one that's different.

So, we'd better come up with some ks to plug in on this handsome question with variables in the choices. Twelve and 24 are multiples of 12 that are not multiples of 9. But we can't use 36, since that is a multiple of 9, even though it's the next multiple of 12. Let's play with 12 and 24 and see where we are. If we use $k = 12$, then A equals 4. That's an integer. So A is okay. If we use 12 in B, then we get 3, so that's an integer too. We should put checks next to A and B so we know that whatever they are, they're the same as each other (either both work or both don't). When we try 12 in C it doesn't work (for now, don't put a check next to it). But that doesn't mean it doesn't ever work. We'll come back to it. Put $k = 12$ into D and we get 1, definitely an integer (check it off). Try $k = 12$ in E and we get junk (don't check it off). So, we have C and E as holdouts. Can we come up with a multiple of 12 that's not a multiple of 9 that will make one of those choices an integer? Let's try some more possible k values. Forty-eight and 60 are okay; 72 is not. Plug $k = 60$ into C, and we get 6, an integer. Check off C. We're left with E. And guess what? We will never find an acceptable value for k that will be divisible by 36. That's why E is the odd man out, and thus the answer.

6. **A** This question is a bit of work. We're asked how many of the categories of workers had a 30% or higher increase from 1975 to 1980. One way to do this would be to start with the 1975 figures, add 30% to each, and see how that compares with the 1980 figures. For Region X nongrads, 1975 was $7,500. Find 30% of this using translation, then add it to the 1975 amount. That would be 30% higher. Is the 1980 amount that or larger? $\frac{30}{100}$ times 7,500 = 2,250. Added to the original, that would be 9,750. And the 8,500 in 1980 is less than that. So that's one of the four groups that DIDN'T have a 30% increase. Repeat for Region X grads. They went from $10,000 to $12,800. Thirty percent of the $10,000 would be $3,000, adding that on gives us $13,000, but the 1980 amount falls short of this by about $200. Oh well, no 30% increase here. For Region Y nongrads, 1975 was $7,800. Thirty percent of that would be $2,340. Added to the $7,800, that would give $10,140. But 1980 was only about $9,300. So, no 30% increase here either. Last chance is for Region Y grads. They made about $13,200 in 1975; an increase of 30% would be $3,960, yielding a total of $17,160. But they were really only making $16,100 in 1980. So, none of the groups saw an increase of 30% or more between 1975 and 1980. Too bad for them, but that's A.

7. **A** Don't be chumped into messing around with FOIL and factoring here. Best way to do this is to plug in. Pick a value for a, plug it into the original expression, and see which of the choices is equal to the value of the original $(3a - 5)(a + 6)$.

So let's say $a = 2$. Then $(3a - 5)(a + 6)$ is $(6 - 5)(2 + 6)$ which equals 8. Let's see which of the other answers gives us 8 when we plug in $a = 2$. Roman numeral I is $(6 + 5)(2 - 6)$, which is –44. Nope. We can get rid of every answer choice that contains Roman numeral I, which includes C and E. Roman numeral II gives us $-5(8) + 6(8)$ which equals 8. Interesting. We like II. Ditch anything that doesn't have II in it, like B. So what's up with III, then? It gives us $3(4) - 30$, which is –18. So III stinks. Only II worked, so A is the answer.

8. **C** Draw the floor, a rectangle $9\frac{1}{2}$ feet by 12 feet. The tiles are $1\frac{1}{2}$ by 2 INCHES. How many fit along the sides of the rectangle? Suppose we line the $1\frac{1}{2}$ inch sides along the side of the floor that will be 9 feet. In one foot, there will be 8 tiles, because $1\frac{1}{2}$ inches times 8 = 12 inches. So, on that side of the floor, there will be 8 times $9\frac{1}{2}$ tiles. Leave it that way; don't multiply it out. If you wanted to multiply it, looking at the ugly numbers in Column B should discourage you. Multiplication is not what this test is about. Okay, back to the floor. The 2-inch sides will be along the side of the floor that will be 12 feet long. There will be 6 tiles in each foot, so 12 times 6 tiles along that side. In order to find the number of tiles in the whole floor, we need to multiply the number in the length times the number in the width. This will be 8 times $9\frac{1}{2}$ times 12 times 6. Again, don't multiply it all out. We can knock the same numbers out of both sides of the question. Here's what we have:

Column A	Column B
$(8)(9\frac{1}{2})(12)(6)$	$(6)(48)(19)$

We can certainly divide 6 out of each side, knocking that out. So now we have:

Column A	Column B
$(8)(12)(9\frac{1}{2})$	$(48)(19)$

We can divide each side by 12 now, getting rid of a 12 on the left, and changing the 48 on the right to a 4. So now there's:

Column A	Column B
$(8)(9\frac{1}{2})$	$(4)(19)$

We can also divide both sides by 4 again:

$(2)(9\frac{1}{2})$	19

Now it's not so annoying to actually do the multiplication, and lo and behold, we find that Column A and B are equal. So C it is. Careful canceling sure beats multiplying all that junk out, doesn't it?

9. **D** This question is asking how many small groups can be drawn from a larger group, and order doesn't matter. That's a combination, and the formula is $\frac{n!}{r!(n-r)!}$. In this case, n, which is the total number in the group we're drawing from, is 10, and r, the number in the group we're selecting, is 4. So, let's put those numbers into the formula: $\frac{10!}{4!(10-4)!}$. That can be rewritten as:

$$\frac{10 \cdot 9 \cdot 8 \cdot 7 \cdot 6 \cdot 5 \cdot 4 \cdot 3 \cdot 2 \cdot 1}{4 \cdot 3 \cdot 2 \cdot 1 \cdot 6 \cdot 5 \cdot 4 \cdot 3 \cdot 2 \cdot 1}.$$

Don't start calculating until you reduce! We're left with $\frac{10 \cdot 9 \cdot 8 \cdot 7}{4 \cdot 3 \cdot 2 \cdot 1}$, which can be reduced further: $5 \times 3 \times 2 \times 7$, which equals 210. That's D.

10. **C** We're not going to be able to get away without doing some arithmetic here. We need to find out what k is. Just do it carefully, remembering PEMDAS. So, parentheses and exponents first: 3 to the third power is 27. Now multiply: 9 times 27 = 243. That plus 4 = 247. Eek. But that's k. Now we need to find its factors, since that's what they're talking about in Column A. Trial and error is the way to go here. 247 is not divisible by 2, or any even number, for that matter. Anyway, we need prime factors. Try 3—no good. Doesn't end with 5 or 0, so not 5 either. Keep going. Seven's no good, and 9 isn't prime so there's no need to even try it. Eleven is useless. Thirteen is the first thing we find that goes in. In fact, 247 is 13 times 19. Those are the prime factors. Pretty hideous ones, too. Okay: Column A asks us for the average of the prime factors of k. Add 13 and 19—that's 32. Now divide by 2; we get 16. It's C. Just bite the bullet here, and take the time to get it right.

11. **B** It's FOIL time in Column A! We've got $(6 + \sqrt{10})(6 - \sqrt{10})$, which is (6×6) $-(6\sqrt{10}) + (6\sqrt{10}) - (10)$. The middle terms cancel each other out, and we get $36 - 10$, which is 26. Column B is 27, so B is the answer.

12. **C** Write down A, B, C, D! We've got variables, so Plugging In is the way to go here. First, pick a set of easy numbers for a and b. The values $a = 5$ and $b = 3$ work with the information we're given. Now evaluate Column A. a^2 is 25, $-2ab$ is $(-2)(5)(3)$ which equals -30, and $b^2 = 9$. So $25 - 30 + 9 = 4$. That's Column A. Column B is $2(5) - 2(3) = 10 - 6 = 4$. Column B is also 4. They're equal this time, so cross out A and B. But you have to make sure to plug in at least twice. Let's pick a wackier set of values for a and b. We can make $a = 0$ and $b = -2$. Column A is $0^2 - 2(0)(-2)$, which is 0, plus $(-2)^2$, which is four. Column B is $2(0) - 2(-2)$, or $0 - (-4)$, which is also 4. They're equal again. It's beginning to look a lot like C.

13. **E** We are being asked for the answer that CANNOT be the sum of the surface areas of two sides of the solid. How do we find surface area? Surface area is the areas of the sides of the box added together. But that's not necessary to do here. We just want to know which of the answers can be two sides added together. We will have two sides that will have dimensions 5 by 6, two sides with dimensions 6 by 7, and two sides with dimensions 5 by 7. So, we have two sides of area 30, two that are area 35, and two that are 42. Now let's take each of the answers and see if we can make them by adding two of the same or different sized sides. Sixty, or Choice A can be made with $30 + 30$. B can be made with $35 + 35$. C can be made with $42 + 35$. D can be made with $42 + 42$. But E CANNOT be made with two sides. The largest number we can get that is a sum of two sides is 84. So E is the bad seed and, therefore, the answer.

14. **B** Remember, average is equal to total divided by number, so always think TOTAL. First, we're told that Tommy has an 84 average after 8 tests. To get his total, multiply the average, 84, by the number, 8. We get 672. Then we're told if one test score is taken away (they tell us it's the most recent just to be obnoxious; we actually don't care which one it is!), Tommy's average is an 85. Let's figure out his new total: Multiply his new average, 85, by his new number, which is 7 (8 minus the score that was dropped). That's 595. The difference between his old total, 672, and his new total, 595, will be the score that was dropped (his "most recent test score," or Column A). So, 672 minus 595 is 77. Column A is 77, Column B is 83, and the answer is B.

15. **C** We're given two of the three dimensions of the box, and asked about the third. We also know the surface area of the box. We find surface area by finding the areas of the six sides of the box (top, bottom, left side, right side, front, and back) and adding them together. Here, we really only know the area of the front and back, which are each 5 times $5 = 25$ square feet. The whole box has a surface area of 190, so the front and the back account for a total of 50 of that 190. That leaves another 140. Each of the long sides of the box—the top, bottom, left, and right sides—has dimensions of 5 times ℓ. And four of these must equal the 140 square feet we have left. If we take the 140 and divide it by the four equal sides, we find that each has an area of 35. We know one dimension of each of those sides is 5. In order to get area to equal 35, the value of ℓ must be 7. So it's C, since Column A and Column B will both be 7. Phew!

16. **C** If the median (middle number) of these five numbers is 16, and none of the other numbers can be 16 (because they're "distinct"), and the numbers can't be negative, we have to plug in numbers that will make the sum of the five numbers the smallest. The smallest that the two numbers less than 16 could be is 1 and 2. The smallest that the two numbers larger than 16 could be is 17 and 18. Now we add: $1 + 2 + 16 + 17 + 18 = 54$. That's C.

17. **C** There's no reason to visualize this problem in your head. Make this hard problem easy by simply drawing a quick sketch of a cube on your scratch paper. Now take a look—each face of a cube shares an edge with four other faces. The value of Column A, therefore, is 4. And how about Column B? A square clearly has 4 sides. The values of the two columns are the same. The answer is C.

18. **E** Notice that this question is not asking for the value of m, n, or p. These are simultaneous equations, so let's stack them and see what happens. Might as well try adding first—if it doesn't give us anything we can use, we'll just try subtracting:

$$\begin{array}{rl} m+n & =24 \\ \underline{m-n+p} & \underline{=15} \\ 2m\quad +p & =39 \end{array}$$

So, the answer is C, right? Wrong. The question is asking for $4m + 2p$, not $2m + p$. If $2m + p = 39$, then what does $4m + 2p$ equal? Twice as much, or 78. That's E.

19. **D** What, no diagram? Just draw one yourself. But here's a way to make this tricky question easier: A square is a type of rectangle (just a rectangle with four equal sides), so just draw a square with perimeter 16 and one with perimeter 20. Now finding the diagonals is easy—think Pythagorean Theorem. In Column A, each side of the square is 4, so the diagonal is $4\sqrt{2}$. In Column B, each side of the square is 5, so the diagonal is $5\sqrt{2}$. So far the answer is B, and we can eliminate choices A and C. Now, you know we're not done yet—we always have to plug in at least twice on Quant Comps. Let's try to disprove our answer by making the diagonal of the rectangle in Column A bigger. Think of "weird" numbers for the sides of the rectangle. How about sides of 1 and 7? What's the diagonal of this rectangle? It's the square root of 50, which equals $5\sqrt{2}$! That proves that B is wrong, too, so the answer must be D.

20. **A** Let's deal with Column B first, because it's easier. We can add whatever's under the radical sign and get $\sqrt{64}$, which is 8. Now, to Column A. We can't add these, but remember: On Quant Comps, it's not what it *is*, but which is *bigger*, so let's approximate using perfect squares. The square root of 13 is somewhere between the square root of 9 (which is 3), and the square root of 16 (which is 4). Let's call it 3-ish. The square root of 51 is somewhere between the square root of 49 (which is 7), and the square root of 64 (which is 8). Let's call it 7-ish. Now, let's add: 3-ish + 7-ish = 10-ish. Which is bigger, 10-ish or 8? 10-ish, so the answer is A.

22

Analytical Writing Practice Sets and Sample Essays

ANALYTICAL WRITING PRACTICE

Now it's time to practice writing the essays for the Analytical Writing section. Before you begin, you may want to briefly review the templates you created and the steps involved in preparing your outline and then writing the essay. Once you've done that, you're ready to get started.

Make sure you have enough uninterrupted time. You'll need 45 minutes to write an Analysis of the Issue essay and 30 minutes to write an Analysis of the Argument essay. Unplug the phone, and tell your roommates or family not to bother you until you're done writing the essay. Remove any other distractions, like the TV or radio.

Turn on your computer and start a word processing program. You may want to use a very rudimentary one (like Notepad) because it will be closest in feel to the program you'll use during the real test. Do not use a program that automatically underlines words you've spelled wrong. You need to practice proofreading your own work before you're done writing.

Get out several sheets of blank paper and a pencil, for brainstorming. Set a timer for the correct amount of time, and then look at the practice question and begin. When you're done writing the essays, take a break and then flip to the back of this chapter to assess your essay and see a sample essay written on the question topic.

We're giving you the choice between two Issue topics (like you'll see on the GRE). Later, be sure to practice writing an essay for the topic you didn't choose the first time. We've also numbered the essay topics, even though they won't be numbered on the GRE, so you can match them up with the sample essays we've provided.

PRACTICE ESSAY QUESTIONS

Present your perspective on the issue below, using relevant reasons and/or examples to support your views.

1. If I cannot have freedom, I'd rather not be alive.

OR

2. Some parenting experts feel that parents should be completely honest with their children, even when this would force them to admit to behaviors they don't wish their children to engage in. They cite, in particular, the issues of experimentation with drugs and sexual activity.

Discuss how well reasoned you find this argument.

3. The university requirement committee recently changed the foreign language requirements for all undergraduates, requiring them to take a full two-year course of a primary language and a one-year course in another language. The head of the committee released the following statement:

"We are convinced that this change will increase the number of students who receive full-time job offers before graduation day. This language requirement is now stricter than that of our competitor university across town, so companies will hire our graduates over theirs, because our graduates are clearly harder workers. The current economy favors multinational corporations, who will be desperate to hire students who have studied multiple foreign languages. In addition, many studies show a correlation between strong language skills and strong mathematical skills, so high-tech companies will also be eager to hire our students."

Present your perspective on the issue below, using relevant reasons and/or examples to support your views.

4. An author should be judged on the complete body of his or her work, rather than on one outstanding example.

OR

5. Every cloud has a silver lining.

Discuss how well reasoned you find this argument.

6. A leading doctor said:

"High-tech surgeries should be funded by public tax dollars instead of by patients or insurance companies. All high-tech surgeries are by some measure experimental, even after they become standard, so performing these surgeries always contributes to the body of medical knowledge. The ability to perform these surgeries benefits everyone, since any person could need a high-tech surgery in the future. And investing in high-tech surgeries would be a much better use of tax dollars than paying for many current so-called public health programs, like welfare and food stamps."

Present your perspective on the issue below, using relevant reasons and/or examples to support your views.

7. The value of art lies exclusively in the finished work.

OR

8. Any revolutionary political movement is bound to lose momentum as soon as the general population recognizes its views as being valid.

Discuss how well reasoned you find this argument.

9. A large corporation recently changed its policy on parental leave upon the birth or adoption of a child to give as little time off as the law allows. The head of Human Resources released the following statement:

"We believe that by discouraging employees from taking excessive time off to care for the children they themselves choose to have, we will make our staff both happier and more productive. Without the burden of having to choose how much time to take off, they will have an easier time balancing work and home responsibilities. In addition, the more time they spend at work, the more loyalty they will feel toward the corporation. Studies show that employees who spend more time at work advance more rapidly within the company structure, so our new policy will create a company of ultra-loyal, ultra-achieving employees."

Present your perspective on the issue below, using relevant reasons and/or examples to support your views.

10. Some economists argue that smoking should be made illegal, since it is not merely a matter of public health, but also of national wealth, because smoking-related illnesses and deaths cost billions of dollars annually.

OR

11. Many analysts argue that population growth is causing most of the Earth's major problems. They recommend that nations impose mandatory restrictions on the number of children that their citizens can have.

Discuss how well reasoned you find this argument.

12. A new testing procedure would reduce the number of flawed parts that make it to the market by catching these parts before they are packaged and shipped to retailers. Proponents of this new procedure argue that it should be instituted in all of ABC Company's factories because it will increase the efficiency, and therefore reduce the costs, of manufacturing these parts. They argue further that reducing the costs would allow them ultimately to manufacture many more parts, and to increase ABC Company's profits exponentially.

SCORING GUIDE

Use the following lists of questions to help you score your essays. Be critical but not overly picky. Remember that the official essay readers don't have very much time to read your essay, so concentrate on the larger issues.

ANALYSIS OF AN ISSUE (1, 2, 4, 5, 7, 8, 10, 11)

Set a timer for two minutes. Read the essay carefully but quickly, so that you do not exceed the two minutes on the timer.

Now ask yourself the following questions about the essay:

1. Overall, did it make sense?
2. Did you address the topic directly?
3. Did you address the topic thoroughly?
4. Did the introduction paragraph repeat the issue to establish the topic of the essay?
5. Did the first paragraph make your position on the topic obvious?
6. Did you have three strong paragraphs supporting your position?
7. Did your examples make sense?
8. Did you flesh out the examples?
9. Did the examples apply directly to the topic?
10. Did the essay have a strong conclusion paragraph?
11. Was the essay well-organized?
12. Did you use language that made the organization of the essay obvious?
13. Did you use correct grammar, spelling, and language, for the most part?
14. Was the essay of an appropriate length?

If you could answer "yes" to all or almost all of those questions, congratulations! Your essay would receive a score in the 5-6 range. If you continue to practice and write an essay of similar quality on the Analysis of an Issue essay of the real test, you should score very well.

If you answered "yes" to fewer than 12 of the questions, you have room for improvement. Fortunately, you also know which areas you need to work on as you continue to practice.

If you answered "yes" to fewer than 5 of the questions, your essay would not score very well on a real GRE. An essay of this quality would not help you in the admissions process and could raise some red flags in the minds of the admissions people. You need to continue to practice, focusing on the areas of weakness that you discovered during this scoring process.

ANALYSIS OF AN ARGUMENT (3, 6, 9, 12)

Set a timer for two minutes. Read the essay carefully but quickly, so that you do not exceed the two minutes on the timer.

Now ask yourself the following questions about the essay:

1. Overall, did it make sense?
2. Did you address the argument directly?
3. Did you critique the argument thoroughly?
4. Did the introduction paragraph repeat the argument to establish the topic of the essay?
5. Did you avoid injecting your opinion into the essay?
6. Did you have three strong paragraphs critiquing the arguments?
7. Did your critiques make sense?
8. Did you flesh out your points to make the weaknesses of the argument explicit?
9. Did the examples apply directly to the topic?
10. Did the essay have a strong conclusion paragraph?
11. Was the essay well-organized?
12. Did you use language that made the organization of the essay obvious?
13. Did you use correct grammar, spelling, and language, for the most part?
14. Was the essay an appropriate length?

If you could answer "yes" to all or almost all of those questions, congratulations! Your essay would receive a score in the 5-6 range. If you continue to practice and write an essay of similar quality on the Analysis of an Argument essay of the real test, you should score very well.

If you answered "yes" to fewer than 12 of the questions, you have room for improvement. Fortunately, you also know which areas to work on as you continue to practice.

If you answered "yes" to fewer than 5 of the questions, your essay would not score very well on a real GRE. An essay of this quality would not help you in the admissions process and could raise some red flags in the minds of the admissions people. You need to continue to practice, focusing on the areas of weakness that you discovered during this scoring process.

SAMPLE ESSAYS

These essays are not perfect. They are realistic, flawed essays that would still receive high scores on the GRE because they answer the question completely, are organized, make good use of the English language, and are of an appropriate length. Your essays do not have to look exactly like these (obviously), but you can use them as guides for how to approach writing the essays in general. If you're looking for examples of perfect essays, there are some on the GRE website, www.gre.org.

1. If I cannot have freedom, I'd rather not be alive.

"If I cannot have freedom, I'd rather not be alive." This statement encapsulates the views of many of our founding father in the United States. In other countries with different traditions, this statement might be seen as ridiculous and naive. However, I will argue that it is true in this essay.

Without the freedom to act and think as we want to, there's no real difference between humans and animals. Humans have the ability to think about higher things like philosophy, art, and truth. But without the freedom to think about these things, talk about these things, and act on our thoughts about these things, we might as well not have this ability at all. We might as well spend our lives in cages or on leashes.

Although some people feel that any existence at all is preferable to death, this does not make sense. Those who have lead severely physically restricted lives, such as Stephen Hawking, enjoy their lives because they have the freedom to think and create as they please. If a person loses both physical freedom and mental freedom, what is left? Whether a person believes in any form of an afterlife or not, death would be a release from an existence of total restriction.

This does not mean that we do not need rules or laws. On the contrary, part of what creates freedom is the common agreement we have to abide by certain guidelines for living. However, when a given society has a rule that is not just, it is the responsibility of the citizens of that society to change that rule to preserve freedom. This, in the long run, will create more freedoms for the people, which will, in turn create a more productive, happier society.

To sum up, death is preferable to a life lived in physical and mental captivity. Although rules and laws are necessary, they should be used to maintain freedom for all, not to restrict freedom. Only in this way can society reach its higher goals.

2. Some parenting experts feel that parents should be completely honest with their children, even when this would force them to admit to behaviors they don't wish their children to engage in. They cite, in particular, the areas of experimentation with drugs and sexual activity.

Some parenting experts urge parents to tell their children the truth about their past experiences with drugs and sex, even when they don't want their children to do what they did. Others think parents should censor what they tell their children. I will demonstrate that it is better for parents to censor what they tell their children until the children are old enough to understand.

One of the primary duties of parenting is to impart the parents' moral views to their children. Moral views are developed throughout a lifetime. This means that the activities that a parent engaged in, especially with drugs and sex, long before he or she was a parent, formed his or her moral views. This does not mean that they conformed to these views, but that they helped to shape the parent's views. For instance, a woman who experimented with drugs as a teenager and regretted it will probably have developed the moral view that teenagers should not take drugs, based on (not despite) the fact that she did it herself. This is something that children and young teens can't understand, so it would be harmful for the parent to have to confess her drug use while telling her children not to try drugs.

Children have such a black and white view of the world that they cannot understand that a person could do something and then regret it later. Confessing all of one's youthful indiscretions would make a parent's discussions with their children about drugs and sex counterproductive. In fact, many parents might choose not to discuss these subjects at all, rather than risk confusing their children or revealing facts their children are too young to know.

Opponents of this view might argue that once a child learns the truth about his or her parents' activities, he or she will lose respect for the parent and will no longer see the parent's views as credible. However, this is not a logical assumption, since by the time the child finds out the truth, he or she will be old enough to understand why the parent lied. A 22-year-old who finds out that her mother smoked pot in college will understand why the mother did not tell her that when she was 12. And a 20-year-old who discovers that his father had premarital sex will most likely feel very differently about that than he would have when he was 11.

To conclude, parents need to adjust what they tell their children to fit the child's age and developmental stage. When the children are young, they should be less concerned with telling the absolute truth about their own experiences than they should be with making sure their children know what their own moral views are. Later, once the children are old enough, the parents could choose to reveal the truth of their own experiences, but at this point the children will be past the danger point.

3. The university requirement committee recently changed the foreign language requirements for all undergraduates, requiring them to take a full two-year course of a primary language and a one-year course in another language. The head of the committee released the following statement:

"We are convinced that this change will increase the number of students who receive full-time job offers before graduation day. This language requirement is now stricter than that of our competitor university across town, so companies will hire our graduates over theirs, because our graduates are clearly harder workers. The current economy favors multinational corporations, who will be desperate to hire students who have studied multiple foreign languages. In addition, many studies show a correlation between strong language skills and strong mathematical skills, so high-tech companies will also be eager to hire our students."

The argument that increasing the foreign language requirements for undergraduates will increase the number of students who receive full-time job offers before graduation is not complete. There are gaps in the logic that render it unconvincing. The following essay will expose these flaws and demonstrate how the argument could be made more convincing.

The committee begins the argument by comparing university requirements with those of the university across town. Without more information about this "competitor university" we cannot fully assess the validity of this comparison. For instance, if the university across town does not have the same admissions standards or academic reputation as the university in question, the increased language requirements will have no effect on the difference in hiring rates from the two universities.

Additionally, it is a large flaw to say that students from the university in question are "clearly harder workers" simply because the foreign language requirements are increased. The students may or may not be hard workers, but this has nothing to do with language requirements. In fact, increasing the language requirements could lower students' work loads if the classes that are being replaced with language classes are harder than the language classes themselves.

Moreover, the claim that high-tech companies will want to hire students with more language classwork simply because there is a correlation between talent for languages and talent for math does not make sense. If the students have not studied math at higher levels, they will not have the training necessary to work for these high-tech companies even if they are very talented at languages. The correlation would only be relevant if students were required to take high-level math courses in addition to the increase language classes.

The argument could be strengthened if the committee could demonstrate that multinational corporations were specifically interested in students who had studied the languages that university students will study. Without this additional information, this point does not strengthen the argument. If all the university students, for example, take Ancient Icelandic but none of the multinationals are looking for Ancient Icelandic, this statement is not relevant. Without closing this gap and fixing the other problems discussed in this essay, the argument is simply not convincing.

4.   An author should be judged on the complete body of his or her work, rather than on one outstanding example.

It has been said that an author should be judged on the complete body of his or her works, rather than on one outstanding example. Others, however, feel that an author should be judged instead by the best example of his or her work. This essay will demonstrate that it is better to judge one fine example of an author's work than to look at the entire body of work to make a judgement.

To begin, as an author grows older and experiences more of life, his or her work changes. Each piece he or she writes can be seen as an encapsulation of his or her experience at that point in time. Some authors are particularly talented at expressing one mood or feeling very well, but are not as good at others. It is not fair to expect that an author can have the same facility in describing different periods in his or her life.

Additionally, authors may experience other problems that inhibit (or enhance) their ability to write. Some authors are particularly motivated by poverty. Others are motivated by either love or heartbreak. Sylvia Plath was motivated by depression, while many other authors are paralyzed by it. Authors shouldn't all be judged by the same criteria when they don't respond to life in the same ways.

Moreover, authors sometimes write simply to practice their craft. Many of these exercises are simply that—exercises to keep their creative juices flowing. Judging authors by the entire body of everything they've ever written is like saying that they should remain idle until a brilliantly-worded phrase jumps into their heads and they hurry to write it down. Without the discipline of constant practice, writers would not be able to produce their greatest works. The mediocre makes the brilliant possible.

To conclude, an author should be judged not on the entire body of his or her works, but on one or two examples of his or her best works. After all, the best works of a writer are really a culmination of all the works, both good and bad, that he or she has ever written.

5. Every cloud has a silver lining.

The statement "every cloud has a silver lining" is a common platitude. However, the fact that it is an overused statement does not mean it is not true. On the contrary, this statement is almost always valid. The following essay will show that if one looks for a silver lining one will almost always find it.

The statement "every cloud has a silver lining" is merely a poetic way to say that something good can always be found in a situation that looks bad. Some common examples of this would be a person who loses a job and then is forced into another career which they end up excelling at. Or the person who is betrayed by a romantic partner but ends up finding a soul mate they would never have met if not for the betrayal. Looking at the statement as a perfect balance between bad and good, however, could lead one to believe that it is too simplistic and is not realistic at all, since bad things continue to happen.

The statement does not mean that the good in a situation is equal to or greater than the bad in a situation. It simply means that there is always at least some small good thing in the presence of a bad situation. For instance, the Holocaust resulted in the death of millions of Jews and others in Europe. Despite this, there were thousands of examples of good in the midst of the Holocaust, from the large scale (like Oskar Schindler's list that saved hundreds of people) to the tiny scale (like the concentration camp prisoner that found a raspberry and gave it to her friend). Of course these acts of kindness did not outweigh the atrocity of the Holocaust. But they did exist.

Those who believe that there is nothing good in a bad situation have decided that that is true. Then, even if something good happens, they are unable to see it because they have decided that it can't exist (or that it isn't really good). So, in essence, this statement wouldn't be true for a real pessimist. But for anyone willing to open their eyes, there will almost always be some small good thing even in the face of a large bad situation.

I have shown that the statement "every cloud has a silver lining" is true because it is not the simplistic sentiment many people believe it is. It does not depend on a perfect balance or equality of good and evil in the universe, but instead depends on a person's willingness to accept even small kindnesses. Looking at the statement in this light, it cannot be anything but true.

6. A leading doctor said:

"High-tech surgeries should be funded by public tax dollars instead of by patients or insurance companies. All high-tech surgeries are by some measure experimental, even after they become standard, so performing these surgeries always contributes to the body of medical knowledge. The ability to perform these surgeries benefits everyone, since any person could need a high-tech surgery in the future. And investing in high-tech surgeries would be a much better use of tax dollars than paying for many current so-called public health programs, like welfare and food stamps."

The argument that high-tech surgeries should be funded by tax dollars instead of by patients or insurance companies is not entirely convincing. There are several logical flaws in the argument, which prevent it from being effective. The following essay will expose these flaws and suggest ways to improve the argument.

The first problem with the argument is that the author never defines the term "high-tech surgeries." Without this definition, there is no way for the average reader to assess the validity of the author's claim, or even to follow the argument completely. The argument would have been significantly strengthened with the addition of a straightforward, uncomplicated definition of "high-tech surgeries."

The author claims that "all high-tech surgeries are by some measure experimental" and that they "always" contribute to medical knowledge. Again, without a definition of "high-tech surgeries," there is no really way to evaluate this statement. However, it is unlikely that all surgeries are experimental. This statement is too extreme to be true It is also unlikely that high-tech surgeries always contribute to the body of medical knowledge. Again, the extreme nature of the statements call their truth into question.

Another gap in the author's argument s the claim that high-tech surgeries benefit everyone because "any person could need a high-tech surgery in the future." Again, depending on the definition of "high-tech surgeries," this statement is probably not true. There are many rare disorders that are a result of genetic flaws or diseases which only affect certain parts of the general population. Also, there are other conditions that develop only as a result of certain activities (like smoking or repetitive movements) that would only affect people who engaged in those activities.

The author could improve his or her argument by giving statistics or reasoning to support the last statement of the argument, that funding high-tech surgeries is a better use of public health funds than supporting welfare or food stamps. This could be true, but without more evidence there is no way to evaluate this statement. In addition, the author should provide a definition for "high-tech surgeries," eliminate unprovable extreme statements, and remove the statement that these surgeries benefit everyone equally.

7. The value of art lies exclusively in the finished work.

Some people claim that the value of art lies exclusively in the finished work. However, I would argue that the value of art lies not in the final product, but in the process used to achieve that product. I will outline my reasons below.

First, the argument that the only value of art is the finished work betrays the very concept of the artist. One definition of an artist is a person who creates something expressing truth. This definition is very specific in that that the person must create something. It is no specific at all about what is created. This means that the creation is the important part of the artistic equation.

Speaking more practically, the value of the artist and his or her process is not destroyed if the finished product is destroyed. Think about all the pieces in a museum. If the museum burns down and all the finished works inside it are destroyed in the fire, are the artists no longer artists because their finished works are gone? Did the process they spent creating these works not take place simply because the pieces no longer exit? The obvious answer to these questions is that the artists are still artists because they created the pieces, whether the pieces still exist or not.

Last, a widely-held view is that the purpose of art is to "transform." If this is true, then there is no way to judge the value of a given piece of artwork, since that piece may or may not transform any individual viewer. However, it is much more likely that transformation of one sort or another will have occurred to the artist as he or she was creating the piece. Therefore, the purpose of art is most likely achieved in the process of creation rather than in the finished product.

In conclusion, I have demonstrated in the preceding essay that the value of art lies in the process of creating it, not in the finished work. The act of creation is more important than the object being created, because it transforms the artist. Without this process, society would suffer.

8. Any revolutionary political movement is bound to lose momentum as soon as the general population recognizes its views as being valid.

The statement that "any revolutionary political movement is bound to lose momentum as soon as the general population recognizes its views as being valid" is true. Others could argue that movements do not always lose their strength, but this view is not accurate. The following paragraphs will demonstrate that a revolutionary movement cannot maintain momentum after it is recognized by the general population.

The heart of this statement is the word "revolutionary." Revolutionary means that the movement goes against the status quo and seeks to enact radical change. By its very nature, a truly revolutionary movement cannot be accepted by the majority of the people or else it wouldn't be revolutionary anymore. Once it becomes part of the accepted and is a component of the status quo, it is no longer radical.

A movement could still be revolutionary even if everyone in a society was aware of it. But the statement specifically says that the general population recognizes the movement's views as "being valid." An example of this would be radical environmental groups that destroy property and kill humans in their efforts to stop pollution. The majority of Americans are aware that these groups exist, yet few feel that their actions and beliefs are valid. Therefore, they are still a revolutionary movement with radical views.

The reason that a revolutionary movement cannot maintain momentum once its views are accepted as being valid is that much of the power of a revolutionary movement comes from its ability to shock. If the general population is not surprised or dismayed by the actions of the group, it will no longer be newsworthy and it will lose the power it once enjoyed. Without this power, the movement will have a harder time publicizing and advancing its views to the point that a society embraces them and makes the changes that the movement originally sought.

It is evident that the statement that "any revolutionary political movement is bound to lose momentum as soon as the general population recognizes its views as being valid" is correct. For the reasons outlined above, a movement needs to maintain its outsider status to retain power and strength. Once this status is gone, the movement cannot continue to function effectively.

9. A large corporation recently changed its policy on parental leave upon the birth or adoption of a child to give as little time off as the law allows. The head of Human Resources released the following statement:

"We believe that by discouraging employees from taking excessive time off to care for the children they themselves choose to have, we will make our staff both happier and more productive. Without the burden of having to choose how much time to take off, they will have an easier time balancing work and home responsibilities. In addition, the more time they spend at work, the more loyalty they will feel toward the corporation. Studies show that employees who spend more time at work advance more rapidly within the company structure, so our new policy will create a company of ultra-loyal, ultra-achieving employees."

The corporation's argument that restricting the amount of time a parent can take off work upon the birth or adoption of a child will create more loyal, productive employees is inherently flawed. The argument's reasoning is not convincing, and there are many logical gaps that need to be addressed. In the following essay I will expose these flaws and suggest ways in which the argument could be made more convincing.

The first argument the corporation makes is that employees will have an easier time balancing work and home responsibilities if they do not have the ability to choose how much time to spend with their families. While this may technically be true, it's incredibly one-sided. Of course the employees won't have problems with balance—the scale will be tipped entirely in favor of the corporation. Instead of relieving stress and breeding loyalty, however, removing the employees' choice will merely cause resentment toward the company. In fact, it would not be surprising if many of the corporation's employees looked for jobs with other companies as soon as they found out that they would become parents.

The corporation's second argument is that the more time employees spend at work the more loyalty they will feel toward the corporation. This, again, may be technically true—there are some famous examples of people taken hostage who developed a strong sense of loyalty to their captors. In fact, this psychological phenomenon is called "The Stockholm Syndrome." However, this form of loyalty is considered to be a form of mental illness, and is not something that a wise corporation would want to encourage in its employees.

The corporation's third argument, that forcing employees to spend more time at work will create a company full of super-achievers, is also not supported. Studies do show that the more time an employee spends at work, the faster he or she will advance in the company. However, if all employees are forced to work long hours, then how will any of them separate from the group to advance more rapidly? Instead, they will continue to advance at the same rate, even as they work longer hours. The corporation's argument does not hold up.

The flaws in reasoning in the corporation's argument make it logically unconvincing. Since the company's logic is based on a position that is unlikely ever to be accepted by employees, it would be virtually impossible to improve the argument substantially without changing it radically. Instead, the corporation may want to reexamine this new policy, if it truly wants to breed loyalty in its employees.

10. Some economists argue that smoking should be made illegal, since it is not merely a matter of public health, but also of national wealth, because smoking-related illnesses and deaths cost billions of dollars annually.

The issue of whether or not smoking should be made illegal is a controversial one. Some economists argue that it should be because it causes a financial drain on society. Others argue that smoking should be a matter of personal choice, and that money should not be an issue. This essay will argue that smoking should be a matter of personal choice and should not be made illegal.

If economists want to make smoking illegal because it costs the nation money from illness and death, they will have to make dozens of other common practices illegal, too. Some examples of these dangerous practices would be drinking alcohol, driving cars, crossing the street, eating fatty foods, and not exercising. It may sound ridiculous to make eating fatty foods illegal, but this is no more ridiculous than making smoking illegal is. Eating fatty foods has been proven to cause heart disease, high cholesterol, stroke, and death, and yet no one is suggesting that we make it illegal. Why, then should smoking be held to a different standard?

The economists are not taking into account the wealth that smoking and smoking-related industries contribute to the national economy. Tobacco is the largest cash crop of many of the Southern states, and cigarette factories provide thousands of jobs. If smoking was made illegal, this revenue would be lost. The economists don't seem to have taken this into account. It is possible that making smoking illegal would cause a loss of wealth for the country, even if disease and death from smoking stopped.

The best argument against making smoking illegal, however, is that this would be a violation of human rights. The United States Constitution guarantees the right to life, liberty, and the pursuit of happiness. Smoking makes many people happy, and to make it illegal would be a violation of the very principles upon which this country was founded. Without our outstanding freedoms, we would not have the strong, economically healthy country we have today.

To conclude, the argument that smoking should be made illegal for financial reasons is invalid. The arguments that smoking should not be treated any differently than other matters of personal choice, like eating fatty foods, cannot be overlooked. In addition, smoking contributes wealth to the nation, and making smoking illegal would be a violation of the principles upon which this country was founded.

11. Many analysts argue that population growth is causing most of the Earth's major problems. They recommend that nations impose mandatory restrictions on the number of children that their citizens can have.

Analysts argue that "population growth is causing most of the Earth's problems" and that nations should "impose mandatory restrictions on the number of children their citizens can have." It could be argued, however, that restrictive policies would cause more problems than they solve, so that restrictive policies would be counterproductive. In the following essay I will argue for the latter point, that mandatory restrictions on the number of children families are allowed to have would cause larger problems than those the Earth is facing currently.

First of all, there is evidence that restricting the number of children that families can have causes societal problems. China has had restrictions in place for years which limit families to only one child. This has led to a strong societal preference for male children, since traditionally, males took care of their families in old age. Many families opted to find out the sex of their unborn children and aborted them if they were girls. This practice was so widespread that it is now illegal for doctors or hospitals to tell parents the sex of their unborn children. The restriction to one child per family has lead to a gender imbalance in China, which is causing violence in some areas of the country. Girls are being kidnapped or raped because there are not enough girls to marry the boys that every family wants to have.

Moreover, this strong gender preference can lead to an imbalance in the numbers of men and women in a society. If restrictions were enacted on a larger scale, it is possible that eventually there would be a serious gender imbalance in the world. Without both sexes in relatively equal numbers, women could become a weak underclass. In extreme cases, it is possible that they would be forced to become pregnant to provide heirs for the dominant males. In a more realistic scenario, women would lose all the advances they have made socially and politically over the last few hundred years.

Without equal numbers of women, violence in society would be likely to increase. Traditionally, societies in which men have been strongly dominant over women have been societies ruled by violence that use violence to subdue their enemies. Since many of the problems analysts point to as being caused by overpopulation are a result of violence and scarcity of resources (which can also be caused by unchecked violence) restricting population growth would only solve these problems in the short term.

Some may argue that the sex selection technologies available in the United States are used primarily to have girls, but this fact does not necessarily apply to the question at hand. First of all, this statistic takes into account the United States only, not the entire world. Secondly, and most importantly, sex selection technologies are being used by people who do not have governmental restrictions on the number of children they can have. The people who are trying to have girls already have at least one boy. There is no way to know if they would still want girls if they were only allowed to have one child.

In conclusion, the argument that strictly controlling population by restricting the number of children a family can have will reduce the Earth's problems is not valid. Restricting family growth will lead to a gender imbalance that is problematic in itself. However, a gender imbalance will also cause larger-scale problems that may be worse than the problems we have now.

12. A new testing procedure would reduce the number of flawed parts that make it to the market by catching these parts before they are packaged and shipped to retailers. Proponents of this new procedure argue that it should be instituted in all of ABC Company's factories because it will increase the efficiency, and therefore reduce the costs, of manufacturing these parts. They argue further that reducing the costs would allow them ultimately to manufacture many more parts, and to increase ABC Company's profits exponentially.

The argument that implementing a new testing procedure for flawed parts in all of ABC Company's factories will allow them to manufacture more parts an increase profits is not logically convincing. The gaps in the argument are major flaws. In the following essay I will expose these flaws and suggest ways to improve the argument.

The author of the argument claims that implementing the new testing procedure will increase the efficiency of manufacturing the parts. However, the test only catches the parts before they are shipped to retailers, not before they are made. This means that the manufacturing process is just as efficient with the testing procedure in place as it was without it. If a procedure could be developed to stop these flawed parts from being made in the first place, that would increase the efficiency of the process.

Since the efficiency of the process will not actually be affected, then the cost of producing the parts will not be affected either. The author's argument continues to fall apart, because it is based on the premise that the testing procedure will increase efficiency. Since costs will not be reduced, they may not be able to manufacture more parts, which may prevent an increase in profits.

The author could improve the argument by pointing out that costs will be saved by implementing the new testing procedure because no more money will be wasted on costly returns of flawed parts from retailers. In turn, the savings they realize from not having to pay for return may allow them to manufacture more parts and increase profits.

As it is written, the argument that instituting a new testing procedure will increase production and profitability for ABC Company is inherently flawed. The entire argument could be redeemed if the author removed the claim that the testing procedure will increase efficiency, and instead pointed out that the company will save money by reducing costs associated with accepting return of flawed parts from retailers.

GRE Diagnostic Software

ABOUT THE SOFTWARE

The diagnostic tests on the CD-ROM are designed to help you practice your test-taking skills, pacing, and techniques in a setting that is very much like the real GRE. We want to make sure your testing experience is as realistic as possible. Each test has a pool of questions, and each question drawn from that pool depends on how you answered the previous question—just like an actual GRE.

In addition to the four full-length GREs on the disc, you can practice specific question types with drills. The drill questions come out of a pool of questions that will not show up on the tests. However, when you have completed all four full GREs, the entire question pool (over 2,000 questions) is opened into the drills. So, although you may see some repeat questions at that point, you can drill as much as you need to. We've even included some suggestions for using the drills (see below).

Although the software allows you to take a single section of the test on its own, we recommend trying an entire test in one sitting. Remember—you want to simulate real testing conditions. And don't forget to use scratch paper—that screen-to-scratch paper conversion is very important. We also advise that you make good use of the review features—look at the explanations for questions you missed, and determine which sections are giving you the most trouble.

SYSTEM REQUIREMENTS*

WINDOWS™

166 MHz or higher

Windows 95, 98, 2000 ME, XP

32 MB RAM

12 MB Hard Disk space

256 Color Monitor (640 × 480 pixels)

Windows compatible sound device

MACINTOSH®

Power PC, 166 MHz or higher

System 7.6.1 or higher

32 MB RAM

12 MB Hard Disk space

256 Color Monitor (640 × 480 pixels)

* This software will not operate with Windows NT.

INSTALLATION AND START-UP

WINDOWS:

Close all other applications.
Check that your monitor is set to 256 colors.

1. Insert the CD in your CD-ROM drive.

2. From your Start Menu, select **Run**.

3. Type **D: setup** and press **Enter**. (If your CD-ROM drive is not drive D:, type the appropriate letter.)

4. Follow the onscreen instructions until installation is complete.

5. Once setup is complete, if you want to begin immediately, you can check "Yes, I want to run GRE Diagnostic now" and select **Finish.** Otherwise, just select **Finish**.

Note: If onscreen instructions don't appear, open the file setup.exe on your D drive. This should initiate installation.

To run the software later, make sure the CD is in your CD-ROM drive, and simply select **GRE Diagnostic** from *The Princeton Review* folder in Programs from the Start Menu.

MACINTOSH:

1. Insert the CD in your CD-ROM drive.

2. Double click the GRE Diagnostic Installer icon.

3. Follow the onscreen instructions until installation is complete.

To run the software, make sure the CD is in your CD-ROM drive, and simply double click the *Tester* icon located in the *GRE Diagnostic* folder on your hard drive.

USING GRE DIAGNOSTIC TESTS

THE MAIN MENU

Each time you launch your GRE Diagnostic, you will begin with the main menu screen. From this screen, you can **Take a Test**—one of four GRE Diagnostics (which can be taken section by section or as a whole test), **Review a Test** you've already taken, or **Practice a Section** with drills. You can also exit the software by clicking **Quit** on the upper-right corner.

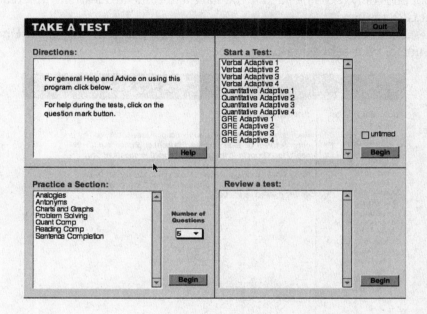

TAKING A TEST

Each full-length GRE consists of four sections: Verbal, Quantitative, Analytical, Writing, and an unscored Experimental section. In an actual GRE, you will not know which section is experimental, but in this software you do. You can skip this section by clicking Exit Section—see TOOLBAR for explanation.

If you choose to take an individual section, you can only take the corresponding sections separately as well. Likewise, if you take a full test, the corresponding sections become unavailable.

You also have the option of taking an untimed test by clicking the "untimed" box above the Begin button. This option is only recommended if you have a documented learning difference and will be taking the real GRE untimed.

To start a test, select one from the list and click **Begin**. You will go directly to the Directions screen of the first section of your selected test.

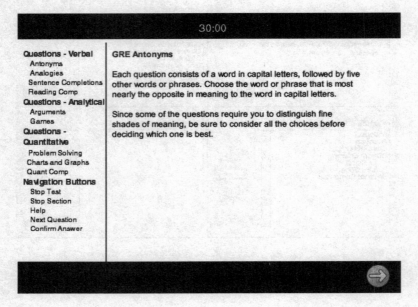

This is also the **Help** screen. If you need to review the directions for any type of question or the functions of any of the buttons on your screen, simply click the **Help** button at the bottom of any active testing screen and this screen will reappear. You can then click on the topic with which you need help.

Since the timer starts as soon as you click **Begin**, you should not spend unnecessary time on the Directions screen. Please review all of the section directions (provided in the book) before taking the diagnostic tests. The buttons on the actual GRE are also explained in the book in chapter 2, but please read the TOOLBAR section below because the buttons on these diagnostic tests are slightly different.

Unlike the actual GRE, there is no warning that you are nearing the end of a section, so pay attention to the timer.

Here is a sample test question screen:

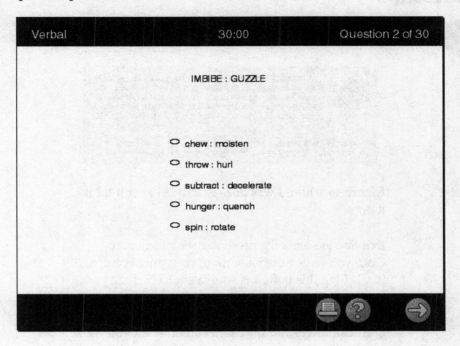

IMBIBE : GUZZLE

○ chew : moisten

○ throw : hurl

○ subtract : decelerate

○ hunger : quench

○ spin : rotate

To select an answer, click on the oval next to the answer or the answer itself, and then click the **NEXT QUESTION** button, which will turn into a **CONFIRM ANSWER** button. Click that button again to move to the next question. Remember, once you click **CONFIRM ANSWER,** you cannot return to that question.

THE TOOLBAR

 Clicking **STOP TEST** will give you the following warning:

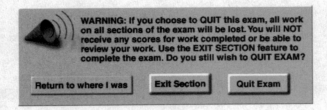

Return to where I was does exactly what you think it does.

Exit Section ends the present section of the test. Once you have exited a section, you cannot return to it. Clicking this button is equivalent to clicking **Section Exit** from the toolbar of an actual GRE.

Quit Exam will end the exam and erase all your results. We have included this button for emergency purposes, but we recommend that you never use it because you will not be able to review any of your work on that test. Furthermore, when you start a new test, it is possible that there will be questions repeated from the test that you quit, which will compromise the validity of your score. Clicking this button is equivalent to clicking **Test Exit** from the toolbar of an actual GRE.

The **Stop Test** button does not appear until after you select an answer and click the **Next Question** button. It does not appear at all on the first question of any section.

 Clicking **PRINT** will print the question presently on the screen. You cannot print out the entire test. This feature is not available during a real GRE.

 Clicking **HELP** will bring you to the Directions screen (see above), just as it does on an actual GRE.

 Clicking **NEXT** will change the button into **CONFIRM.** In the actual GRE, these are two separate buttons.

 Clicking **CONFIRM ANSWER** will record your answer and bring you the next question. Before confirming, you have one last chance to change your answer.

ENDING A SECTION AND FINISHING THE TEST

When you reach the end of a section, you will see this message:

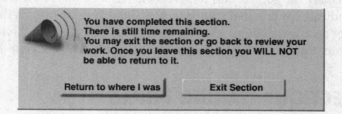

Return to where I was allows you to continue working on the last question in the section only. You cannot review the test at this time.

Exit Section will end your time on the section. Choose this option if you are finished with the section. If you have another section remaining, you will have a short break (2 minutes after sections 1 and 3, 10 minutes after section 2) and then the computer will start the next section. (In an actual GRE, you will only have 1 minute after sections 1 and 3.) If you would like a longer break, you can also wait until time runs out on this section.

When you reach the end of the last section of the test and choose **Exit Section**, you will receive a message that reads, "You have reached the end of the exam." Select **Exit** to proceed.

THE SCORE REPORT

When you have completed a test, you will see a screen that asks you to wait while your exam is scored. Then you will see your **SCORE REPORT**. This report gives you detailed information about your test. You can view the results of each section by selecting a section from the pull-down menu in the upper-right corner, or you can print the full report by clicking the **Print** button.

SCORE REPORT				Print		Exit Review

Exam Name Computer Adaptive Test 1 **Date** 3/12/99 **Subject** Verbal
Scores Verbal=220

Section Performance (Click on a question to review.)

Q#	Corr Ans	Your Ans	Category	QID	Time Spent
1	D	E	ANT	9052	00:17
2	B	E	ANA	9024	00:14
3	A	A	ANA	9070	00:06
4	C	D	ANT	9106	00:10
5	E	D	SC	9016	00:03
6	D	A	ANA	9023	00:01
7	A	C	RC	9036	00:02
8	A	D	RC	9035	00:01
9	B	C	RC	9034	00:01
10	C	C	ANA	9021	00:18
11	A	C	ANT	9047	00:02

Performance Summary

Category	#Right	#Wrong	%Right	Average Time
Antonyms..(ANT)	2	6	25	00:06
Analogies..(ANA)	5	3	62	00:06
Sentence Completion..(SC)	1	5	16	00:03
Reading Comp..(RC)	1	7	12	00:02

You can view this **SCORE REPORT** at another time by selecting this test from the **Review a Test** section of the Main Menu.

REVIEWING YOUR TEST

You may review any question from your test by clicking on the question number in the **SCORE REPORT**. This will display the correct and incorrect answers. The review mode will show you a green checkmark to indicate the credited response, and show your answer as the darkened oval. To view an explanation for an answer choice, click on the answer (the words in the answer, not the oval). These explanations do not print. To return to the **SCORE REPORT**, click on the **STOP SECTION** button.

PRACTICE A SECTION—TAKING DRILLS

To take a drill, select a question type from the **Practice a Section** menu, select whether you want 5, or even 30, questions, and click **Begin.**

The drill screens look the same as the testing screens, with the following functional differences:

- The questions are untimed.

- You are shown the correct answer as soon as you select an answer. So, while there is no need to confirm answers, you cannot change answers while using the drills.

- You can view explanations immediately after you've answered by clicking on the answer choice—not the oval. But unlike **Reviewing a Test**, you cannot go back to a question once you have moved onto the next.

We've designed our drills so that you will not jeopardize the accuracy of any of your practice tests by seeing questions early. We have secured a group of about 400 questions for you to drill before you complete the tests. Once you have completed all four tests, you may see questions you saw previously in a test or drill (we want you to be able to drill to your heart's content), but at this point seeing questions again will not affect the utility of these drills. Remember that questions tend to fall into predictable patterns—that's part of what makes the GRE a standardized test.

You can use the drills to increase your familiarity with a particular question type, to target specific weaknesses, or to increase your speed or accuracy. Here are some suggestions:

Building accuracy

After you've taken a test, look at the **Performance Summary** on your **Score Report** and find a question type you need to improve on. Note the average time per question. To increase your accuracy on that type of question, double the average amount of time spent per question and try to get each drill question right. Then decrease the time slightly, while staying at 100 percent accuracy. This drilling method helps you improve your performance in the first third of the test, where accuracy is more important than speed.

Building speed

From the **Performance Summary** of your **Score Report**, choose a question type on which you do well. Note the average time spent per question. When drilling that question type, decrease that time slightly and challenge yourself to maintain the same level of accuracy. This drilling method helps you build speed for the middle of the test, where you need to move more quickly without sacrificing accuracy.

Practicing pacing

You can choose the appropriate number of drill questions to simulate the pacing of an actual test. For example, if your target score is 700 on the Math section, aim for 100 percent accuracy on the first 10 questions in the first 15 minutes of the test. You can simulate this in a drill by doing 5 Quant Comp questions and 5 Problem Solving questions in 15 minutes.

Mini-test

You can simulate the experience of taking a portion of the test by choosing an assortment of questions and working them within a set amount of time. A Verbal Mini-test might consist of 5 of each of the four question types in 20 minutes. You can use a Mini-test drill to help build your stamina through the most crucial part of the test.

TO UNINSTALL

Windows:

Select "Remove GRE Diagnostic" from *The Princeton Review* folder in Programs in the Start Menu. Or use the following procedure:

1. Select Control Panel from your Start Menu.
2. Click on "Add/Remove Programs."
3. Select GRE Diagnostic.
4. Click on the Add/Remove option.
5. Delete your user files. They can be found in C:\Program Files\The Princeton Review\GRE Diagnostic. Simply delete the folder "GRE Diagnostic."

Macintosh:

1. Select the GRE Diagnostic folder from your hard drive.
2. Click and drag to the trash.

If you have any questions, please call our Technical Support Center at 800-546-2102.

ABOUT THE AUTHOR

Karen Lurie lives in New York City. The world of the Graduate Record Examination has been orbitting her for about ten years. She has written six books, including the *LSAT/GRE Analytic Workout* and *GRE Crash Course*.

www.review.com

The Princeton Review Admissions Services

At The Princeton Review, we genuinely care about your academic success, which involves much more than just the GRE and other standardized tests. Review.com is the premier online resource available to help you search for, apply to, and figure out how you're going to pay for graduate school.

The main page of the Graduate Center on Review.com acts as a portal, sending you directly to our free information and services. When you register, you gain access to even more free services tailored to your profile.

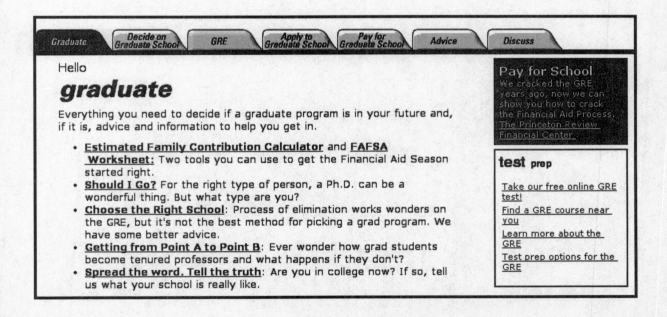

APPLYING ONLINE

Applying to grad school online is faster and easier! Just ask any of the over 450,000 students entering college and graduate school in the fall of 2002 who applied online using our Embark technology. Every line that you scrawl by hand on a paper application has to be hand-entered by someone at the school's admissions office anyway. If your school's app is available online, why not save yourself and the school some time and trouble by using the more efficient e-application? Here are just a few of the perks: You can stop and save your app at any time, you don't have to fill out basic information more than once for multiple applications, and there's no need for a postage stamp. Did we mention that there's no fee to apply online with The Princeton Review? Yes, it's free.

The Princeton Review and Embark are pleased to offer online applications from schools such as Columbia University's Graduate School of Arts and Sciences, Harvard University's Graduate School of Design and John F. Kennedy School of Government, Dartmouth College's Thayer School of Engineering, Tufts University's Graduate School of Arts and Sciences, Syracuse University's S.I. Newhouse School of Public Communications, and Yale University's School of Music.

FINANCIAL CENTER

Our revamped Financial Center is a unique resource for students. You'll find everything from helpful tips on saving money, tax forms, aid, loans, and scholarships to tools that allow you to compare aid packages and calculate your expected family contribution. We also offer advice on managing your personal finances—tips on credit cards, debt, and insurance. For those of you who are completely lost, we can show you the way: We have a straightforward financial timeline telling you exactly what to do and when to do it so you can get the maximum amount of aid.

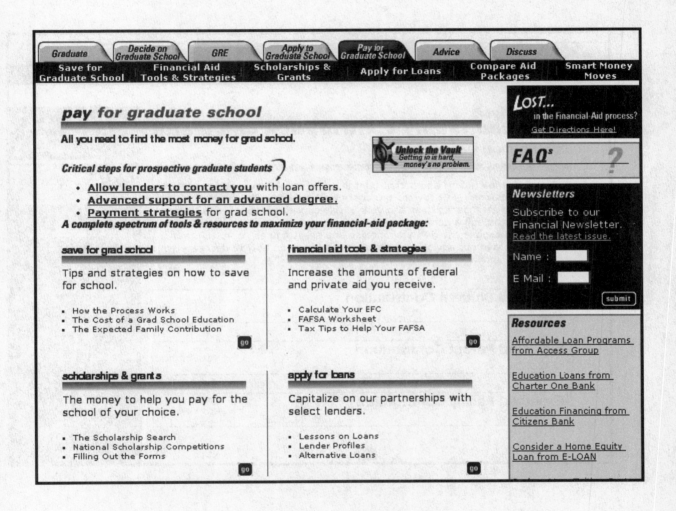

Two outstanding financial tools you'll find on Review.com are the EFC Calculator and the FAFSA Worksheet. The Need Analysis/Expected Family Contribution Calculator allows you to calculate your approximate Expected Family Contribution (EFC), which both schools and the federal government use to determine what they think you should be able to pay for a year's worth of higher education. This is an essential starting point for financial aid, as it helps you understand the federal methodology and gives you a ballpark figure with which you can start the financial aid process.

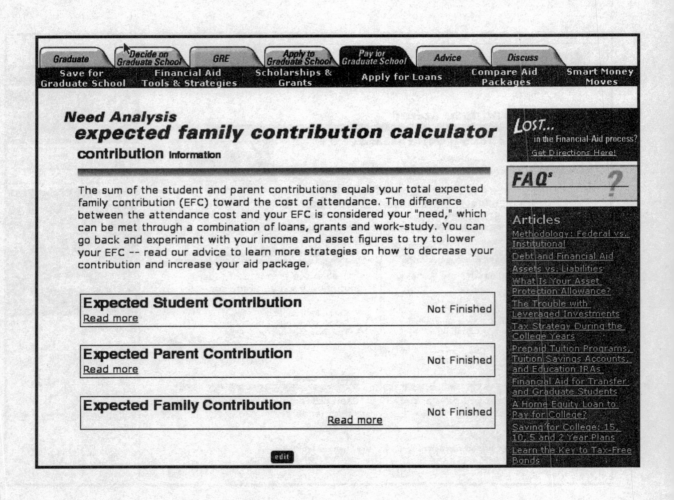

The FAFSA Worksheet is a virtual dress rehearsal for the official FAFSA form. You will *have* to complete the FAFSA if you want any federal financial aid at all. Each question on the worksheet has its own pop-up window with a detailed explanation and tips for entering the response that will benefit you most.

Note: This worksheet has been known to radically reduce the likelihood that students will suffer from the panic attacks and financial nightmares often attributed to filling out the FAFSA.

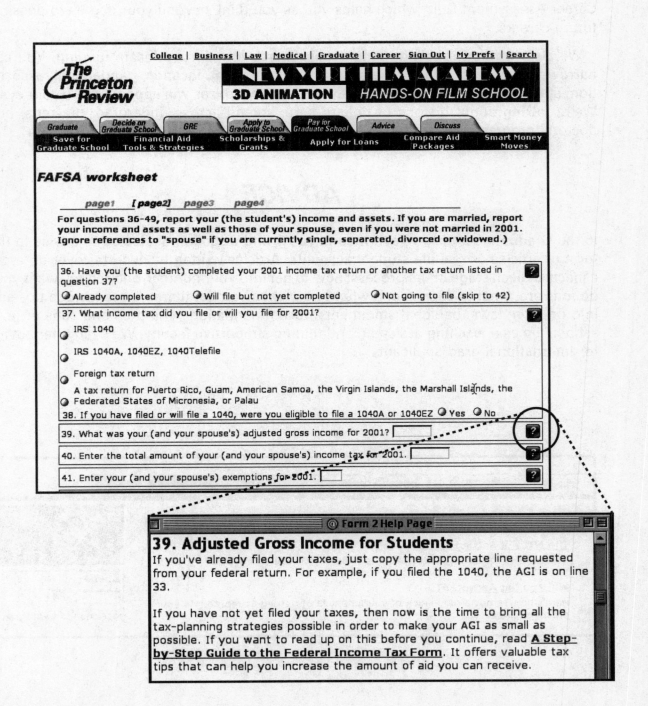

SEARCHABLE DATABASES

Visitors to Review.com can search for graduate schools using our Embark technology. They'll have access to thousands of grad school profiles, which include contact information and links to each school's website and online application, if available.

If you don't mind filling out a bit of information about yourself (don't worry—registration is simple), you have even more services at your fingertips. One such feature is the Career Assessment Quiz, which helps you as you think beyond your degree to possible future careers.

We also have an excellent Scholarship Search to help you locate funding. You can narrow your search with criteria such as dollar amount, location, gender, club association, ethnicity, athletics, and talent, and prospective prizes will appear before your eyes. We're talking about billions of dollars here, spread across undergrad, master's, and doctoral programs, so opt in.

ADVICE

In the Graduate Center on Review.com, you'll find a section dedicated to advice in the form of articles or real-life student accounts. Articles written by experts cover different aspects of each stage of the process: how to get into your number-one school, what your options are, what to expect, and what to do when you get there. These include tips and info on interviews, personal statements, recommendations, the pros and cons of grad school, life as a teaching assistant, and finding supportive faculty. We even offer advice for international grad applicants.

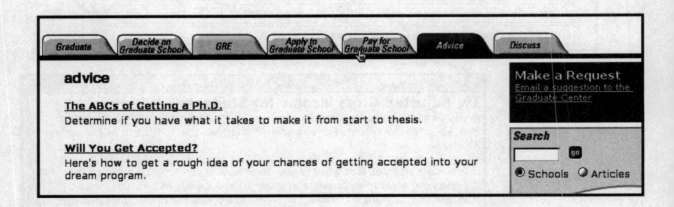

BOOKS

Admissions Services publishes great data and advice books on undergrad, graduate, and professional schools, as well as careers. Just a few of the titles we offer are *Guide to Your Career*, *The Internship Bible*, *The Complete Book of Distance Learning Schools*, *Why Won't the Landlord Take Visa?*, and our *Job Surfing* series. For a complete listing of our available titles, check out our books page at *www.review.com/college/booksandsoftware.cfm?books=0*.

TUFTS UNIVERSITY

BENDETSON HALL, MEDFORD, MA 02155 • ADMISSIONS: 617-627-3170 • FAX: 617-627-3860

CAMPUS LIFE

Quality of Life Rating	87
Type of school	private
Affiliation	none
Environment	suburban

STUDENTS

Total undergrad enrollment	4,869
% male/female	47/53
% from out of state	77
% from public high school	60
% live on campus	80
% in (# of) fraternities	15 (10)
% in (# of) sororities	3 (3)
% African American	7
% Asian	14
% Caucasian	60
% Hispanic	7
% international	7

SURVEY SAYS . . .
Campus feels safe
Great library
Beautiful campus
Campus easy to get around
Great off-campus food
Student publications are ignored
(Almost) no one listens to college radio
Students are cliquish
(Almost) no one smokes

ACADEMICS

Academic Rating	89
Calendar	semester
Student/faculty ratio	9:1
Profs interesting rating	85
Profs accessible rating	96
% profs teaching UG courses	100
% classes taught by TAs	1
Avg lab size	10-19 students
Avg reg class size	10-19 students

MOST POPULAR MAJORS
international relations
biology
English

STUDENTS SPEAK OUT

Academics

Known for stealing the Ivy wait-list population, Tufts University offers rigorous academics that keep the school's hard-working, career-driven students on their toes. With its small class size, ample funding, and noteworthy professors, Tufts offers a wide variety of solid departments. Of particular renown is the international relations major, which draws in students from all over. Notes one student, "The best part of academics at Tufts are the small classes, the accessible faculty and staff, and the fact that NO classes are taught by TAs." Another opines, "Academically Tufts is impressive. The teachers are always available and ready to help, and if you look well, there are some really interesting classes: History of Reggae, Negotiation and Conflict Resolution, and Yoga." Requirements for first-year students are stiff, and some freshmen are hung up on "pointless requirements," but says one older and wiser student, "As an incoming freshman, it was good to have some idea of what to take. The advising program is excellent." Professors are highly regarded: reports one student, "My professors are incredible! From an astronomy professor who was late to class because he was rushing back from a NASA meeting in Houston to a political science professor who accidentally caught Justice Sandra Day O'Connor with food in her teeth, I have had fantastic and knowledgeable professors throughout my Tufts career. They're all open, honest, and enthusiastic educators with whom it is a pleasure to learn." Administrators "are great. . . . The president takes a very personal interest in the lives of the students. He is one of three professors leading a community dialogue/class on Leadership for Active Citizenship." On the downside, "Classrooms are ugly at best. . . . On the outside the buildings are pretty, but our lack of a large endowment has allowed many of them to become somewhat dilapidated on the inside."

Life

Tufts students describe an active campus life, one cram-packed with both class-related activities and extracurriculars. Writes one, "Even though most people are very focused on academics, most find plenty of time to be active in several of our 150-plus diverse activities. We have fantastic volunteer organizations, for example." Agrees another, "School spirit lies primarily in the 150 student activities groups. Within these groups, the most incredible bonds are formed. From the moment I arrived on campus, I joined everything! The daily newspaper, film series, debate team, tutoring, musical theater, etc. There's so much to do, my parents often question when I do my work." Students report that "everyone at this school is either dating someone here or someone at another school. This is far from a 'frat party and hook up' school." As for the Greeks, students explain that "although the fraternities and sororities make up only a fraction of the student body, they are pretty much the center of freshman life on campus. Once you become an upperclassman, though, you realize there is life beyond the Greek system." That life usually takes students into Boston, fortuitously "nearby to offer an outlet for students to live life. A lot of people go to Boston for fun, movies, dinner, and dance clubs." Then it's back to the beautiful campus, secluded in the suburban hills just a short commuter train ride away.

Student Body

Assessing his peers, one Tufts undergrad offers these observations: "Tufts students are very intelligent but not extremely competitive, which creates a nice learning environment. People are generally pretty nice and normal. The students are racially diverse, but the vast majority are rich and wear J.Crew." Perhaps it is this last characteristic that leads some students to offer that "The Tufts stereotype is a reality: a lot of nice, average guys from the New York tri-state area named Dave." Overall, Tufts students consider themselves "ambitious" and "energetic." Political personalities vary from the "'cause-of-the-week' types" to the "apathetic." "People often talk about campus politics," writes one student, "but not as much about national or international politics."

More Books from Admissions Services...

NOTES

NOTES

NOTES

NOTES

NOTES

NOTES

NOTES

NOTES

NOTES

NOTES

NOTES

NOTES

NOTES

MORE EXPERT ADVICE FROM THE PRINCETON REVIEW

If you want to give yourself the best chances for getting into the graduate school of your choice, we can help you get higher test scores, make the most informed choices, and make the most of your experience once you get there. We can also help you make the career move that will let you use your skills and education to their best advantage.

CRACKING THE GRE
2003 EDITION
0-375-76247-7 $20.00

**CRACKING THE GRE
SAMPLE TESTS ON CD-ROM**
2003 EDITION
0-375-76248-5 $31.95

CRACKING THE GRE BIOLOGY
4TH EDITION
0-375-76265-5 $18.00

**CRACKING THE GRE
CHEMISTRY**
2ND EDITION
0-375-76266-3 $16.00

**CRACKING THE GRE
LITERATURE**
4TH EDITION
0-375-76268-X $18.00

CRACKING THE GRE MATH
2ND EDITION
0-375-76267-1 $18.00

**CRACKING THE GRE
PSYCHOLOGY**
6TH EDITION
0-375-76269-8 $18.00

**VERBAL WORKOUT
FOR THE GRE**
0-679-77890-X $16.00

**THE BEST GRADUATE
PROGRAMS: ENGINEERING**
2ND EDITION
0-375-75205-6 $21.00

**THE BEST GRADUATE
PROGRAMS: HUMANITIES
AND SOCIAL SCIENCES**
2ND EDITION
0-375-75203-X $25.00

**THE BEST GRADUATE
PROGRAMS: PHYSICAL
AND BIOLOGICAL
SCIENCES**
2ND EDITION
0-375-75204-8 $25.00

GUIDE TO YOUR CAREER
4TH EDITION
0-375-75620-5 $21.00

**GUIDE TO CAREERS IN
THE HEALTH PROFESSIONS**
0-375-76158-6 $24.95